Ying Zhan
Child Agency in Family Language Policy

Contributions to the Sociology of Language

Edited by
Ofelia García
Francis M. Hult

Founding editor
Joshua A. Fishman

Volume 122

Ying Zhan

Child Agency in Family Language Policy

Growing up Multilingual and Multiliterate

DE GRUYTER
MOUTON

ISBN 978-3-11-162809-7
e-ISBN (PDF) 978-3-11-100309-2
e-ISBN (EPUB) 978-3-11-100358-0
ISSN 1861-0676

Library of Congress Control Number: 2023933706

Bibliographic information published by the Deutsche Nationalbibliothek
The Deutsche Nationalbibliothek lists this publication in the Deutsche Nationalbibliografie;
detailed bibliographic data are available on the internet at http://dnb.dnb.de.

© 2024 Walter de Gruyter GmbH, Berlin/Boston
This volume is text- and page-identical with the hardback published in 2023.
Cover image: sculpies/shutterstock
Typesetting: Integra Software Services Pvt. Ltd.

www.degruyter.com

Acknowledgements

This book could not have been published without the support of many people. Particular appreciation is owed to Professor Fred Anderson and Professor Mary Noguchi, who helped me as I revised this book manuscript and treated me like a friend. I have benefited greatly from discussing various questions with them and listening to their insightful comments.

Furthermore, I am grateful to Professor Demin Tao and Professor Katsuhiro Yamazumi, who carefully evaluated the merits and demerits of my study.

I must thank the two series editors of the Contributions to Sociology of Language (CSL) book series of De Gruyter Mouton, Professor Ofelia García and Professor Francis M. Hult, for offering me this enormous opportunity to turn my dissertation into a book. Without their approval and helpful suggestions, I would not have been able to take the first step to achieve my dream of sharing my family's multilingual experience.

I also thank the first anonymous external reviewer, who conveyed his/her appreciation of my work through stimulating and kind comments. I am very grateful for his/her understanding of the inconsistency between my original research direction and the story that emerged from my data. I had not anticipated how powerful child agency could be when my daughter was born. I hope that now that I have reorganized and re-focused my work, the phenomenon of child agency is more readily apparent in the wealth of examples provided in this book.

I also thank the second anonymous external reviewer whose careful analysis encouraged me to make my revisions with great enthusiasm. The reviewer specifically guided me to think more about child agency in literacy-driven practices and its relation to language socialization and multilingual parenting, as well as family language policies. Taking his/her advice, I was able to reorganize some parts and focus the research more clearly.

I want to sincerely thank Dr. Natalie Fecher, Kirstin Börgen, and Tharani Ramachandran for their help with my book project.

Finally, I want to thank my husband who has been my good friend over the last 19 years. I also want to thank Y, my daughter and playmate, who always thinks and acts kindly, cheerfully, sensibly, and independently. Without the participation and support of both my husband and daughter, the present study would not have been filled with so much joy, laughter, happiness, and love.

Contents

Acknowledgements —— V

List of figures and charts —— XI

List of symbols —— XIII

1 Introduction —— 1
1.1 A study of the trilingual child, Y —— 2
1.2 Features of this book —— 5
1.3 English, Japanese, and Mandarin —— 6
1.4 Overview —— 8

2 Family language policy —— 11
2.1 Studies of family language policy —— 12
2.2 Factors influencing family language policy —— 14
2.3 Literacy in language socialization —— 16

3 Child agency in family language policy —— 19
3.1 Negotiating and reshaping parents' language policy and practices —— 20
3.2 The bidirectional influence between parents and children —— 22
3.3 At what point can children have an influence on family language policy? —— 23

4 An ethnographic case study —— 26
4.1 Ethnographic case studies of family language policy —— 27
4.2 Data collection —— 30
4.3 Data transcription —— 34
4.4 Data analysis —— 36
4.5 Limitations and considerations —— 38

5 A journey from being socialized to being the main socializing agent in family language policy —— 40
5.1 Overall patterns of language use in Y's family —— 40
5.2 Dynamic language practices guided by parents —— 44
5.2.1 Learning one language in one context —— 44
5.2.2 Parents' code-switching —— 50
5.2.3 Establishing a multilingual space through translanguaging —— 53

5.3	From participant to child leader in family language practices — **56**	
5.3.1	Taking advantage of different linguistic resources — **57**	
5.3.2	Code-mixing and code-switching: from unintentional to intentional — **59**	
5.3.3	Socializing in dual-lingual conversations — **66**	
5.3.4	Collaborative translating — **67**	
5.3.5	Translanguaging — **71**	

6 From parent facilitators to child manager — 75
- 6.1 Parents as language facilitators — **75**
- 6.1.1 Adopting a flexible one-parent-one-language policy — **76**
- 6.1.2 From monolingual-like discourse strategies to bilingual-like discourse strategies — **79**
- 6.2 Child as language manager — **85**
- 6.2.1 Redefining the one-parent-one-language policy — **85**
- 6.2.2 Reshaping adults' discourse strategies — **87**
- 6.2.3 Becoming a language teacher to parents — **92**
- 6.2.3.1 Pronunciation — **95**
- 6.2.3.2 Vocabulary — **98**
- 6.2.3.3 Grammar — **99**

7 Metalinguistic, cultural awareness, and evolving identity — 102
- 7.1 Parents' flexible language ideologies — **102**
- 7.1.1 Parents' attitudes to trilingualism — **103**
- 7.1.2 Parents' invisible ideologies and factors affecting them — **105**
- 7.2 Y's emerging agency: from birth to 8;1 — **108**
- 7.2.1 Assessing general language proficiency — **108**
- 7.2.2 Distinguishing relative language proficiency — **111**
- 7.2.3 Distinguishing literacy skills from language skills — **112**
- 7.2.4 Associating language ability with language practices — **113**
- 7.2.5 The development of linguistic and ethnic identity — **114**
- 7.3 Y's consistent agency: from Japan to Scotland — **118**
- 7.3.1 Language preferences — **118**
- 7.3.2 Consistency between beliefs and actions in the non-societal languages — **121**
- 7.3.3 Learning language and culture in native and non-native environments — **123**
- 7.4 Cross-linguistic influence and child agency — **125**
- 7.4.1 Language dominance — **125**
- 7.4.2 Developmental errors — **127**

7.4.3	Parental modelling —— **128**
7.4.4	Home language mode —— **128**

8 Creativity and literacy-driven language socialization —— 131
8.1   Creativity in childhood —— **131**
8.1.1   Play —— **132**
8.1.2   Artistic and musical creativity —— **134**
8.2   Creativity in literacy —— **137**
8.2.1   Acquiring three linguistic systems —— **138**
8.2.2   Making cross-linguistic associations among written forms —— **143**
8.3   Reading as a means of language socialization —— **146**
8.3.1   Becoming an independent reader —— **147**
8.3.2   Imagination and using language from books in daily speech —— **148**
8.3.3   Narrating —— **150**
8.3.4   Translating books —— **152**
8.4   Writing as a means of language socialization —— **154**
8.4.1   Guided writing —— **155**
8.4.2   Creative writing —— **156**
8.5   Adding Spanish and Japanese sign language to trilingualism —— **178**
8.6   Reading newspapers and publishing articles —— **181**
8.7   Doing research —— **183**

9   The contribution of this research —— 186

Appendix 1: Videos taken between 2;0 and 5;10 —— 191

Appendix 2: Transcription conventions in the example of two coded transcripts —— 193

References —— 195

Index —— 207

List of figures and charts

Figures

Figure 1 Learning place value (4;11) —— **72**
Figure 2 A drawing of a classic Chinese novel (4;9) —— **134**
Figure 3 A piece of artwork (5;7) —— **135**
Figure 4 Composing music (7;1) —— **136**
Figure 5 Handwriting (3;7) —— **138**
Figure 6 Handwriting (4;4) —— **139**
Figure 7 P1 homework in the Scottish school (5;2) —— **139**
Figure 8 Practicing *pīnyīn* (4;3) —— **140**
Figure 9 Practicing IPA (4;11) —— **141**
Figure 10 Practicing Chinese characters (7;0) —— **142**
Figure 11 Plotting a story with her father (3;10) —— **155**
Figure 12 The story of Peppa Pig (4;6) —— **157**
Figure 13 The story of *Huī gū niang* [Cinderella] (4;6) —— **157**
Figure 14 The story of うさぎのやま [Rabbit mountain] (4;6) —— **158**
Figure 15 The story of Snow White (7;8) —— **159**
Figure 16 A page from a chapter book (7;1) —— **160**
Figure 17 A page from a chapter book (7;1) —— **160**
Figure 18 One day of Peppa Pig (7;3) —— **161**
Figure 19 Y's diary (5;5) —— **162**
Figure 20 Y's diary (4;6) —— **163**
Figure 21 A piece of writing (6;2) —— **163**
Figure 22 Y's diary (7;9) —— **164**
Figure 23 A Mother's Day card (5;11) —— **166**
Figure 24 An invitation card (6;7) —— **166**
Figure 25 A card to her mother (6;7) —— **167**
Figure 26 A shopping list (5;5) —— **167**
Figure 27 A text message to her grandfather (7;9) —— **168**
Figure 28 An email to her father (4;11) —— **169**
Figure 29 A text message to her mother (4;11) —— **169**
Figure 30 A time schedule (5;9) —— **170**
Figure 31 A time schedule (7;1) —— **171**
Figure 32 Good or bad chart (7;2) —— **171**
Figure 33 Y's story (5;10) —— **173**
Figure 34 An argumentative essay (7;9) —— **174**
Figure 35 A piece of writing: how to pass (7;8) —— **174**
Figure 36 An English poem (7;4) —— **175**
Figure 37 A published Japanese poem (7;3) —— **176**
Figure 38 A published Japanese poem (7;11) —— **177**
Figure 39 A published Japanese poem (8;4) —— **177**
Figure 40 Teaching Spanish to her parents (6;10) —— **179**
Figure 41 Giving her mother a Spanish test (7;6) —— **179**
Figure 42 A published Japanese article (8;1) —— **180**

Figure 43 A self-administered spelling test (5;9) —— **183**
Figure 44 Research data (8;1) —— **184**
Figure 45 Research data (8;1) —— **185**

Charts

Chart 1 Y's language exposure in and outside the home —— **42**
Chart 2 Y's language exposure in the home —— **42**
Chart 3 Y's language exposure outside the home —— **43**

List of symbols

BBC	British Broadcasting Corporation
CHI	child
CLI	cross-linguistic influence
CNN	The Cable News Network
FAT	father
FLP	family language policy
GrF	grandfather
GrM	grandmother
IPA	International Phonetic Alphabet
L1	first language
LP	language policy
MOT	mother
N	noun
NHK	The Japan Broadcasting Corporation
NP	noun phrase
OPOL	one-parent-one-language
P1	Primary 1
P2	Primary 2
PP	prepositional phrase
PPV	prepositional phrase verb
SVO	subject verb object
V	verb
VPP	verb prepositional phrase
[ ]	English translation to non-English texts is shown in square brackets.
( )	general comments are shown in round brackets

1 Introduction

Due to globalization, immigrant populations growing rapidly and international marriages having become common, the language situation in linguistically mixed families is often complex. Language is an important part of child development. Language skills are invaluable for children to achieve success both in their academics and future career. This may be why more and more parents are drawn to the idea of giving their children the gift of bilingualism and multilingualism (Baker 2000). Although multilingualism has numerous advantages, raising multilingual children is believed to be more complicated than raising their monolingual peers (Shin 2017).

It is well-known that when some languages are learned and maintained at home, others are lost. The language choices negotiated in daily interaction are related to which languages are maintained or lost. Some parents assume that language acquisition is beyond their control, whilst others believe that family language activities can be planned and managed. Grosjean (1982) refers to childhood bilingualism as a conscious decision made by parents; extra efforts, patience, and persistence are generally required to ensure the acquisition and the maintenance of two or more languages.

There are many incentives for children to acquire two or more languages. One common one is that immigrant parents wish their children to acquire both the heritage language (a native, home, or ancestral language) and the societal language (a language commonly used in public life in a society). Immigrant families may employ the policies that favor a heritage language to "enable its members to maintain a connection with their past, strengthen a family bond across generations, and protect through adaptation the integrity of the family in response to external forces" (Tannenbaum 2012: 62). In this instance the home environment and parents are the best and often the only sources for transmitting the heritage language and culture to the younger generation which, otherwise, would be deemed to be lost (Fishman 1991).

How parents perceive different languages and how they negotiate the use of the totality of their linguistic repertoires directly affect their children's acquisition of each of these languages. Making decisions is especially necessary when children are involved in a family where each parent speaks a different native language (King and Fogle 2006). Thus, the linguistic characteristics of multilingual families have aroused a keen interest in the growing field of family language policy (FLP) (King, Fogle, and Logan-Terry 2008).

1.1 A study of the trilingual child, Y

I became interested in the topic of family language policy because I am part of a multilingual family, being a Chinese married to a Japanese. I met my husband in Scotland and we spoke only in English with each other in this foreign land. In addition to the fact that we were in an English-speaking country, neither of us spoke the other's native language, so English was the natural default language. When we started to live together as a family in Japan, I was granted many opportunities to learn Japanese and become trilingual. Although we continued to share our thoughts and hobbies using English in Japan, for the first time, we felt a need to establish a language policy (LP) among ourselves if we were to continue speaking the language that we used with each other in the place where we first met. This desire became even stronger when our daughter, Y, was born. We often discussed and argued about what kind of language policies would be best for her and for the whole family. In the meanwhile, I decided to go back to graduate school and research multilingual child development and family language policy.

This book is an extension of the study done for my doctoral dissertation, which was an ethnographic[1] case study of the trilingual development of Y from birth until the age of 5;10 (5 years; 10 months). I have now followed her development for eight years. We do not live very close to any of our extended family members and therefore I, my husband, and Y are always the main participants in the study. Y's Chinese grandparents visited Japan and lived together with us for about three months when she was two years old (2;6–2;9). This is the only occasion when outside participants were closely involved in this study.

Although the original focus of the doctoral research was family language policy, as Y developed, she exerted unexpected influence on our family's policies. For example, she expressed a desire to acquire Chinese language, culture, and identity, including the reading and writing of Chinese characters, when she was two years old, though my previous expectation was only for her to be able to make daily conversations in Mandarin. In addition, Y picked up International Phonetic Alphabet (IPA) at age four as she looked up words in a dictionary. She also memorized the lyrics of one version of Disney's *Frozen* song – "*Let it Go*" (a song sung by 25 singers in 25 languages)[2] as a five-year-old. This achievement gave her a lot of motivation to add Spanish to her trilingualism. What Y had done

---

[1] In FLP studies, ethnography is a research method used when a researcher studies in a real-life environment through an insider's perspective.
[2] Every singer is from a different linguistic background and the singers take turns, each singing a line of lyrics in a his/her native language.

had gone far beyond my imagination and this led me to become increasingly aware of *child agency*.[3]

Y reads and writes above grade level in English and Japanese at the present time. She has been reading Penguin Classics (e.g. *A Tale of Two Cities*[4]) and *Oxford School Shakespeare: Romeo and Juliet*[5] since she was six years old. Her favorite authors include William Shakespeare, Jane Austin, Victor Hugo, Charles Dickens, Louisa May Alcott, and Conan Doyle. In addition to classic novels, she is keen on reading about world history, particularly English, Scottish, and French history. Y also reads extensively in Japanese. She could read both fiction and non-fiction books listed for Primary 5 students and above when she was only in Primary 1. Some of the fiction and history books that she reads in Japanese overlap with the contents that she reads in English. She is critical about the facts that are retold in Japanese if they originate from English. She also started to read Japanese newspapers designed for primary and secondary school students every day from six years old. As for Mandarin, she enjoys learning from the Mandarin textbooks that are widely used in primary schools in China. She also loves Chinese storybooks and classic novels, particularly a well-known one called *Three Kingdoms*.

Y began to learn Spanish on her own at six. She has done this by using Spanish language textbooks for adult beginners, listening to the books' audio recordings, and watching their online lessons. She also reads bilingual stories written in English and Spanish and memorizes the lyrics of Spanish songs. Furthermore, she started to learn Japanese sign language from seven years old. She reads newspaper articles and books introducing this language. She also teaches the language to her parents, uses it in daily conversations (e.g. using one of her three languages and Japanese sign language at the same time when singing or talking), and makes storybooks about it at home. Her teacher reported that Y created a sign language corner in the classroom and encouraged her peers to make sign language booklets and posters together with her. Y's suggestion of using Japanese sign language together with the Japanese spoken language in routine greetings (e.g. formulaic phrases said before starting a lesson and eating school lunch) was also adopted by her teacher and classmates.

In addition to reading in her three main languages, Y also enjoys writing creatively in all of the three. She has developed writing as a hobby and a habit from four, thinking of herself as an "author" and producing at least one piece of writing

---

3 Ahearn (2001: 112) defines child agency as "socioculturally mediated capacity to act".
4 This edition uses the text as it appeared in its first serial publication in 1859.
5 *Romeo and Juliet* is a set text for KS3 in England.

every day. She published two essays and three poems in the first and second grades in a Japanese daily newspaper called *Mainichi Shougakusei Shinbun* [Daily Primary School Newspaper].[6] I was surprised to find that Y was categorizing her work into six main types and that she had prepared six notebooks, one for each type of writing: fairy tales, chapter books, poems, Y's diary, general essays, and argumentative essays. I noticed some of these notebooks when she was four and gradually found the others after she turned five.

What surprised me more was that she started to read my research diary and check the mistakes in my notes (from age three). For example, she would correct the name of a book that she had read which I had referred to, or the words that she said in a conversation. She also kept a field journal occasionally, recording her own activities and observation on her classmates' learning (from age five). Moreover, she was "proofreading" my doctoral dissertation and book manuscript in its various stages (from age four). Y's support for my research has thus been both multilingual and multimodal. In the course of the study, she developed from an infant participant to a child ethnographer, studying herself and the data on herself.

Although I myself do not feel that I have done anything exceptional or that my daughter is particularly exceptional, many people have remarked at how exceptional she is and suggested that she might be called a gifted child. I admit that Y's achievements deserve loud applause; however, what I respect in her the most are the great continuing efforts that she has made in each of her activities, as well as the positive attitude that she holds when facing both success and failure. I personally believe that it is her good nature and good habits that make her special or, somehow, "gifted", rather than her IQ. For this reason, I have not had her tested to see if she would actually be classified as gifted.

It should be pointed out that the first eight years of Y's language development cannot be considered as representative of every multilingual child: her parents came from different language backgrounds and her three acquired languages included one that was not native to either of her parents. Nevertheless, her case does offer useful, if limited, insights into the role of children and their agency in multilingual families' language policies. In attempting to understand how Y's family realized, negotiated, and modified its FLP in the process of face-to-face interaction, Spolsky's (2004) triangulated LP model as well as related literature on FLP serve as a flexible guide. Spolsky's model incorporates the analysis of three interrelated but independent components: language ideology, language practices, and language

---

6 The newspaper's main readers are primary school students and their parents.

management. However, rather than looking only at the top-down decisions and actions taken by parents, the present study highlights the child's bottom-up efforts and reveals a set of agentive strategies that she has used to shape family interactions and language policies.

1.2 Features of this book

This is a case study of a multilingual child's near simultaneous language and literacy development and her parents' efforts to accommodate and support her from birth to age eight in their family environment. The child's learning processes and her family's language use are shaped by her specific interests and skills related to language and literacy acquisition. The study is unusual in four major ways.

First, what makes Y unique and an especially interesting case is her early literacy and the ways in which she used literacy as a springboard for further language development, as well as seeing herself as "teacher" and "researcher" in her family. While research on FLP originally tended to focus on explicit and overt planning in relation to language use within the home domain among family members (Curdt-Christiansen 2013a), recent approaches attend to home language[7] and, less frequently, literacy practices (King and Lanza 2019). The present study clearly furthers this extension of the field.

Second, it is unusual in its examination of the impact of child agency on family language policy. As noted by Gafaranga (2010) and Gyogi (2014), children sometimes challenge and reshape adults' choices and strategies; however, such agentive behavior has not been widely addressed for nursery-age children. Y's powerful agency in her language, especially literacy, did not only influence the parental decisions, but also enabled her to make new language policies and become a leader in the family. The family's language policies thus shifted in response to the child. The present study can be seen as a further development of the existing FLP studies. It offers new perspectives on the research on language socialization; that is, children switch from mere participants to family language policy co-makers and co-managers.

Third, longitudinal case studies on infant trilingualism in the language constellation of English, Japanese, and Mandarin cannot be found in the research on FLP. What is more, the family's lingua franca, English, was a language non-native to her parents and a foreign language in the Japanese society where Y was mainly raised. Nevertheless, she was able to reach a high level of competency in English,

---

7 Home language is a language that is not commonly used in public life in the region where a family lives. In the present study, English and Mandarin are Y's home languages.

speaking this language with age-appropriate fluency from the age of two, reading both fiction and non-fiction books from three, and writing meaningful sentences, paragraphs, and essays before she turned five. Y's communication skills and academic abilities in English were confirmed and further developed during the year that she was educated in Scotland.

Fourth, multilingual development occurring in contrasting sociolinguistic environments (Japan and Scotland in the present study) has been taken up little, if at all, in research of a similar nature. For the first four years and ten months (0–4;10), the family lived in their home country, the predominantly monolingual and monocultural society of Japan. Then for one year (4;10–5;10), they relocated to Scotland, an English dominant society where Y was a preschooler for four months and then a first grader for eight months.[8] They returned to Japan when Y was 5;10. This seemingly short Scottish stay proved to be significant to the development of Y's linguistic, cognitive, and social abilities. The sojourn is also noteworthy because the data from these two societies illustrate both continuing family language policies and policies that varied according to the situation. Moreover, the influence from the two divergent cultures on Y and her parents' thinking and behaving cannot be ignored.

1.3 English, Japanese, and Mandarin

Y was born and raised in Japan, but while her father is Japanese, her mother is Chinese. Her parents use English to communicate with each other and with Y when the three of them are together. In addition, the father speaks English to her when they are alone together, but the mother speaks Mandarin to her in this kind of situation. Japanese is also used in the home, but in specific situations, such as in her reading, writing, and learning time. In this way, Y grew up simultaneously acquiring English, Japanese, and Mandarin from birth.

These three languages are from different language families and have radically different typologies: English is from the Indo-European family, Mandarin is from the Sino-Tibetan family, and Japanese is a language isolate. English is the third most-spoken native language in the world, after Mandarin and Spanish, and the most widely accepted and learned second and foreign language, as well as a common lingua franca between speakers from different language backgrounds whose native languages are mutually unintelligible.

---

8 Y's father had a sabbatical year in Scotland.

Although Japanese is not clearly related to any other extant language, modern Japanese incorporates a large number of loanwords, the majority of which come from English and are written in *katakana* phonetic script.[9] Moreover, English plays an important role in the Japanese education system. From 2020, the Japanese government lowered the age of English education in primary schools, making "English activity" classes compulsory for third and fourth graders and a required exam subject for fifth and sixth graders. In fact, many Japanese parents start sending their children to English cram schools even before their children enter primary school. Nevertheless, although there was a great deal of implicit English in Y's environment while growing up, English conversations were rarely heard in her neighborhood and fluent English speakers were rare among her acquaintances.

Y's mother, the researcher, is Chinese and grew up in an area where a southeastern Chinese dialect is spoken, although she also speaks Mandarin Chinese. As China's economic and political power have strengthened in recent years, its official language, Mandarin, has come to play an important role on the international stage. Unlike English, the Chinese logographic writing system is independent from its speech system. Therefore, a child's literacy skills in Mandarin need to be developed separately from acquiring the spoken form of the language.

Although the Japanese language is historically and structurally completely different from Chinese, its orthography and lexicon are deeply influenced by Chinese. In fact, the Japanese language did not originally have its own writing system; instead, it borrowed and adapted written characters from Chinese (referred to as *kanji*, or Chinese characters, in Japanese). Until the late ninth century, the written Japanese language used only *kanji*. After that, two Japanese syllabic writing systems, *hiragana* and *katakana*,[10] were developed. Although both syllabaries were adapted from Chinese characters, unlike *kanji*, the *kana* symbols[11] are used to convey phonetic sounds. *Hiragana* is normally the first form of writing Japanese children learn and can be used to write complete stories. *Kanji* symbols are inserted into sentences written in *hiragana* to make the meaning clearer. *Katakana* tends to be reserved for onomatopoeia and loanwords. Nowadays, Japanese incorporates a great number of loanwords adapted from English as well as from other European languages, and these are usually written in the *katakana* phonetic script. As a result, Japanese is written in a mix of *kanji* and the two types of *kana* symbols.

---

9 *Katakana* and *hiragana* are Japanese syllabic writing systems. *Katakana*, *hiragana*, and *kanji* (Chinese characters) are the three components of the overall Japanese writing system.
10 See Footnote 9.
11 *Kana* symbols include *hiragana* symbols and *katakana* symbols.

Nevertheless, the pronunciation of each Chinese character in Mandarin and Japanese is different, the meaning varies, and the form is simplified to different levels. Even though their scripts are related, the ability to read Mandarin does not translate into the ability to read Japanese, or vice versa. Thus, the child, Y, at the center of the present study acquired literacy skills in three different languages with three different scripts.

1.4 Overview

This book takes a close look at how the trilingual child, Y, acquired her three first languages from birth to eight years old in two different sociolinguistic environments (Japan and Scotland). Chapter 1 is an introductory chapter which provides an overall vision of the study. It introduces the trilingual child, Y, and her family. It also explains the background and uniqueness of the study. It sketches out the basic context for each of the three languages used.

Chapter 2 presents a literature review of one of the two key concepts relevant to this research – family language policy. Within this field, it overviews the studies of child multilingual acquisition and analyzes the factors influential in the making of a family's language policies. It highlights the role of literacy and suggests that literacy activities can provide new contexts and patterns for language socialization, as well as reverse the social relationships among family members.

Chapter 3 centers on the other key concept – child agency. It reviews how children negotiate and reshape parents' rules and sometimes their opinions through actual practices. It explains how and to what degree parents can actually be influenced by their children. This provides evidence for bidirectional impact among family members and, moreover, the growing power of children over parents when their agencies are exercised and accommodated.

Chapter 4 focuses on the methodology that guides the present work. It describes how the data were collected, presented, and analyzed in this longitudinal ethnographic case study. A large amount of data were collected in order to provide a thorough account of the family's language and literacy practices.

Chapters 5 through 7 illustrate Y's journey from being the object of socialization to being the main socializing agent in the family with regard to the three aspects of FLP – family language ideologies, family language practices, and family language management. What is unusual about Y and her family's language policies is not her acquisition of three languages or the strategies her parents used to support that acquisition (since many of these are similar to those described in other studies), but rather a shift from a parent-directional focus to a child-directional focus. To be more specific, Chapter 5 begins with an overview of Y's language use, and the practices organized for her by her parents over time and space before the age of three. It then describes how, while parents and other input sources acted as language models, Y understood and cooperated in the parents' expected ways of using languages, but eventually came to socialize them into new practices that she had developed. Since these language use patterns and strategies did arise from her parents' interests and experience in the first place, it can be seen that the family socialization was bidirectional.

Chapter 6 looks at the influence of child agency on the aspect of family language management. While her parents initially directed the family's language choice using the one-parent-one-language (OPOL) policy and a variety of discourse strategies, Y challenged the parents' authority with her emerging ideologies concerning language and identity, and eventually took a lead in family socialization. Examples where Y directed the language choice and where she monitored and corrected her parents' language use, as well as of her teaching different languages to her parents, are included.

Chapter 7 goes into the concept of language ideology of Y and her parents and examines its relationships with their language choice and language use. The parents' attitudes to their three languages and to child multilingualism, as well as to their harmonious family bonds, are first taken up. The chapter then discusses Y's metalinguistic awareness, her evolving conceptions of language ability and language choice, and how these ideas fit into her dynamic orientations towards the different languages in her linguistic repertoire. The chapter attempts to explain Y's agentive behavior through the lens of her developmental psychology. Change in the parents' way of thinking and acting is regarded as a result of the influence of Y's agentic behaviour on parents.

Chapter 8 is a discussion related to a new trend in FLP in the matter of literacy-driven socialization. The chapter describes Y's precocious literacy and the way it is seen to have influenced her language development, her agency, and her family's language policy. Y's special interest and skills in written language shaped her learning processes and communication that she had with her other family members. This is different than what we see in most studies of multilingual children.

Finally, Chapter 9 centers on the contribution of this research. It argues that children can use their specific skills to direct their own learning processes and take the lead in the family's language and literacy-driven practices. It also emphasizes the importance of a harmonious environment and intimate intergenerational bonds for children's language and cognitive development. These new features that emerged from the present study should contribute to our understanding of future research on family language policy, especially in respect of child agency and literacy.

It is expected that this book will be enjoyed by readers who are specially interested in early childhood language development, as well as by those who are simply interested in the three languages involved in the study. The book endeavors to exhibit how children's creativity can be supported (or not supported) by the learning environments in different sociocultural milieus. It is hoped that Y's long journey as a trilingual from her birth to the age of six, and then into polyglotism (adding Spanish and Japanese sign language) after that age, will offer insights for parents and teachers of multilingual children.

I would now, in Chapter 2 and Chapter 3 respectively, like to build on my introduction by reviewing previous research on family language policy and child agency. It would be possible, however, for readers who are more interested in the case study itself (rather than the background research) to skip directly to Chapter 4.

2 Family language policy

Most people do not live in a purely monolingual community. We need to consider who speaks what to whom where and when in order to make appropriate language choices in our daily lives (Fishman 1965). Choices about why, when, and how to use a language variety are subject to the specific rules of a society. Language policy (LP) is all about such choices of language (Spolsky 2004). LP may be the choice of a specific sound, a lexical term, or a speech style; it may also be selection of a specific language or a language variety (Spolsky 2004).

Language policies are normally made by an individual speaker or a group of speakers who are recognized as members of a particular speech community, or whose authority controls or influences other individuals or groups (Spolsky 2004). Language policies are made on the basis of rule-governed patterns, such as beliefs and behavior (Spolsky 2004). Spolsky (2004) views the concept of LP as being composed of three interrelated but independent components – language ideology, language practices, and language management.

It is not easy to define the language policies of a speech community (McCarty 2011). They can be made explicitly "in the formal and organized management" or be decided implicitly "in the informal and simple management" of language (Spolsky 2004: 217). Sometimes an explicitly stated policy may not be entirely implemented and an implicit policy may contradict the stated policy of a community (Spolsky 2004). Spolsky (2004: 8) points out that no matter whether a policy is explicitly established by the authorities, or formal or written, or informal or unwritten, its effect on language practices "is not guaranteed or presumed to be consistent" if no efforts have been made to enforce it.

Although studies of language policy tend to focus on the activities of the central state and local communities, events in families where language shift occurs cannot be ignored (Spolsky 2012). As a general trend, languages of lesser power in a community tend to give way to more powerful languages (Spolsky 2009). Language choice across generations, or intergenerational transmission, is seen to be a crucial factor in language shift (Fishman 1970). Language shift is often the norm in family practices because it is rather difficult to establish language rules in immigrant families, despite parents' strong desires to do so (Spolsky 2009). Caldas (2012) notes that most parental decisions tend not to be strategically plotted; instead, they are made naturally, determined by circumstances beyond the family's control. Some government policies may influence the language choices of families, while others have few practical effects on FLP if they contradict the interests of families (Spolsky and Shohamy 1999).

Early investigations on generational transmission in immigrant families generally explored effective macro level factors such as the influences of politics and the community; recently, more studies in this field have started to focus on different types of multilingual families and attend to micro level factors such as parents' discourse strategies in response to children's language use (Lanza and Curdt-Christiansen 2018). Family provides an immediate context for studying the nature of language policy (Spolsky 2012). Shin (2017) notes that children who become bilingual and maintain bilingualism are often from families where particular languages are spoken as a matter of policy. Family has thus come to be viewed as an invaluable and independent domain relevant to language policy, and family language policies have come to be studied as an entity in themselves (King, Fogle, and Logan-Terry 2008; Siiner, Hult, and Kupisch 2018; Spolsky 2012).

2.1 Studies of family language policy

Research on FLP describes explicit and overt planning in relation to language use within the home domain among family members (Curdt-Christiansen 2013a). It provides a frame for examining "the child-caretaker interactions, parental language ideologies and child language development" (King and Fogle 2018: 316). The interdisciplinary field of inquiry into FLP joins two independent fields – language policy and child language development – and encompasses topics from language policy and language socialization to literacy studies and child language acquisition (Fogle 2012; Lanza 2007; Smith-Christmas 2014). Drawing on the LP model, studies of FLP combine sociolinguistic, anthropological and language socialization approaches to link family with societal institutions (Curdt-Christiansen 2013a). Studying FLP leads to a deeper understanding of the complex and dynamic processes involved in family language planning and management (Spolsky 2009).

There are three significant foci of FLP study. First, family language ideology describes the values that family members attach to languages and language use. Language ideology is the driving force behind language practices and language management. Second, family language practices are what members actually do with a language, which includes the varieties and patterns of language use that are established in the context of particular language ideologies. Third, family language management refers to the efforts that members make to modify the language practices and language ideologies of others (King, Fogle, and Logan-Terry 2008). Such efforts focus to a large extent on parents' authority in planning and shaping children's activities and language use, and less on children's own perspectives and actions.

Although FLP research has existed for just a couple of decades or so as a defined research field, the study of bi- and multilingual development at the family level can be seen as dating back more than a century (King and Fogle 2018). The development of FLP can be seen to have begun with two separate diary studies, those of Ronjat (1913) and Leopold (1939–1949) (as cited in Barron-Hauwaert 2004). Based on these two classic diary studies by linguist parents, much work in this field took issue with psycholinguistic questions related to child language acquisition, such as those of language differentiation and language mixing, which are now regarded as natural behavior among multilingual speakers (Fantini 1985; Saunders 1988; Taeschner 1983). Taking Döpke's (1992) and Lanza's (1997) studies as examples, although neither of the researchers explicitly used the term "family language policy", these two milestone studies and their discussion contributed to our understanding of how bilingual practices and child language development are shaped by family language policies.

Researchers continue to focus on the role of parents in child language acquisition and on language production in bilingual and, to a lesser extent, trilingual settings (De Houwer 1999, 2009; Hoffmann 2001, 2010; Lanza 2004, 2007; Stavans and Hoffmann 2015). Questions regarding the influence of parental ideologies and parent-child interactions on child language outcomes have been investigated (Chevalier 2015; Okita 2002). For example, the field seeks to understand why some children grow up to be bilinguals and others monolinguals, and how this is related to the ways in which parents promote or neglect children's use of a particular language (Curdt-Christiansen 2013b).

FLP emerged more recently as a formal field of enquiry, using a more sociolinguistic approach, with an emphasis on "the balance between and use of languages within the family unit" rather than targeting children's language use alone (King and Fogle 2013: 172). Studies on FLP have aimed to "draw clear causal links across ideologies, practices, and outcomes" (King 2016: 731). Studies have also examined issues of multilingual repertoires, meaning-making, lived experiences, child agency, and identity constructions in multilingual families (Lanza and Curdt-Christiansen 2018; King and Lanza 2019). Two trends in current FLP research have been identified. The first trend is paying attention to demographic changes "seen through a lens that draws on notions such as migration, mobility and transnationalism to better understand multilingual practices" (Gomes 2018: 57). The second trend in FLP research shows a shift from focusing on the connections between language input and its outcomes to investigating the contexts in which family communication takes place (Gomes 2018).

The family has traditionally been considered a private domain that contains sets of relationships; it implies that there are parameters for family members to use languages within the space of the home (Fishman 1991). Lately, the notion of the family has been expanded from the focus on the nuclear family, which exists in the home space, to include extended formations where family members from across the world are involved in daily multilingual communication (Van Mensel and De Meulder 2021). Studies of families in different contexts have been conducted in order to present a more holistic understanding of how families manage languages (Mensel and Meulder 2021). For instance, in an examination of a transnational family in Ireland with a strong pro-Polish FLP, Smith-Christmas (2021a) illustrates how the autochthonous Irish language acts as a neutral, third space and provides a means for the parents to mitigate the potential language shift caused by the power of the children's stronger language, English. Using a third voice is another strategy that is adopted in multilingual family talk (Van Mensel 2018). In this strategy, a family member speaks to another member with the voice of a third party, typically the child's (Van Mensel 2018). This is referred to as *ventriloquizing* by Tannen (2004). The third voice may come from any object and this object may be given a role in a scenario, such as during play, reading, or writing.

2.2 Factors influencing family language policy

Even though family is "the most common and inescapable basis of mother tongue transmission, bonding and stabilization" (Fishman 1991: 94), it is not an enclosed neutral space but rather is "porous, open to influences and interests from other broader social forces and institutions" (Canagarajah 2008: 171). Consciously developing an FLP is often associated with social prestige, educational empowerment, and economic advantages (Curdt-Christiansen 2016). It has been pointed out that families may face various challenges in bringing up children multilingually – negative effects from government language policies and conflicts between language planning and sociocultural identity to name a few (Curdt-Christiansen 2016). Family language practices thus operate at a local, micro scale in interaction and language policies at a societal, macro scale (Curdt-Christiansen 2013a).

Political decisions on national language policies and language education policies appear to have an essential influence on the family's choice of a particular language to use at home. However, research before the 1990s did not consider the connection between these policies and children's multilingualism (Curdt-Christiansen 2016). While some parents believe that maintaining a heritage language is a right and an obligation, others see it as an obstacle in gaining access to a new society (Skutnabb-Kangas 2000). In a study of 20 Chinese-English bilingual families in Singapore, Curdt-Christiansen (2014a) found that parents' ideologies and practices in the heritage language, Chinese, were closely related to the school's bilingual language education policy (i.e. English used as the medium of instruction and Chinese taught as a language subject). Although Chinese parents appreciated and believed in the cultural benefits of their children's Chinese development, educational achievement in English was highly promoted and therefore parents unconsciously held lower expectations for the children's Chinese language proficiency (Curdt-Christiansen 2014a). The language ideologies of these parents are described as power-inflected and their language practices as value-laden (Curdt-Christiansen 2016).

Curdt-Christiansen (2016) also discusses how family members translated their beliefs into policies in a Chinese, a Malay, and an Indian family in Singapore, identifying inconsistencies between adults' language ideologies and family language practices. Bilingual education policy in Singapore recognizes both the heritage languages and English as the country's official languages; however, only English is used as the medium of instruction in school education (Curdt-Christiansen 2016). The author (Curdt-Christiansen 2016) explained that although maintaining the bond with the heritage language and culture was strongly desired in all three families, the family members' preference for another language was convincingly confirmed in their everyday practices. Analysis of these clear preferences revealed that family policies were guided by the instrumental value of English due to the educational opportunities it provided. In contrast, the heritage language had symbolic value for cultural maintenance. Examples of adult–child exchanges in these families showed that the efforts made by the adults in communication were incongruent with what they professed to believe (Curdt-Christiansen 2016).

The value of a language is also enhanced by the economic advantage it brings and the higher social status of its speakers. This is evident in Curdt-Christiansen's (2009) study of ten Chinese families in Québec, Canada as related to their FLP for Chinese, English, and French. The author (Curdt-Christiansen 2009) found that these Chinese parents' spontaneous and invisible planning was sometimes contrary to the state's visible policies. Although French was recognized as the only official language of the province, the parents shared beliefs that English is a lingua franca in the world, making it important to learn in order to achieve socioeconomic goals, that French is a basic socializing tool in Québec, and that the influence of Chinese is increasing in the world's economy and politics. Acknowledging the socioeconomic opportunities and impact associated with each of these three languages greatly influenced these parents' decisions and subsequent actions to rear their children trilingually (Curdt-Christiansen 2009).

Similarly, Ren and Hu (2013) studied the language practices of Chinese-English bilingual families in Singapore and suggested that the members' positive attitudes toward the heritage language (Chinese) practices were related to the growing economic power of China. Also, in an ethnographic study of three diasporic Chinese families living in Britain, Zhu and Li (2016) found the families' positive attitudes toward Mandarin education were partly driven by the parents' expectations of the economic power of Mandarin skills in terms of their children's future career.

It should be noted that the economic strength of a family can ensure access to private learning. Elite families have the economic and educational resources to establish a language policy that allows them to value and practice their languages (Stavans 2012). For example, Ethiopian mothers in Israel used their economic resources to provide for complementary literacy practice in the heritage language (Stavans 2012). Curdt-Christiansen (2014b) also discussed how Chinese-English families in Singapore deployed available economic resources, for example, by sending their children to private classes to learn Chinese.

In contrast, families that do not have ample educational and economic resources are more likely to abandon the heritage language in favor of the societal language for the sake of children's scholastic and social success (Stavans 2012). The socioeconomic opportunities and the privileged social status tied to English language proficiency are particularly appreciated. As a result, language shift from the heritage languages towards English has been observed in linguistic minority families (Curdt-Christiansen 2016).

2.3 Literacy in language socialization

A language variety is hard to maintain without resources in its written form. Saunders (1988: 198) notes that "it is psychologically important for children to be aware that their parents' language is also, like the majority language, a fully-fledged medium of communication, with its own literature, its own writing conventions, etc." Some parents have a strong desire for their children to achieve a high level of literacy skills in the socially and academically valued languages, while also expecting them to acquire their heritage language (Curdt-Christiansen 2016). Despite parents' expectations and efforts, literacy skills are normally first built in the societal language under the systematic and institutional education implemented in mainstream schools. Thus, formal schooling that offers instruction in all of a family's languages is probably the most effective environment in which to rear multilingual and multiliterate children; however, it is not available to everyone (Baker 2000; Caldas 2012). Early literacy, however, can be developed in the majority and the minority language before children start any formal schooling (Caldas 2012). As pointed out by Mason (1984), children begin to write at the same time as they begin to recognize words. Multiliteracy development thus goes beyond the school context and school-based programs, and how language and literacy are practiced in the family domain needs to be understood (Fishman 2001).

Multilingual families adopt various strategies to help their children to learn non-societal languages at home. Applying the OPOL policy, each parent can help the child read and write in his/her native language. Collier (1992) claims that the stronger a child's academic ability in their heritage language, the faster they will learn the society's majority language. Even when children become bilingual consecutively, their reading proficiency in the first language will transfer to some degree to the second (Cummins 1991). Nevertheless, it is normal to expect a steadier increase in a child's reading and writing skills in the majority language once they are enrolled in a local school (Noguchi 1996a).

A so-called literacy event is "any occasion in which a piece of writing is integral to the nature of participants' interactions and their interpretive processes" (Schieffelin and Ochs 1986: 93). Heath (1983) described how young children in the setting of "mainstream" families were routinely involved in literacy events as part of daily interaction with adults. Activities, such as reading and writing, are not taken as a set of technical skills, but "a way of taking meaning from the environment" (Schieffelin and Ochs 1986: 49). Kenner (2004) finds that literacy practice through reading and writing is an ideological practice which reflects an individual's values, beliefs, and culture. For example, children from Chinese, Arabic, and Spanish immigrant families in the UK, who studied different writing systems using different resources at home, expressed "their sense of living in multiple social and cultural worlds" (Kenner 2004: 118).

Children's first experiences in literacy are usually through interacting with story and picture books with their caregivers. Story reading is an interactive negotiation during which sequences of interaction are required and ways of organizing narrative are displayed. The relationship between speaking and writing is also a consideration in oral language use and literacy, that is, the ways in which competencies in one mode can facilitate the development of interest and skill in the other mode (Schieffelin and Ochs 1986). It has been found, for example, that young children within specific social relationships carry out meaningful communication through writing letters and dialogue journals (Schieffelin and Ochs 1986).

It is important to consider literacy activities in relation to a wide range of social and cultural skills and knowledge, and also to focus on the consequences of literacy for the structure of child/adult relationships and individual identity issues (Schieffelin and Ochs 1986). It is also important to recognize that the structure of literacy events is closely related to the form, function, and content of the discourse itself (Schieffelin and Ochs 1986). It is best to think about socialization for literacy in the home situation within a larger family language policy framework concerned with how children and caretakers are presented with information, and the modes of negotiating or interpreting it.

To conclude, this chapter examined a concept of family language policy that views language socialization as primarily deterministic, unidirectional, and goal-oriented toward adulthood (Vygotsky 1986). In other words, the language ideologies and strategies of parents generally determine children's language use and impact their language development. However, parent-child interactions are not entirely controlled by parents in either the domestic or the wider social context (Mishina-Mori 2011). Although parents are commonly the authoritative members who make rules and policies, the desires of children may be accommodated as well. Children have their own opinions about language and language use which can influence parents' opinions and decisions. Children can also make their own rules and monitor parents' language use through literacy routines. As the role of literacy in the research on FLP has come to be addressed more and more, the child agentic acquisition of literacy skills, including independent reading and creative writing skills, have been influential in reshaping the conceptual framework of FLP. Close attention needs to be paid to the new patterns of social relationships and interactions in literacy socialization related to child agency in order to understand the processes of language learning in the family setting.

3 Child agency in family language policy

Language socialization is the process through which children and novices are socialized through language to use language appropriately and meaningfully (Schieffelin and Ochs 1986). However, it is not a static, top-down process of knowledge transmission but rather dynamic and dialectic (Goodwin 2006). While many socializing situations involve adults as experts and youths as novices, the reverse is also commonplace, especially as rapidly emerging technologies show the inadequacy of existing ways of thinking (Ochs and Schieffelin 2011). Children and youths are no longer passive recipients of sociocultural knowledge but rather active contributors to the meaning and outcome of interactions (Ochs and Schieffelin 2011). Family socialization is thus no longer seen as a unidirectional process led by parents but an interactional network of cooperative intervention. All parties involved in socializing practices, including parents and children, are agents in the formation of competence (Ochs and Schieffelin 2011).

Not only do children learn languages and values from adults, they also exert influence on the adults' language practices (Gafaranga 2010; King and Fogle 2013). This socioculturally mediated capacity to make sense of the environment, initiate change, and make choices is referred to as agency (Ahearn 2001). Child agency appears in multiple forms, is flexible, and is contextual (Fogle 2012). It is usually exercised in two dimensions: *sense of agency* (a child's agentic feelings for general or specific contexts) and *behavior of agency* (a child's agentic behavior as participation or action, or deliberate non-participation or non-action) (Mercer 2012).

Traditionally, child agency was assumed to be minimal and its role remained largely unexamined (Luykx 2005). Recent contributions on the role of child agency have extended the scope of FLP research from focusing solely on one-directional, parent-dominated influence to bidirectional, mutual parent-child influence on child language development (Fogle 2012; Fogle and King 2013; Gafaranga 2010; Gyogi 2014). This chapter emphasizes the agentive role of children in language socialization. It looks at the insights gained from child agency studies within the larger field of FLP. It attempts to illustrate the significant influence that children assert on parents' thoughts and behavior as well as on the family's language policies and practices.

3.1 Negotiating and reshaping parents' language policy and practices

Although parents may decide on and demand the use of a certain language, actual family language use patterns may not match the explicit policies put out by the parents. Children are active agents in forming and negotiating parents' policies and they influence parents' socialization practices to different extents (Luykx 2005). Fogle and King (2013) identify three aspects of agency in parent-child discourse: children's resistance strategies used to shape the conversational context and negotiate the communication codes, children's enactments of family external ideologies about race and language, and children's metalinguistic comments. Lanza (1997), in her study of parental discourse strategies, explains how some parents accepted the responses from the child made in a different language, and how some even gave up their own language and switched to the child's preferred or dominant language. Lanza (1997) thus argues that children's attitudes of rejection towards a parent's language could change the parent's language choice.

Fogle (2012) also focused on children's resistance to parental language policy, categorizing three different types of contestations made by children to resist adults' language choices: not responding, interacting using high frequency "Wh-" questions, and influencing the language choice of adults. A study conducted by King and Logan-Terry (2008) showed how an English-Spanish two-year-old's response to the mother's passive discourse strategies were acknowledged by the mother. When the bilingual mother started with an open-ended question in Spanish, the child did not respond. The mother then moved to an either-or question. When the child eventually answered in English, the mother confirmed the answer using the child's language ("Okay") and continued the conversation in that language. The mother eventually switched to the child's code following the child's strategic replies, which nudged the mother's response toward the child's preferred language in a step-by-step process (King and Logan-Terry 2008).

Fogle (2012) reports that children in transnational adoptive families (American parents and Russian children) negotiated family language practices by initiating metalinguistic questions about the target language. Those children were reluctant to use their parents' language and hence persuaded adoptive parents to accommodate their strategies. In this way, the children constructed part of their language identities as well as social identities as members of transnational families.

Moreover, children implicitly or explicitly negotiate and reshape family members' language choices (Fogle and King 2013). In negotiating language use, children always need to think about the relationship between a language and the context in which it is embedded (Lanza 1997). There is interplay between societal and familial factors in the negotiations. For example, in a study examining the relation between cultural norms and bilingual practices in overseas Asian families, Zhu (2008) reported that Chinese children in the UK strategically switched codes with parents and siblings to negotiate, mediate and manage conflicts over cultural issues and family relations. Similarly, in an ethnographic study of Ethiopian and Columbian refugee families in New Zealand, Revis (2016) identified five strategies employed by the children to negotiate languages and culture with their parents. Revis (2016) considers, on the one hand, how children might be influenced by the language ideologies that their parents have absorbed from the dominant society and the language policies and practices that were specific to the parents; on the other hand, children might promote change in the language and cultural practices of the parents.

It has been found that children's ideologies related to the higher status of a language may result in their contestation of parents' policies. One example is shown in Gafaranga's (2010) study of the interactions between parents and children of Kinyarwanda-French families in Belgium. Gafaranga (2010) explained how the children negotiated their parents' language practices, their agency leading their parents to change their language choice from Kinyarwanda (the heritage language) to French (the dominant language in the society). Gafaranga (2010) reported that these parents were persuaded to accommodate their children's preferred language, French; when the parents did not conform to the child's choice, a parallel conversation would be carried out in each party's preferred language. Gafaranga (2010: 264–266) thus highlighted the importance of child agency, arguing that through *medium requests* (asking for translations of parents' Kinyarwanda to the child's preferred language, French), family members "talked language shift into being" (adopting French as the main medium of family interactions).

Moreover, children have been found to make planned decisions, give deliberate performances, and change adults' multilingual practices by redefining their language beliefs (Fogle 2012; Gafaranga 2010; Gyogi 2014). In an example focusing on the second language socialization in adoptive families, Fogle (2012) explored how parental ideologies and family language practices were negotiated and constructed in everyday activities that were influenced by their children's emerging self-motivated learning behavior and strategies.

Similarly, in a study of two English-Japanese children negotiating and constructing bilingual space at home in London, Gyogi (2014) found that the children were aware of their own bilingual identities and were able to give deliberate performances to resist their parents' monolingual policies. For instance, one child resisted her mother's monolingual Japanese use and flexibly used English and Japanese with her mother. Gyogi (2014) took the view that the girl's negative agency was not a complete contestation of the mother's language beliefs since she consistently used Japanese when addressing the Japanese researcher. The other child in this study used English to construct her social identity as a good English learner and negotiated the mother-child relationship, taking into account the mother's attitude toward English (Gyogi 2014). Through this positive agency, the second girl seemed to provide herself with further flexibility to use both languages (Gyogi 2014). The results suggest that the responses of both children to their mothers' policies were not controlled by the mothers' beliefs but were "an exercise of children's agency through contestation, negotiation and redefinition" of the adults' beliefs (Gyogi 2014: 749).

Studies that attend to family language practices thus show that there is a considerable "gap between the parents' role as language planners and managers who are expected to insist on minority language use and the reality within authentic families" (Schwartz 2010: 185). Child agency and children's language practices therefore constitute a crucial area in examining how family language policies are implemented or transformed in family interaction (Fogle and King 2013).

3.2 The bidirectional influence between parents and children

The influence between parents and children in a relationship context is bidirectional (Kuczynski, Pitman, Ta-Young, and Harach 2016). Parents may see children as a part of their living environment. Engaging in a long-term parent-child relationship constantly exposes parents to the direct and indirect influence of their children. Therefore, people who become parents and have children in their environment present a different developmental trajectory than those who do not have the responsibilities of parenthood (Kuczynski, Pitman, Ta-Young, and Harach 2016). It has been found that involvement in the child nurturing and socialization processes presents parents with challenges, emotional experiences, and opportunities for problem-solving and self-reflection (Kuczynski, Pitman, Ta-Young, and Harach 2016).

Why do parents, who have more power in the family, comply with their children's requests and change their own way of thinking and behaving in response to the children's behavior? One explanation is that an interdependent, close parent-child relationship mediates the influence between parents and children (Kuczynski and De Mol 2015). In other words, parents and children interpret and respond to each other and children's responses matter to parents on an emotional level, which in turn make parents receptive and vulnerable to influence from their children (Kuczynski 2003).

The concept of child agency offers another explanation for parents' receptivity to influence from their children. Children tend to use two particular strategies, persuasion and coercion, to try to get their parents to comply with their wishes

(Kuczynski, Pitman, Ta-Young, and Harach 2016). Undoubtedly, children are often skillful enough at persuasion to get their parents to cooperate in fulfilling their wishes. For example, a child persuades her mother to stay at the park longer or allow her to go to bed later than usual to watch a special TV program. In such transactions, children may successfully persuade their parents to change their behavior, suggesting that children's influence has implications for the development of the adults (Kuczynski, Pitman, Ta-Young, and Harach 2016). However, the degree of influence of a child's verbal and non-verbal cues largely depends on the parent's interpretation of the importance of the child's request through a transactional process (Kuczynski, Pitman, Ta-Young, and Harach 2016). Parents who appreciate their children's independent ways of thinking and actions are generally comfortable being influenced by their children and see children as actors and agents (Kuczynski, Pitman, Ta-Young, and Harach 2016).

In addition to children's communication skills, another explanation for why children persuade and coerce their parents into changing their behavior might be that parents perceive their receptivity to their children's request as a means of promoting *parent-child intimacy* – a mutual, positive, and open communicative relationship (Oliphant and Kuczynski, 2011). Overall, it has been found that mothers tend to receive more direct influence from their children than fathers, in that mothers are more engaged with child-rearing and the mother-child relationship tends to be more intimate (Oliphant and Kuczynski 2011). By maintaining an intimate and interdependent relationship with children, adults are also provided with challenges as well as opportunities to improve themselves as grown-ups (Kuczynski, Pitman, Ta-Young, and Harach 2016). In this way, child-adult collaborative development can be realized.

3.3 At what point can children have an influence on family language policy?

There has been a great deal of discussion about what agency means and how humans achieve agency in various sociolinguistic environments (Bourdieu 1997). Several different ways of treating child agency are found in childhood studies; these include taking the view that "children have agency" as a mantra within the field, as well as the tendency to interpret agency as "a mere expression of 'resistance' or 'resourcefulness'" (Abebe 2019: 8), and as accepting ambiguity in the notion of "competence" within discussion of child agency (Smith-Christmas 2020).

Asymmetries in power pervade socializing interactions; even when children challenge adult authority in the seemingly neutral sphere of play, adults tend to come out as winners, in that they are stronger in the parent-child tie or more in the know (Ochs and Schieffelin 2011). Smith-Christmas (2021a) explains how, in Irish negotiation, the power/solidarity equilibrium within the family and, albeit more indirectly, the constant renegotiation of policies come into being. Smith-Christmas (2020) argues that the relationships between children and their caregivers need to be framed in terms of "interdependence" when examining child agency exerted on practices over time and space. Based on Kuczynski's (2003: 9) definition of agency as "individuals as actors with the ability to make sense of the environment, initiate change, and make choices" and Fogle's (2012: 41) key question of "at what point can children have an influence on the construction of family language policies?", we need to think about how children's linguistic choices in family socialization can be considered agentive. Smith-Christmas (2020) takes four dimensions into account when conceptualizing child agency in FLP: compliance regimes, linguistic norms, linguistic competence, and *generational positioning* (generational order).

As an illustration, Smith-Christmas (2020) explains how the caregiver reported in Lanza's (1997) study may pretend not to understand the child if the child uses the societal language; the caregiver may also provide the equivalent word in the home language. Such compliance – speaking the minority language – may lead to certain linguistic norms, which are conceptualized as the shared expectations that interlocutors have when they interact with each other (Smith-Christmas 2020).

However, Smith-Christmas (2020) specifies that a key question in building a compliance/non-compliance paradigm is to determine at what point linguistic choices influenced by a norm are agentive or not. Taking Gafaranga's (2010) examinations of language choice and child agency as an example, the author notes that Rwandan caregivers in Belgium did not mark their child's choice as non-compliant when they spoke in Kinyarwanda (the minority language) and the child replied in French (the majority language). The Rwandan parents either continued in Kinyarwanda or switched to French themselves. Smith-Christmas (2020) points out that when both practices become norms in child-caregiver interactions, questions such as whether the children's use of French should be explained as "resistance" or as a norm of interaction have remained.

Smith-Christmas (2020) points to children's command of grammatical structures and lexical items as another issue related to language choice and child agency. Seeing that children in Gafaranga's (2010) case study had lower linguistic competence in Kinyarwanda compared to their French skills, Smith-Christmas (2020) asks the following question: to what extent can the child's reply in the majority language be seen as agentive if the child does not have the linguistic competence to answer in the minority language, even if the child wanted to?

Finally, Smith-Christmas (2020) specifies that generational positioning shapes language choice in families. The parent-child asymmetrical positions of power and status are usually age based; younger, less experienced, and less skilled members are commonly socialized into the cultures and languages of the older ones (Luykx 2005). By exercising their agencies, children can redefine general positioning in the traditional language socialization processes. For example, benefiting from their greater competence in the majority language, children in immigrant families often act as *language brokers*,[12] thus subverting the expected generational roles, as well as causing conflicts in transnational families (Antonini 2016; Smith-Christmas 2020). These four dimensions proposed by Smith-Christmas (2020) highlight the relational, negotiated nature of child agency and they will be employed in the discussions of language choice in the present case study.

To conclude, although child agency has been extensively investigated in the research on child language acquisition, most existing studies embed child agency within the previous literature on FLP. Analyses foregrounding child agency and interpreting the role of children as equal to that of adults in the making, implementing, and managing of language policies are still scarce. Child agency is affected by the structure of a family's practice through time and space. There is a certain discourse typical of home practice, which places participants in different subject positions and roles during the practice (Bergroth and Palviainen 2017). Children being socialized into the use of target language at home do not automatically change the family's language policies and practices. However, once children understand the family's practice structure, they can no longer be seen as simply being socialized in the family's norms (Bergroth and Palviainen 2017). They can challenge these norms by responding through their own actions.

---

[12] Antonini (2016) refers to language brokers as children of immigrants who translate language and interpret cultural practices for their parents.

4 An ethnographic case study

The child, Y, was born in 2014 in Japan to a Mandarin speaking mother, who was also the present researcher, and a Japanese father. English was the lingua franca of the family. Y's mother had learned English as a foreign language since she was young. She picked up Japanese as her second foreign language after settling down in Japan. Y's father had also learned English as a foreign language in the Japanese schools and now regularly read and wrote in English as a university researcher. Both of Y's parents received postgraduate education in the UK and were fond of English language and literature, as well as British history and culture. Since Y was born, she had been exposed to three languages: Mandarin, spoken by her mother; English, by her father and in family conversations; and Japanese, by both parents for reading and doing other activities related to this language. After spending nearly five years in Japan (0–4;10), Y moved to Scotland with her parents for one year (4;10–5;10). The same language use pattern was adopted when the family relocated to Scotland. Y returned to Japan at the age of 5;10. She turned 8;1 at the time of this writing. The majority of data on Y and her parents were collected from 0 to 4;10 in Japan and from 4;10 to 5;10 in Scotland. Data revealing the home reading and writing practices continued to be collected until she reached the age of 8;1 (5;10–8;1). Y produced a great amount of writing over this duration.

The naturalistic data used in the present study to describe Y's development and her interaction with her parents were collected using ethnographic case study methods. By analyzing data collected through participant observation, the mother's diary entries, video and audio recordings, and metalinguistic conversations among family members, the research aims to contribute to a deeper understanding of child agency with a particular focus on the child's participation and language choice, and most importantly, her leading role in family socialization. The present chapter first provides an overview of the ethnographic method. It then explains the multiple approaches used for data collection and describes the procedures for data transcription and analysis. Finally, it addresses ethical considerations and other issues related to the study.

Ethnography was originally developed within the field of anthropology, but it is now widely used in both anthropology and social sciences more generally (Pole and Morrison 2003). An ethnography is a situated exploration "based upon sharing the time and space of those who one is studying" (Riain 2009: 291). By drawing on methods such as participant observation and field notes, ethnography attempts to create a thick description of the culture of the group (Creswell and Poth 2018). In doing so, ethnographers provide detailed accounts of the complex, critical elements that are observed in a real-life environment through an insider's perspective, including the domain, participants, processes, goals, or contexts of use, etc. (Berg 2001; Cruz-Ferreira 2006; Pole and Morrison 2003).

Case study, meanwhile, is as an approach "that facilitates exploration of a phenomenon within its context using a variety of data sources" (Baxter and Jack 2008: 544). As Schwandt and Gates (2018: 341) explain, "[A] case is an instance, incident, or unit of something and can be anything–a person, an organization, an event, a decision, an action, a location" at the micro, meso, or macro level. The choice of a case study approach is seen as appropriate to the present research. It enables the researcher to gather information through personal and social interaction with the participants; it also allows the researcher to describe the phenomenon from the perspectives of participants (Berg 2001). Involving both the parents and the young child in the present research made it possible to describe the language ideologies, language practices, and language management of all three family members and how these potentially influenced their language choices.

Ethnography has "a case study character" and is intimately related to case studies (Riain 2009: 291). In essence, ethnographic case studies are case studies "employing ethnographic methods and focused on building arguments about cultural, group, or community formation or examining other sociocultural phenomena" (Schwandt and Gates 2018: 344). However, ethnographic case studies differ from other types of case studies primarily in their focus, methodology, and duration; in particular, ethnographic studies are typically of long duration as per the demands of ethnographic work (Schwandt and Gates 2018). Choosing this blended research design is not coincidental but determined by the nature of the phenomenon of FLP under investigation. That is to say, ethnographic tools are employed to attend to the perspectives of family members including the beliefs and values that underlie and organize their utterances and other language and literacy activities. Meanwhile, case study methodology was employed to investigate the empirical and theoretical aspects of phenomena in a natural family context.

4.1 Ethnographic case studies of family language policy

One of the main issues with FLP research involves obtaining and analyzing language use in the very intimate setting of the family (Smith-Christmas 2017). In order to do this, a wide array of approaches is used to investigate how factors at the social and familial levels potentially influence family language choice (Caldas 2006). Analysis relies heavily on: (1) participant observation and field notes which are critical to gaining divergent and in-depth understandings of relationships, symbols, and other context-embedded information, (2) elicitation of members' reflections and interpretations (e.g. interviews, conversations, and language background surveys), (3) systematic audio and visual documentation (e.g. audio and video recordings of family activities), and (4) collection of relevant texts and other artifacts (e.g. photographs, drawings and other creative tasks, and written diary entries) (Geertz 1973; Mensel and Meulder 2021).

In case studies where a researcher's own family is studied, family members are asked to make their own field notes and self-recordings, and are involved in the generation of data; such an approach grows into a form of collaborative autoethnography (Student, Kendall, and Day 2017). When the researcher is the parent of the child, the language diary is an invaluable means to record parents' and child's language use, as well as the parent-researcher's reflections on his/her own language use with the child.

The development of FLP as an explicit area began more than a century ago with two separate diary studies, those of Ronjat (1913) and Leopold (1939–1949) (as cited in Barron-Hauwaert 2004). Ronjat applied one-parent-one-language (OPOL) strategy as a means to promote his son's bilingualism by speaking only French to the child and the child's mother speaking only German (Barron-Hauwaert 2004). Leopold gave a detailed description of the links between bilingualism and cognitive attributes such as metalinguistic awareness (Barron-Hauwaert 2004). The language diary was also used as a procedure by De Houwer and Bornstein (2003) for their study of French-Dutch bilinguals in Belgium.

It is certain that the language diary provides considerable opportunities for researchers to understand child language acquisition and production (Cruz-Ferreira 2006). However, there are some considerations to be made when using this method, one of which is that keeping diary entries largely depends on the diligence and sustained efforts of caregivers. Diary studies often document the earliest signs of language comprehension and production in children, possibly with extensive details such as the new words appearing in a child's lexicon. It is unlikely that this research activity could be conducted better by anyone other than a child's parents who live in the same household as the child. Another shortcoming of diary studies is that handwritten notes cannot be verified by other researchers. A possible solution to this issue is to complement handwritten notes with other data collecting methods such as audio or video recordings, as described, for example, by Cruz-Ferreira (2006), in a study of her three children acquiring Portuguese in a trilingual environment.

The multifaceted foci of FLP research require a variety of methodological approaches (Montanari 2009). In the majority of ethnographic case studies, where the researcher is not the child's parent, participant observation, interviews, and recordings of caregiver-child interactions are commonly employed by the outsider researchers to obtain live data (Caldas 2006; Cruz-Ferreira 2006; De Houwer

1990; Döpke 1992; Fantini 1985; Saunders 1988; Taeschner 1983). Using a combination of the above methods can produce an in-depth understanding of FLP.

In participant observation, the researcher experiences social life along with the participants in a real environment while gathering information through interaction with the participants (Cruz-Ferreira 2006). Observation of this type fulfills two main aims. First, rather than relying entirely on the family members' reported policies, observing the actual language practices in the course of the fieldwork allows cross-checking of the authenticity of the reported data. For instance, even if a OPOL strategy is firmly reported by parents, code-switching behavior is nevertheless sometimes observed. In this sense, observation is a valuable tool to complement the parents' self-reports. Second, observation is important to find out not only which languages are used by parents but also for what purposes the languages are employed in the actual interactions. In that respect, parents' intentions could be obtained through observation.

The interview method is used to draw out the speaker's language ideologies regarding their own and others' language use. This is exemplified in Curdt-Christiansen's (2009) study of the language policies of Chinese families in Montreal, in which she combined interviews with weekly visits, recordings, and participation in the community. One more example is seen in Chevalier's (2015) case study of two trilingual children in German-speaking Switzerland, in which interviews, recordings, and regular observations were made every three months. Moreover, other studies have employed surveys in assessing family language use (King and Fogle 2006).

In order to address questions of the quality of language use, it is necessary to obtain recorded samples of evidence from actual language practices in addition to parents' self-reported practices. Data from recordings is the most reliable type of data for sociolinguistic studies of this kind (Genesee, Nicoladis, and Paradis 1995). Recording allows the researcher to refer back to the data and in some cases to not be present, therefore avoiding the observer's paradox (Kendall 2008). The recorded verbal interactions can also be used to assess children's input and many aspects of child language skills.

Parent-child conversations provide valuable insights into family language practices. Language conversations are opportunities for family members to exchange their language knowledge and ideologies. By talking about specific issues, reliable data emerge, particularly those describing speakers' attitudes and beliefs that cannot be easily obtained through other approaches. Parent-child conversations thus help validate the evidence presented in parents' reports.

It must be pointed out that few studies on FLP have collected data from both parents and children; however, incorporating a child's perspectives alongside the parental data are believed to be important (Okita 2002). Using children's reports and observing their language socialization strengthen the validity of data collected from parents, as well as emphasize the importance of considering children as agents in the implementation of family language policies (Schwartz and Verschik 2013).

4.2 Data collection

Data collection is time-consuming and relatively unstructured. Multiple approaches were adopted to collect more than one type of data, which provided different perspectives on the complex phenomenon of Y's family's FLP over time. Data that showed how family members perceived, negotiated, and modified their policies were gathered in the course of actual interactions, based on the researcher-mother's diary, video and audio recordings, participant observation, and parent-child metalinguistic conversations. Moreover, instead of being interviewed by an outside researcher, Y's mother self-reported her opinions in her language diary, insofar as they had a bearing on language and language use. During data collection, a single phenomenon was cross-recorded by more than one means; for instance, Y's mother sometimes observed a particular moment while it was simultaneously video recorded.

The mother's diary

Diary studies give us information about how language acquisition actually takes place. A parent's diary entries provide a direct measure of this process, validating children's language experience when it is also recorded through other measures (Hoff and Rumiche 2012). In the present study, Y's mother's diary entries played a large role in the continuous collection of data. She kept a diary in English every couple of days in a notebook, recording facts and opinions which were difficult to report through other data collection methods. For example, she noted down how many hours Y spent in speaking, reading, and watching television in each language in a single day. In addition, instances of monologues and dialogues regarding different language aspects were recorded in the diary. These included, for example, Y correcting the languages and language choices of herself and others. Moreover, the mother recorded her interpretations, as well as those of Y and her father in the diary, which thus served as a self-report in the written form.

Recordings

Y started to make understandable utterances from two years old. Her mother collected 80 video clips (one video clip lasted for a couple of minutes), recording her activities before her second birthday. From 2;0 to 5;10 recording took place in the form of monthly sessions, normally on the first weekend of a month.[13] A typical recording was made over a period of 40 minutes. Recordings were primarily videotaped before Y's third birthday but mainly audiotaped after that age.

There were two considerations in making the change from video to audio. First, with the natural background noise in the home, it was difficult to decipher the two-year-old's utterances without referring to her body language, as the sounds were not clearly distinguished and the grammar not clearly structured. However, Y had become highly fluent in all of her three languages and excelled in verbal expression by her third birthday. For this reason, it took little effort to understand or decode her audio-recorded speech from that age on. Second, as Y became more active, it was impossible to have her stay in one fixed place. Therefore, audio recording had become more convenient and produced fewer distractions as her mother did not have to pay attention to her positioning and move the recording equipment during the sessions. The audio recorder would simply be put in a place that was not distracting to Y and her parents such as on the floor, and this ensured that they were more relaxed and yet the quality of the recording was not affected.

The researcher-mother recorded one interaction per month for each of the following three situations: child-mother, child-father, and family time. English was generally used in daily conversations between Y and her father, among the three family members, or in an English learning context. Mandarin was mainly adopted in communication between Y and her mother and sometimes purposefully employed with the father as a way to encourage him to learn this language. The third language, Japanese, was primarily used between Y and her father for reading, learning, and doing other activities related to this language. However, it was common to use more than one language when explaining something or having a discussion about something.

In general Y's mother spent more time taking care of her than her father did. The mother was always present during the recording sessions either as a participant or as an observer taking part in the conversations. Among the total 48 videos, 22 videos recorded child-mother interactions, 11 videos showed conversations between Y and her father, and 13 videos demonstrated family communication (as

---

[13] From 5;10 to 8;1, the researcher-mother continued to collect data using a variety of methods, but recordings were no longer made regularly.

shown in Appendix 1). The Chinese grandparents visited and stayed in Japan for about three months when Y was aged 2;6 and they were participants in the two videos taken in that duration.

The recorded verbal interactions were useful in assessing Y's language input and many aspects of her language skills. However, recordings also have drawbacks, such as the potentially low quality of a recording (where sounds are indistinguishable in a particular environment), or problems related to the types of recording (in an audio recording there is only sound, no visual data, and in a video recording things may happen away from the direction in which the camera is pointed).

Participant observation and field notes

Language practices occurring in Y's family were mainly explored through observation of face-to-face child-parent interactions (i.e. what they actually do) rather than through parents' self-reports (i.e. what they believe they are doing). Most of the time, observations in the present study were unstructured, although they were sometimes selective and focused on particular situations. General and descriptive observations in daily gatherings were useful to get a general idea of the family's language practices. The mother tried to keep an eye on Y when she had no household chores, making written notes of what she had observed. Focused and selective observations were carried out, not only focusing on the family's language use, but also seeking to provide complementary perspectives that explain the FLP. In this way, it seemed valuable to use more than one measure to collect data on the same language practice.

With this in mind, observations were made and field notes were recorded even when an activity was video or audio recorded. For example, her mother observed and took notes while recording Y and her father doing activities, particularly reading or working on something involving materials with written texts. The mother found this integrated method helpful because observations and associated notes supplied a background description of a recording, summarized its content, and highlighted special language phenomena found in the recording.

Descriptions of the observed context and participants' language use can be documented systematically by taking field notes during social interaction (Mackey and Gass 2015). Both descriptive and reflexive notes[14] were recorded by Y's mother.

---

14 Descriptive notes document descriptions of the observed context and of participants' language use (Mackey and Gass 2015). Reflexive notes are taken in the form of memos, which show the development of analytic ideas and systematic monitoring of the research progress (Maxwell 2012).

Descriptive notes were taken during an observation and organized shortly afterwards to describe the participants' verbal and nonverbal language behavior and to provide necessary information about the background and the context (Maxwell 2012). Reflexive notes were taken in the form of memos which showed the development of analytic ideas and systematic monitoring of the research progress (Maxwell 2012). Reflexive notes include the ethnographer's "feelings of personal comfort, anxiety, surprise, shock, or revulsion" (Hammersley and Atkinson 2007: 151). There is often a concern about how notes should be taken without disturbing the usual language practices in ethnographic research (Delamont 2012). In the present study, when it was inappropriate to take notes, Y's mother would make a mental note of the observed issues and write down her comments at a later time.

In addition to recording notes in a notebook, Y's mother also kept notes in a PowerPoint file because she often used her laptop to work when watching Y doing something on her own or together with her parent(s). There were some merits to keeping notes in a PowerPoint document. For example, it was easy to organize data by the slide order. It was particularly helpful to add photographs and samples of literacy artefacts to a slide, such as the pictures showing Y teaching her father Mandarin and math on a whiteboard, or showing her handwritten and typed journals. Photos were taken using the mother's smartphone and were automatically transmitted and saved in her laptop's Google photos. Photos were then downloaded and added to the PowerPoint file.

Metalinguistic conversations

Language socialization across generations is not "a one-way process" but "a dynamic network of mutual family influence" (Luykx 2003: 40). Parent-child interactions provide valuable insights into family practices. In the present study, Y's parents frequently exchanged their opinions on language and language practices. Her parents also chatted about these issues with her. Y demonstrated a good comprehension of some linguistic aspects, such as the phonological and grammatical rules of words and sentences in her three languages. She was also keen on sharing her understanding of language and its usage with her parents. Some conversations of this nature occurred naturally during an activity, while others started unexpectedly. Y's mother jotted down each member's direct comments in her language diary. When it was not possible to note down something immediately during the conversation, she paraphrased the speech, or noted down keywords first and then wrote the original utterances in as much detail as possible when they were still fresh in her memory.

The role of the researcher-mother

Some people may have doubts about parental reports on language practices, concerned, for example, that parents' comments on their language use do not always match their actual practices (Goodz 2006). Nevertheless, parents are those who are most familiar with their children and are provided with the best and most consistent opportunities to participate in and observe family activities, and who can ensure the genuineness of the data (Goodz 2006). This book highlights the researcher-mother's vital role in the design, implementation, and interpretation of the case study. Opportunities and suitability for gathering data are limited in the case of outsider researchers (Goetz and LeCompte 1984). Entering the family group and being accepted and trusted by family members, and especially by children, take a lot of time and effort before any effective data can be collected (Goetz and LeCompte 1984). However, Y's mother was able to combine her two roles – participant and observer – in her observations. That is, she could engage in the same activity as a participant while interacting with other participants to share their perceptions and acts, or simply observing others as a non-participant during an activity without interrupting, The mother was aware that her role as a researcher may be blurred by her identity as the parent and therefore often consciously kept a low profile as a non-participant to view language practices and issues surrounding FLP holistically (Wolcott 2008).

Hence, the observer's paradox, that is, the phenomenon where participants behave unnaturally due to their awareness of the fact that they are being observed or recorded (Zentella 1990), was not considered a prominent issue in the present study. Y's mother invested a considerable amount of time in the house field, observing and socializing with Y and her father while gathering the actual data. The three members were believed to have generally been displaying their natural behavior for two reasons. First, it would be difficult to continue pretend behavior in a case study which encompassed eight years, particularly in one's own home with one's own family members. Second, both Y and her father were comfortable with the mother's observing or recording, such that the observer's paradox would not have had a noticeable impact on the speakers' language use.

4.3 Data transcription

Transcribing is the first stage of data interpretation. Quality transcripts are seen to be important for a meaningful analysis of speech data. A researcher does not need to wait to get all of the data in order to start working with them, but can transcribe and uncover necessary information as the research proceeds (Wray,

Trott, and Bloomer 1998). The data collected in the present study were transcribed and coded from recordings, field notes, and the mother's diary entries.

Transcription of video and audio recordings was made in the CHAT format of CHILDES (MacWhinney 2017). The speakers were coded as CHI (child), FAT (father), MOT (mother), GrM (grandmother), and GrF (grandfather). Utterances were marked as M (Mandarin), E (English), or J (Japanese). Mandarin is coded in Chinese characters, English is coded in roman letters, and Japanese is coded in ひらかな (*hiragana*) and カタカナ (*katakana*). Examples of two coded transcripts are shown in Appendix 2 to illustrate the way a transcript was put together. Each recording and its transcribed data were linked such that the original verbal interactional data could be referred back to easily.

The observation notes kept in the notebooks and PowerPoint slides were also reviewed. First, the researcher-mother read through the handwritten and typed notes and developed brief notes and keywords for the activity episodes during the fieldwork while she had a fresh memory of them. Second, the researcher-mother expanded the brief notes to be as specific as possible, such as describing the order of occurrence of an event and background information of an episode, a member's direct speech, and other members' verbal or non-verbal reactions. Third, photos used in Y's mother's PowerPoint documents were described either as background information or as a supplementary explanation of a phenomenon. Photos containing Y's written text or other learning materials were directly employed in the results where necessary. Fourth, if any video or audio recordings were made during note-taking, the written notes were reviewed together with the transcribed data from the recording. These two types of evidence were compared and cross-referenced in the analysis stage.

Utterances from the mother's diary entries were organized in a way similar to that used in transcribing the observation data. Four types of text were kept in the diary notes: direct or reported speech of a participant, Y's mother's paraphrased speech of a participant, the grammatically-revised utterances of Y, and the mother's opinions. All non-digital data (e.g. diary entries and observation notes) related to the research questions were highlighted and typed in Word files by the researcher-mother.

Notes taken from metalinguistic conversations which were kept in Y's mother's diary were organized in the same way. Her mother's ideas and thoughts (i.e. links among data) were reflected in memos and annotations. Memos were kept at the beginning of each document for recording macro ideas on general data, whereas annotations were kept within the document to record micro-opinions on specific data. Both types of notes began with a date to facilitate later organization in a timeline. Different notes on the same data were thematically classified using color markers.

4.4 Data analysis

Ethnographic research yields numerous and mainly unstructured data, and organizing data into thematic categories is therefore a demanding and reflective process (Hammersley and Atkinson 2007). It is suggested that as soon as an observation or a conversation finishes, researchers should review their raw field notes and write summaries (Miles and Huberman 1994). Data analysis is commonly carried out qualitatively in ethnographic studies. Boyatzis (1998) refers to qualitative analysis as identifying, analyzing, and reporting patterns or themes within the data. Since qualitative data are normally in the form of text, the process of analysis involves a deconstruction of textual data into manageable categories, patterns, and relationships in a systematic search for meaning (Braun and Clarke 2006). In the present study, data gathered through the language diary entries, family metalinguistic conversations, video and audio recordings, and observations were transcribed and compiled, such that they would generate themes and patterns.

Following Yin (2011), the process of analyzing ethnographic data in the present study consisted of four main phases: (1) compiling, (2) disassembling and reassembling, (3) interpreting, and (4) concluding. These phases are not necessarily sequential but rather simultaneous and iterative, which means an ethnographer can return to different phases in a cyclical manner (Delamont 2012). First, guided by the research questions, patterns were looked for and materials were organized into categories. The data collected in Y's study were broken down into smaller, manageable pieces, such as sentences, utterances, or small paragraphs, such that the researcher-mother concentrated on the analytic concepts and categories. Doing this made it easier to understand the phenomena that were central to the research questions. Results, particularly those related to the three broad themes of language ideologies, language practices and language management of Y and her parents, were identified and interpreted in either a narrative or discourse format.

Second, while disassembling primarily focuses on emergent phenomena from small pieces of data, reassembling focuses on "potentially broader patterns in the data" (Yin 2011: 190). The triangulated thematic aspects were explicitly addressed from the perspectives of both Y and her parents according to her three developmental stages (0–3;10, 3;11–4;10, and 4;11–8;1), life in two contrasting sociolinguistic contexts (Japan and Scotland), and her two types of practices (language practice and literacy practice). The process of reassembling provided new insights into the current data and revealed broader dimensions of thematic codes and patterns. For example, "What is Y's mother's attitude toward the heritage Chinese language and culture?" and "How are literacy events surrounding reading and writing related to Y's daily communication?"

Third, a researcher will "develop a comprehensive interpretation, still encompassing specific data, but whose main themes will become the basis for understanding the entire study" (Yin, 2011: 207). Berg (2001) believes that data analysis should be viewed as an ongoing aspect of the research rather than a discrete phase of the research process. To this end, Y's mother concurrently carried out data analysis as the research progressed, identifying common themes and recurring views that needed further inquiry. Her mother aimed to keep an eye on the study as a whole, while simultaneously reflecting on the earlier steps of compiling, disassembling, and reassembling. Finally, the research findings are raised to a higher conceptual level or opened up to a broader set of ideas. For example, the researcher-mother came to challenge widely accepted knowledge, while presenting new concepts and discoveries.

In addition to the general procedure of data analysis described above, two specific methods were employed in the present study: thematic content analysis and discourse analysis.

Thematic content analysis

Thematic content analysis is widely used in qualitative analysis (Braun and Clarke 2006). It entails the organization of data in ways that allow patterns to be interpreted and compared, themes and relations between the themes identified, and theories explained or generated (Braun and Clarke 2006). Berg (2001: 239) considers the interpretive nature of thematic content analysis as allowing a researcher to "treat social action and human activity as text".

In the present study, data gathered through participant observation and field notes, video and audio recordings, the mother's language diary, and family metalinguistic conversations were transcribed and compiled such that they would generate themes and patterns. In particular data related to the three thematic aspects (language ideologies, language practices, and language management) were identified and interpreted. Extra-linguistic variables associated with these three fundamental elements, including sociocultural environment, ethnic identities, educational background, life experiences and language context were also investigated.

The three thematic aspects were explicitly addressed in relation to Y's three developmental stages (0–3;10, 3;11–4;10, and 4;11–8;1). Two types of practices were analyzed through texts that had been transcribed from different sources focusing on Y's daily conversations and learning events surrounding reading and writing. Berg (2001) believes that data analysis should be viewed as an ongoing aspect of the research rather than a discrete phase of the research process. To this end, the researcher-mother concurrently carried out data analysis as the research progressed, identifying common themes and recurring phenomena that needed further inquiry.

Discourse analysis

Johnson (2011: 267) explains that discourse analysis can be incorporated into ethnographic studies of LP to shed light on "how particular policies are recontextualized in particular contexts, how such recontextualization is related to more widely circulating policy text and discourse, and what this means for language policy agents". Discourse analysis uncovers the explicit and implicit meanings in a given setting such as family. It reveals how family members project their meanings with regard to language values and family language policies. In the present study, indexed by key words from the video and audio recorded data, various attitudes and beliefs within Y's family were discussed. Incongruences between her parents' explicitly stated ideologies and their actual implicit behavior were also identified. Utterances were examined in speech turns that consisted of one or more utterances. Speech turns were marked and analyzed to identify whether utterances in a discourse represented an emerging theme (a pattern or a phenomenon) as related to the research questions. Findings from discourse analysis were also organized based on the same three aspects adopted in the content analysis (family language ideologies, family language practices, and family language management), as well as three developmental stages (0–3;10, 3;11–4;10, and 4;11–8;1) and two practice patterns (language practice and literacy practice).

Discourse analysis focusing on negotiation of language practices can deepen one's understanding of the function of a specific space and type of language use in that space (Bourdieu 1990). The present study unveiled the influence of social structure (language ideologies of the wider community, language education policies of the mainstream schools, etc.) on FLP in two sociolinguistic contexts (Japan and Scotland).

4.5 Limitations and considerations

Limitations to the present study must be considered. It is true that this study largely relied on the qualitative approaches for data analysis, including the use of verbatim examples from participants, attempting to show links between the data and interpretation. However, it also adopted what would be considered quantitative techniques (using charts and tables) within the qualitative analysis. These quantitative measurements can provide a snapshot of detailed qualitative narrative text (Denzin 2009). Nevertheless, there were only a small number of participants in the study, such that there would naturally be a greater focus on rich data as opposed to thick data; in other words, quality is valued over quantity. Prolonged engagement in the field and *triangulation*[15] were also strategies that helped develop an in-depth understanding of the phenomena (Creswell 2009). Triangulation also allowed the researcher-mother to view the themes from multiple perspectives when exploring the impact of FLP on child language development. For example, Y's mother's field notes provided rich descriptions for the recorded data and allowed the two types of data to be cross-checked for similar interpretations and conclusions.

Fetterman (2010) points out that the potential ethical issues in ethnographic research are related to the ethnographer gaining access to the field and their building relations with the participants in the field. The ethnographer's respect for the dignity of the participants and their privacy are central to ethnographic research (Creswell 2013). The present researcher, who was also the mother in the family, was aware of ethical and privacy issues, such as the identification of the child and her living environment. For this reason, a pseudonym, Y, was used for the young subject and her parents were referred to as "the father" and "the mother". Conscious steps were also taken to minimize potential threats to the family members' privacy. For example, the researcher-mother had to develop an awareness of the context for judging when it was appropriate to observe the family members' activities.

Finally, it must be emphasized that the objective of this and similar research is to gain a greater understanding of the culture and the features of a particular group of multilingual speakers, like Y and her family in the present study, which is bounded by space and time, rather than transferability.

---

[15] Patton (1999) refers to triangulation as the application of multiple approaches or data sources.

5 A journey from being socialized to being the main socializing agent in family language policy

In much of the research on FLP, "the incorporation of the children's perspectives in the parental data" is rather scarce (Schwartz 2010: 186); relatively few studies have collected data from both parents and children. However, while children are objects of socialization into the language and culture of parents, they can also be agents who socialize parents into their particular language practices (Fogle and King 2013; Luykx 2005). As evident in examples of children's impact on family language policies, there is an evolving understanding of the concept of child agency (King et al. 2008). This chapter shows how Y's perceptions and actions negotiated and reshaped the policies formulated by her parents, and how she socialized them into her own practices and eventually took a leading role in her family interactions. It argues that the switching of generational positioning in Y's family was closely related to her parents' recognition of her agentive abilities, as well as their understanding of the bidirectional nature of family socialization. Y's parents appreciated her higher language, cognitive, and social skills demonstrated in the processes of directing the language choices of herself and other family members. They accepted her as an equal party in the making of the family's language policies and as a language teacher for her parents. Overall, they accommodated the policies and requests made by Y or even followed the child's lead.

5.1 Overall patterns of language use in Y's family

Home is the most common place where children experience languages. It is a critical domain for the practice and transmission of both the societal and heritage language (Spolsky 2012). Language practice is "the habitual pattern of selecting among the varieties that make up a speech community's linguistic repertoire" (Spolsky 2004: 5). It is what people actually do with languages in different situations and for different purposes. Children receive language input from what they hear and produce language output through routine practices (Spolsky 2009).

A lot of data were collected for the present study, which provided a thorough account of the overall language use and general language policies in the first eight years of Y's life. From birth to 1;10, she was cared for by her parents at home. She was taken to play outside every day, for example, attending local nurseries' activities, "reading" in the library, or playing in the neighborhood parks.

These were the main situations for her Japanese input in addition to being read to in Japanese at home. By one and a half, Y started to talk in single words in all of her three languages and soon became an enthusiastic speaker using simple sentences and fixed expressions. Her daily exposure to the three languages between 0;7 and 1;10 was approximately as follows: English for three hours (at home), Japanese for three hours (one hour at home and two hours in the community), and Mandarin for four hours (at home).

For two years, from the age of 1;11, Y attended a small size nursery where English was used in some activities. In the total 12 hours of her time awake, the input of her languages was roughly: English for four hours (three hours at home and one hour in the nursery), Japanese for five hours (one hour at home and four hours in the nursery), and Mandarin for three hours (at home).

From 3;11 to 4;10, Y attended kindergarten where Japanese was the only language of instruction. Her language exposure changed slightly from the previous period during the 13 hours that she was awake: English for four hours (at home), Japanese for six hours (one hour at home and five hours in the kindergarten), and Mandarin for three hours (at home). Her reading skills dramatically developed after the third birthday. It was estimated that she spent an average of two hours per day reading English books independently, while she spent slightly less on Japanese and the least on Mandarin reading.

At the age of 4;10, Y's family relocated to Scotland for one year. She first entered a local preschool for four months and then Primary 1 (P1) for eight months. Her daily exposure (totally 13.5 hours) to the three languages in Scotland was estimated as follows: English for 10.5 hours (four hours at home and six and a half hours at school), Japanese for one hour (at home), and Mandarin for two hours (at home). She continued to read more and higher-level books in English which had been her strongest language during all of the periods, especially in term of literacy skills. While Chinese was used in conversations, reading, and learning in their temporary home in Scotland, Japanese was reserved mainly for reading during this time.

The family returned to Japan when Y was 5;10. She resumed her kindergartener life for one year (5;10–6;10) before again becoming a P1 pupil in a local Japanese school at the age of 6;10.[16] Y's language exposure from birth to 8;1 is shown in the following three charts.

Speaking of language input quality (e.g. language environment and input strategies), input quantity (e.g. the amount of time), and child language output,

---

[16] Japanese schools start on 1st April. Children who enter P1 should be aged between 6;0 and 6;11 before the new term starts.

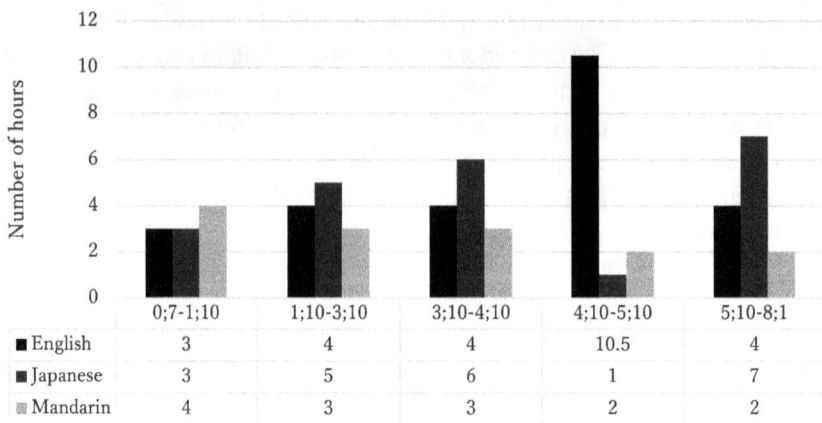

Chart 1: Y's language exposure in and outside the home.

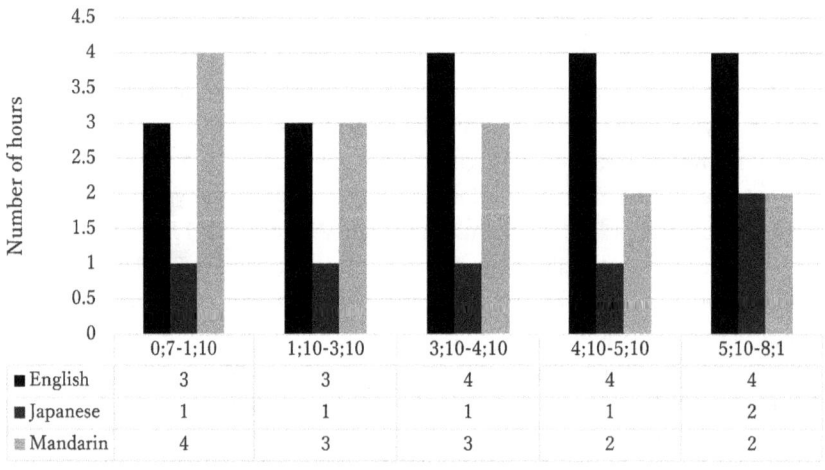

Chart 2: Y's language exposure in the home.

there were no significant differences observed between the data collected in the nursery stage (1;11–3;10) and those collected in the kindergarten stage (3;11–4;10). To that end, these two periods were combined as one in the chapters on data analysis and data discussion.

Examining the temporal dimension of the negotiation process was also considered to be useful. On the one hand, the study explores an eight-year long life story through an examination of moment-by-moment practices at a particular age; nevertheless, it is always important to take the full time-scale into consideration (Goodson, 2013). For example, code-switching was dealt with from different

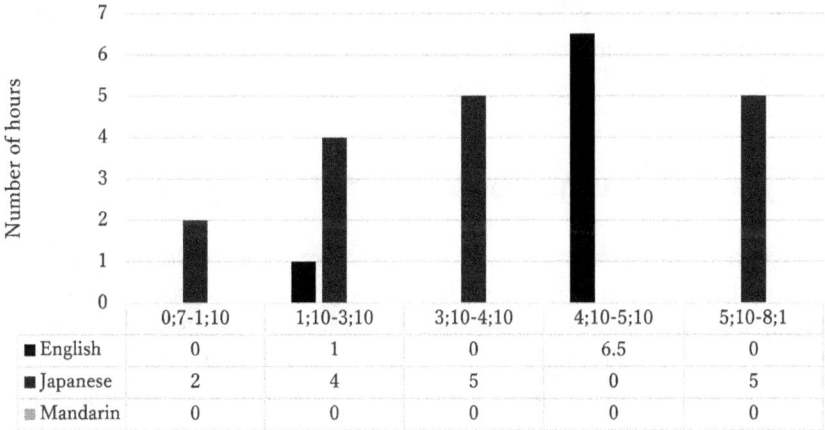

Chart 3: Y's language exposure outside the home.

perspectives at different times. It was believed to be a language proficiency related issue before Y's third birthday, while it was considered as a discourse strategy or a type of language practice after she turned three.

In essence Y's parents were accommodating parents. Since she was born, they commonly adopted child-centered policies to accommodate her desires and needs. They saw language development as a pivotal part of child well-being development and held a strong belief in the advantages of early multilingualism (Rose, Ebert, and Weinert 2017). They also created a variety of contexts to support Y's learning of three languages – communicating overwhelmingly in English and Mandarin, bringing in language and culture-related resources to support the target language, and supporting Y's acquisition of reading and writing skills in all of the three language systems, to name but a few.

However, there was a clear change in her parents' ideologies and input and discourse strategies in response to Y's emerging linguistic and cognitive abilities. To be more specific, before age three her parents were primarily learning facilitators who addressed Y's needs, while after that age they were socialized by Y as participants in the family activities as well as being her supporters. Most of these instances of socialization were related to Y's interests. Although they did arise originally from her parents' preferences and experiences, they eventually became part of Y's passions and daily routines. In this way, while the parents needed to find ways to consciously engage Y in language learning in her earliest years of life, they needed only to cooperate and satisfy her hobbies after that. This explains her parents' changing attitudes and roles in the language socialization process and the different behaviors they displayed as accommodating parents. The parents' changes were reflected in their interactional and discourse strategies and fundamentally their ideologies. These will be discussed in this and the following two chapters.

5.2 Dynamic language practices guided by parents

Researchers of language practices have been interested in exploring how children's multilingual competence is developed in the process of participating in family communication and in the interactional strategies parents use with young children to enhance their bilingual development (Döpke 1992; Lanza 1997, 2004). Y's parents found that child-centered policies would enhance her motivation and was therefore sustainable in terms of developing her language and building family bonds. They considered the quality of parent-child communication to be more critical than the mere quantity of time spent with the child. They thus employed a diversity of teaching techniques, such as modeling, asking choice questions and eliciting answers by providing the initial sound of a key word, and refrained from using ineffective strategies such as giving absolute, one-way instructions. Moreover, they adopted playful child-caring activities, using child-directed speech and being consistent in encouraging the child to speak her home languages.

Y's parents adopted the three languages as resources to clarify meaning and expand her linguistic repertoire. They engaged in complex and contextual language practices like code-switching, translating, and *translanguaging*[17] in both oral and written modes, in ways that are unique to trilingual communication. It is true that family language policies may initially be explicit, but they are also subject to negotiations between parents and children, as contingent on the parents' acceptance of the child's influence on them. Given the enactment of monolingual, bilingual, and trilingual performance, home became a vibrant multilingual space where the three members used their entire linguistic repertoire flexibly and meaningfully.

5.2.1 Learning one language in one context

It is commonplace that some parts of a multilingual speaker's repertoire in one language may overlap with others in another. Such speakers tend not to use all of their languages in any one context, but rather, they generally have a preferred

---

[17] Translanguaging is defined by Baker (2011: 288) as "the process of making meaning, shaping experiences, understandings and knowledge through the use of two languages" in communication.

language at any given time for any given subject (Dodson 1985). A speaker's experience can dictate which languages are likely to be favored in which contexts (Gumperz 1982). Children may routinely confirm meaning in an unfamiliar language by seeking an equivalent in a familiar language, but parents may attempt to make them refrain from resorting to the preferred language in some circumstances and to keep the languages separate by using only one of them in a specific context (Dodson 1985). Despite the fact that Y's spontaneous translating and translanguaging behavior was valued, her parents believed that time and space should be established for each of her individual languages in order for her to develop a mastery of each. Thus, when Y was one and two years old, they promoted the use of specified languages in specific contexts through modeling, indexing and eliciting, and rephrasing and paraphrasing.

Parental modelling and child imitating
Parents are important sources of language input and serve as models for children in language use. Modelling is a common and an effective way to help children acquire vocabulary and learn language structures before they have more access to other language sources and before they can act more independently. As a one-year-old, Y reflexively imitated her parents' speech, as seen in the following example.

Example 1 is from a diary entry (1;6).
1 MOT: 用纸擦一下。
[Wipe with a tissue.]
2 CHI: 用纸擦一下。
[Wipe with a tissue.]
3 MOT: Y好脏。
[Y is dirty.]
4 CHI: Y好脏。
[Y is dirty.]

Such imitation as shown above is believed to have helped Y learn and use languages in conversational contexts (Turns 2 and 4). However, using a language grammatically and correctly in context must be seen in relation to a child's cognitive development. Although Y was able to copy her parents' modelled expressions and use them in her own speech, there were grammar mistakes that could not be corrected through modelling. A typical mistake is found in the use of personal pronouns, as shown in Example 2.

Example 2 is from a diary entry (1;5).
1 MOT: Wash your hands.
2 CHI: Wash your hands.
3 MOT: No, you say, "Wash my hands."

Despite her mother's correction, Y continued to make grammar mistakes similar to that seen in the above. For example, she would say "Wash your hands." when she was about to wash her own hands (Turn 2). The same type of pronoun mistake was also observed in Y's Mandarin utterances and in those of a neighborhood child of similar age who was born to Chinese parents. Y's mother heard the boy say "给你." [Give it to you. (Here you are.)] (2;5) when he asked for a toy from her. The boy probably heard and copied his parents' Mandarin words when they gave him something and said "给你." [Give it to you. (Here you are.)]

Y also enjoyed repeating herself and chanting like any young child does. For instance, when Y's mother told her, "Daddy went to the supermarket to get some coffee, she replied, "Daddy shopping, shopping. Daddy pushing, pushing (a shopping cart). Mummy coffee ok, daddy coffee ok. Y coffee no, no, no." (1;9). Such repetition was a common practice when Y was one and two years old. She used these repeated words to express her opinions, exchange information, and carry on a conversation.

Indexing and eliciting

It is nearly impossible for very young children to separate the meaning field of a word and the visual field of a word in the process of child speech development (Vygotsky 2016). The first function of the word is to signify a particular location in a situation; for example, if an adult says "clock" to a child, the child starts looking and finds the clock in his immediate environment (Vygotsky 2016). Although Y could not speak at 0 years old, her parents would check her responses to short instructions. An instruction might include a word or a combination of words. It might be repeated in the same language, emphasized in body language, or explained by using equivalents from different languages. Encouraging Y to "talk" and involving her in interactive conversations were basic policies made by her parents. It appeared that Y could understand her parents' instructions when they were supported by methods like indexing and eliciting.

Indexing such as pointing to corresponding objects or persons is an explicit way of giving information. When Y's parents talked to her, they would point to the object or the person that was indicated. For example, her mother pointed at father every time she referred to him. This effectively helped Y understand the topic. Indexing also worked well as a non-verbal communication tool for Y when she could not construct grammatical utterances. For instance, she took her mother's hand and pointed at the front door, which was an indication of asking to go outside (1;0). *Eliciting* is the act of drawing out preferred language from a speaker. One example is shown in the following.

Example 3 is from a video clip (1;10).
Situation: Y took off her socks.
1 MOT: 袜子不穿会?
             [If you don't put on the socks, you'll be . . . ?]
2 CHI: 生病。
             [Sick.]
3 MOT: 生病要去?
             [If you are sick, you need go to . . . ?]
4 CHI: 医院。
             [Hospital.]
5 MOT: 医院里有?
             [There are . . . in a hospital.]
6 CHI: 医生。
             [Doctors.]

In the above example, her mother was trying to bring forth from Y the vocabulary required in the conversational context (Turns 1, 3 and 5). While her parents used this technique to elicit appropriate language from her, elicitation was also a technique used by Y to draw out desired content from her parents. She sometimes provided a word of the title of a song or a book as a way to request her parents to join her in singing or reading. For example, holding a toy teapot and saying "tea" was a demand for singing the song *I'm a little teapot* (1;3). She also sometimes prompted her parents by providing the initial sound of a word, as shown in Example 4.

Example 4 is from a video clip (1;8).
1 MOT: What are you cooking? Noodles?
2 CHI: No. Pa-, pa- . . .
3 MOT: Are you cooking pasta?
4 CHI: Yes, pasta.

In the above example, her parents were supportive of Y's vocabulary acquisition and accommodated her interactional strategies since she was very young (Turn 3). The parents' indexing and eliciting skills were copied by Y in daily conversations and this in turn supported her role in leading some family activities as a child teacher. The role of child teacher will be discussed in Chapter 6.

Rephrasing and paraphrasing

Rephrasing is to say or write something again in a different and usually clearer way. *Paraphrasing* is to repeat something spoken or written using different words, often in a simpler and shorter form that makes the original meaning clearer. Both of them are indirect ways of instructing or requiring a speaker to revise their language or language choice. These two types of practices proved to be helpful for Y to acquire new vocabulary and grammatical structures beyond her infancy. In Example 5, her mother rephrased and paraphrased Y's utterances.

Example 5 is from an observation note (1;7).
Situation: A conversation between Y and her mother on their way to *AEON*.[18]
1 CHI: Y *AEON*.
2 MOT: Y is going to *AEON*.
3 CHI: Mama *AEON*.
4 MOT: Mama is going to *AEON*.
5 CHI: Mama Y.
6 MOT: Mama and Y are going to *AEON*.

In the above example, Y's mother used rephrasing and paraphrasing to model how to speak more grammatically correct sentences (Turns 2, 4, and 6). The mother's diary entries recorded that after Y turned three, she had adequate translation equivalents in her three languages. Therefore, parental corrections beyond that age tended to focus more on semantic and syntactic mistakes, such as overextending the meaning of a word, as seen in Example 6, or incorrectly constructing a relative clause, as illustrated in Example 7.

Example 6 is from an observation note (3;8).
1 CHI: 爸爸好凶猛。
         [Daddy is ferocious.]
2 MOT: 为什么?
         [What happened?]
3 CHI: 他很凶猛地骂我了。
         [He told me off ferociously.]
4 MOT: 你是说爸爸很可怕?
         [Do you mean daddy is scary?]
5 CHI: 嗯。
         [Yeah.]

---

18 *AEON* is the name of a department store in Japan.

Example 7 is from an observation note (3;9).
1 CHI: This is Y did it today.
2 MOT: This is what Y did today. This is what I did today.

Extending or narrowing the meaning of a Mandarin word was commonly seen in Y's speech. In Example 6, she picked up the adjective 凶猛 [ferocious] (Turn 1) from a book describing tigers. She used it to describe her father's behavior which seemed scary in her opinion. The incorrect expression was then rephrased by her mother with an appropriate one (Turn 4). In Example 7, her mother indirectly corrected her mistake about an English relative clause by rephrasing the whole sentence (Turn 2). Acquiring complex linguistic structures such as relative clauses before preschool years is considered to be early even for native English speakers (Lightbown and Spada 2013). In her academic studies, Y's mother had learned about how languages were acquired in natural developmental sequences and thus always used indirect corrective methods to help Y with her mistakes.

Similarly, Noguchi (1996b) proposes that when young children are learning to speak, parents often recast the child's utterances. One example of recasting cited by Noguchi (1996b: 257) was from Baron's study; that is, when a child says, "Broom falled down", his mother might respond, "Yes, the broom fell down, didn't it?" Noguchi (1996b: 257) also offered examples of recasting that she used with her own children; for example, when her son made a statement about a piece of play candy, "This don't get the teeth hurt." (a literal translation of the Japanese expression *Kore wa ha wo itamanai*), she simply recast the expression, "Oh, I see. This one's not bad for your teeth." This type of recasting seemed similar to the rephrasing approach that was used by Y's parents. Noguchi (1996b: 257) presumed that the mother in Baron's study might go on to expand her utterance by continuing, "It went bang." or "Let's pick it up." A similar way of practice was also identified in Y's case, as shown in Example 8.

Example 8 is from an observation note (1;8).
1 CHI: ねこ。
         [Cat.]
2 MOT: Where is it?
3 CHI: そこ。
         [Over there.]
4 MOT: Did you see a cat?
5 CHI: Yeah.
6 MOT: What's the color of the cat?
7 CHI: みどり。
         [Green.]
8 MOT: Y saw a green cat. I saw a green cat.

In the above example, when her mother spotted a case of interference, she first expanded the conversation to elicit the expected words from Y (Turns 2 and 6). After failing in her attempt to correct Y's language choice, rather than fussing with her mixed codes, the mother continued the conversation by paraphrasing the whole exchange in English as a model of language and language choice (Turn 8).

Y's parents considered that directly challenging the child's language choice may hinder the flow of a conversation, so they adopted flexible strategies such as those illustrated above to carefully help her acquire all of her three languages. Of the three, Mandarin was a "minority" language in both Japan and Scotland. In addition to explicitly encouraging and entreating Y to speak Mandarin, her mother reported having used a wide range of situational tactics to normalize Mandarin use at home. Those included designating Mandarin-speaking context, watching Mandarin TV programs, reading and writing in Mandarin, playing instruments and singing songs in Mandarin, and taking part in the child-led Mandarin lessons, activities, and games.

5.2.2 Parents' code-switching

In bilingual practices, although one language is normally used as the base code, involving another language is often necessary and in fact unavoidable. Even within a single family, one can find a complex environment involving more than one language. Bilingual speakers' flexible language practices in such an environment have long been described by the notion of code-switching, which refers to the juxtaposition of two or more languages within the same utterance or in the same interaction without syntactical rule violation (Gumperz 1982). Code-switching was traditionally associated with inability to differentiate languages, but here it is investigated within the framework of FLP.

In the present study, even though Y's parents attempted to separate the three languages for instructional purposes and claimed to have consciously adopted the OPOL policy for each specific context, involving different languages in interaction was inevitable and even necessary when conveying meanings. Y's three languages were in fact interwoven into her family's language practices; for instance, they sometimes codeswitched intentionally, as seen in Example 9.

Example 9 is from the mother's diary note (2;7).
1 CHI: Mummy, it's broken.
(The make-up box was broken.)
2 MOT: Who broke it?
3 CHI: Grandma.
(The Chinese grandparents were visiting Y's family in Japan.)

(Grandma suddenly came near.)
4 MOT: 谁弄坏的?
        [Who did it?]
5 CHI: Y.

In the above example, Y's mother switched her language from English to Mandarin (Turn 4) when she became aware of the appearance of the Chinese grandmother. The code-switching seems to have been intentional, because the mother doubted Y's explanation and wanted to call her attention to the grandmother's presence. In this case, parents may employ code-switching within "safe space" as a strategy to gain children's attention, discipline children, and emphasize parents' requests (Schwartz et al. 2010).

Parents may also code-switch to strengthen family bonds. Gyogi (2014) reported that Japanese mothers in London demonstrated code-switching behavior in Japanese conversations with their bilingual children, using English loanwords that were not well-established in Japanese, such as *jeiru* [jail] and *tīchā* [teacher]. The Japanese mothers sometimes switched to the child's dominant language to ensure that the child had understood what was said in the heritage language; the child also sometimes switched to the home language when the mother did not understand what was said in the community language (Gyogi 2014). In such a case, non-code-switching seems unusual as it would impede the flow of family conversations.

Y's mother did not generally switch codes when talking to her bilingual husband or other bilingual speakers. However, she often switched languages in discussions between herself and Y. The mother reported in the following diary entry about why she switched codes with her child:

> One reason for mixing and switching languages was to choose the words that Y was familiar with. Another reason was to provide equivalent words. In order to adapt a mixed code in a base language, I simplified the grammar of a sentence. I soon found that Y knew the three forms well. Thus, I stopped mixing items and started to use grammatical sentences, even though sometimes it can be a very long utterance. (Recorded when Y was 3;5)

Y's mother also reported that she preferred to switch to English in certain situations:

> I couldn't help switching from Mandarin to English in discussions sometimes. I believe English is Y's strongest language. She uses English in various contexts. In addition, I feel more comfortable to talk about some topics in English than doing that in Mandarin, for example, when explaining news or doing math problems. (Recorded when Y was 4;3)

The mother's self-reports show that the parents' use or non-use of switched codes depended on Y's language abilities and on consideration of family bonds. In general, her mother displayed a flexible attitude and was ready to change an existing policy in accordance with Y's language and cognitive development.

Y's father for the most part got used to speaking only English with her in daily conversations. Even when working on a Japanese language or culture related activity, he would naturally switch from Japanese to English when talking to Y. Her mother sometimes thought that it would be better to create a Japanese context in which only Japanese was used. Her father thus tended to elicit equivalents or translate as his most used means to input Japanese, as can be seen in Example 10.

Example 10 is from a video recording (3;5).

Situation:	Y and her father were learning *hiragana* characters using *hiragana* cards.
1 CHI:	こ (*ko*)。I played a spinning top today.
	(こ is a *hiragana* character.)
2 FAT:	Yes, you did. こま (*koma*)。
	[Spinning top]
3 CHI:	こま (*koma*)。す (*su*)。すいか (*suika*)。
	[Spinning top. す is a *hiragana* character. Watermelon.]
4 FAT:	Good.
5 MOT:	にほんご。
	[In Japanese.]
	(The mother reminded the father to use Japanese.)
6 CHI:	せ (*se*)。
	(せ is a *hiragana* character.)
7 FAT:	せ (*se*)。What's the . . . せはなに?
	[Can you find a word that starts with *se*?]
8 CHI:	Cicada.
9 FAT:	日本語でなに。
	[What do you call it in Japanese?]
10 CHI:	せみ (*Semi*)。
	[Cicada.]

In this example, it seems that her father was subconsciously implementing the policy of father speaking English with Y (as part of the OPOL policy) even when learning Japanese *hiragana* characters. Her mother worried about the Japanese input at home and prompted him to use only Japanese (Turn 5). However, he continued to include English in interaction with Y (Turn 7). Thus, even though Y's parents believed they had adopted the OPOL approach and for the most part observed it, they sometimes ended up code-switching either inadvertently or for specific reasons. In such a case, code-switching can be seen as one characteristics of the dynamic language practice found in multilingual language experience.

5.2.3 Establishing a multilingual space through translanguaging

In traditional school teaching circumstances, languages are separated from each other by name. The non-dominant languages of emergent multilinguals are not commonly considered as among the resources that they possess (Cenoz and Gorter 2017). Policies that represent this perspective have been aimed at promoting the learning of a particular language while avoiding cross-linguistic influence (CLI) and discouraging code-switching; this type of policy, however, has now been challenged by multilingual ideologies (Cenoz and Gorter 2017). There is a strong move towards taking a multilingual speaker's entire linguistic repertoire as a reference point in multilingual education rather than dividing the repertoire into different linguistic systems (Cenoz and Gorter 2017).

Fluid language practice can focus on the process of translating and other types of translanguaging (Canagarajah 2013). The word "translanguaging" comes from a Welsh term, *trawsieithu*, which originally refers to a pedagogical practice where two languages are both used to maximize learning in bilingual classrooms (Baker 2011). It has since been developing in different contexts to imply the fluid movement between languages (Cenoz and Gorter 2017). Translanguaging can refer to pedagogical strategies based on the flexible use of a learner's whole linguistic repertoire; it can also refer to spontaneous multilingual practices that are used to enhance pedagogy (Cenoz and Gorter 2017). Translanguaging has gained wide acceptance as a bridge to learning in the area of bilingual and multilingual school education (García and Li 2014). It is understood in different ways and used in different modes in the home context of the present study.

Talking about school life
Language is best learned in context. Multilinguals may prefer a language in the context in which it is learned and in which they can express themselves more accurately. Just as first-generation immigrants find it more tiring to speak a new language than their mother tongue, multilingual children may want to use the school language to describe their school experience. Through the use of translanguaging, learners strategically create and negotiate meanings and, moreover, expand and enrich their learning experience in both academic and non-academic settings (Song 2016).

Y's mother had a flexible policy in conversational situations. She believed that even though one language was used as the base language, other languages could be employed where necessary for content clarification or meaning-making. For example, in a dinner routine in Y's family, everyone talked about their whole day's activities and asked each other questions. During this routine, when

Y was in Japanese preschools, her mother normally brought up topics once in Mandarin between herself and Y and another time in English when the father was involved, but the content might not be exactly the same. In either situation, Japanese and one home language were used for conveying information describing and clarifying meaning. Y and her mother continued using Mandarin and English in Scotland to talk about her daily life in the Scottish schools. In Example 11, Y first told her mother about her school day in Mandarin but then switched to English after trying hard in Mandarin.

Example 11 is from a diary entry (5;7).
妈妈, 我告诉 S1 和 S2, 人不是 . . . . . . 那个什么 . . . . . . [Mummy, I told S1 and S2, human beings are not . . . that . . . . .] Mummy, I told S1 and S2 that people are not made by God, but they didn't believe it. They think people are made by God. I said, "People are from monkeys." They didn't believe it. Only me and S3 believed it.

In this example, Y described her conversation with her classmates, S1, S2, and S3. Her mother waited until she finished describing the school scenario and then started to ask her different questions in Mandarin or English to make sure she understood and could use both languages to talk about the topic. Translanguaging thus helped Y express ideas in her unfamiliar language when talking about what she had read, heard, or watched in her familiar language. In addition to the unavailability of equivalents due to language deficiency or cultural differences, children may also find it a burden to switch from their school language to home language after a long day at school (Noguchi 1996b). Parents insisting on using a home language to talk about children's school and social lives may result in an end to a parent-child conversation. Child well-being and family ties are thus two considerations for parents in adopting flexible language policies.

Likewise, in her research on the bilingual parent acting as model for the bilingual child, Noguchi (1996b) illustrates how she used a similar technique called "debriefing" to encourage her English-Japanese children to talk about their day in Japanese schools. Her children would start out explaining in English but later on seemed unable to stop the flow of Japanese; the American mother (=Noguchi) would clarify the meaning in Japanese as she felt it was important to know what had happened to the children (Noguchi 1996b). To make sure her children eventually learned to express everything in English, she would then go over the story at a later time by asking clarification questions in English; she would also offer English vocabulary (with the Japanese equivalents where necessary) to enable the children to explain most, if not all, of their experiences in their two languages (Noguchi 1996b).

Making meaning in negotiations
Multilingual speakers tend to experience richer and more dynamic linguistic situations in their lives as compared with monolingual speakers. The way in which multilinguals learn and use languages is notably shaped by their life experiences. Y started to learn to read and write in her three languages at the same time as she started to speak them. The language used in family's learning activities therefore differed from the way in which the languages were used in their daily conversations. Y and her parents not only switched between codes for interactional purposes, but also used the totality of their language resources for meaning-making and knowledge transfer in support of her learning of the heritage, academic, and social languages.

Children are said to use their stronger language as scaffolding to understand a text in their weaker language (Creese and Blackledge 2010). In the present study, parent-directed translanguaging of a similar nature played a major role in the learning context. For example, one of Y's languages was used primarily for reading, and so code-switching to a more accessible language was useful for explaining and discussing. Such practice is illustrated in Example 12.

Example 12 is from a video recording (5;4).
盗墓贼 are people. 盗是偷, 墓是坟墓, 贼是小偷。These people are robbers who rob tombs. [盗墓贼 are people. 盗 is stealing, 墓 is tomb, 贼 is thief.]

In this example, her mother clarified the meaning of the Mandarin word, 盗墓贼, and checked Y's understanding using both Mandarin and English. Among Y's three languages, Mandarin accounted for the least input and the fewest context of use. Moreover, expressions in the written Mandarin form were often not decipherable from its speech. For example, when reading a book about World War I, Y asked her mother, "什么是军官?" [What is an officer?] (4;11). Her mother was first about to say, "士兵的领袖" [the leader of soldiers], but immediately realized that the Mandarin explanation seemed even more complex. She then adopted a familiar English equivalent and explained, "军官就是 officer. 军队里的士兵, 但是是 leader of soldiers." [军官 is an officer. He is also a soldier, but the leader of soldiers.] Using translanguaging to clarify content and word meaning might be related to Y's mother's previous working experience as a school teacher in subjects taught in English to non-native English speakers. It might also be related to the mother's high expectations for Y's trilingual competence. Her mother thus purposefully and strategically used more than one language to support her literacy development.

Song (2016) suggests that providing equivalent words helps children become aware of similar meanings in different languages and build potential connections across their languages. Y's mother also often checked Y's understanding of Mandarin using other languages, as shown in Example 13.

Example 13 is from a diary entry (4;3).
CHI: 七个小矮人把白雪公主放在一个杯子里。
 [The seven dwarfs put Snow White in a cup.]
MOT: 杯子? They put Snow White in a . . . ?
 [Cup?]
CHI: Coffee.
MOT: 不是 coffee, 是 coffin。
 [Not coffee, but coffin.]

In this example, Y confused the pronunciations of "coffin" with that of "coffee". Seeing this, her mother asked her to clarify the content of the story through discussions on the story in both English and Mandarin. More generally, the idea of methodological translanguaging has been expanded to include diversified strategies involving a speaker's entire linguistic repertoire as resources. It illustrates the multilingual speaker's abilities to shuttle between languages in a "dynamic and functionally integrated manner to organize and mediate mental processes in understanding, speaking, literacy, and not least learning" (Lewis, Jones, and Baker 2012: 1).

While her mother presumed that Y knew English better and it would be helpful to use translanguaging in discussions, it seemed that Y could understand almost all topics discussed in Mandarin. Moreover, she did not like her mother to use English in their Mandarin conversations. For example, when her mother explained how days and nights were related to the earth's rotation in English and Mandarin, Y contested her languages, "Don't speak English. Speak Chinese. I know Chinese. 太阳光射不到日本, 就是晚上了。" [The sunshine does not reach Japan and it is night (in Japan).] (5;3). Nevertheless, her mother believed that using all available languages was necessary and advantageous for academic learning, and thus she continued this type of practice in topic discussions.

García (2009) has shown that language learners in classrooms also use translanguaging for meaning-negotiation with others in interaction and for knowledge representation. The notion of spontaneous translanguaging broadens the use of translanguaging by embracing discursive practices across a variety of contexts (Cenoz and Gorter 2017). Bilinguals can engage in these multiple discursive practices to make sense of their bilingual worlds (García 2009).

5.3 From participant to child leader in family language practices

So far the role of parents in promoting learning has been emphasized. Although her parents were initially language policy makers, Y's language choice was not a passive response to their expectations and rules but a flexible exercise of her own sense of agency and behavioral patterns. Therefore, rather than looking at the adults' top-down endeavors alone, the present study also displays the child's bottom-up efforts in family socialization. Y was able to carry out particular tasks through guided interaction. Moreover, she adopted and further developed the parents' strategies and created new practices involving both oral and written language. In this way, Y's parents were gradually socialized into the language practices initiated and monitored by the child.

5.3.1 Taking advantage of different linguistic resources

Exposure to the non-community language beyond the parent-child interactional model is important. It may include speaking the language with a friend of a similar linguistic background or attending supplementary schools for language and literacy practices (Chinen and Tucker 2006). In Y's home, resources, such as the media, songs, picture cards and dictionaries, were used to help her become familiar with different languages and cultures. Picture cards were effective tools in the home teaching and learning. Y's mother put up the master alphabet cards on the wall and pointed at each letter when she sang the alphabet song. Y would look at the cards and the printed letters carefully. At one and a half years old, she could recognize all 26 alphabet letters on the cards, saying their names and sounds. She liked touching a letter and chanting its phonics sound. For example, she chanted "/æ/, /æ/, /'æpl/" when saw or heard the letter "a". In addition to English cards, phonetic cards of Japanese *kana* and Mandarin *pīnyīn*,[19] as well as Chinese character cards, were also displayed to help Y learn pronunciations and writing systems from two years old. Playing with cards appears to be common in many families, but it was crucial for Y's early language and literacy development. She also used cards as resources when teaching her parents.

Y frequently looked up English words and Chinese characters in both paper and electronic dictionaries from four years old. Her use of these resources is illustrated in Example 14, in which her mother's response brought out a question about the pronunciations of a Chinese character's retroflex and flat tongue sounds. Similar mistakes are sometimes made by Mandarin speakers from the southern part of China.

---

19 *Pīnyīn* is the romanization of the Chinese written language based on the pronunciation of the Beijing dialect of Mandarin Chinese.

Example 14 is from the mother-child conversation (5;0).
CHI: How to say this in Chinese?
MOT: 防晒霜 (*fáng shài shuāng*) 。
[Sunscreen.]
CHI: 防晒 (*shài*) 霜听起来好像不对。*sh* 不对。
[*shài* doesn't sound quite right. *sh* (a retroflex sound) is not right.]
MOT: Shall we look it up in a dictionary?
(Y then looked up the word in an electronic dictionary.)

In the above example, her mother suggested that Y refer to a dictionary for the correct form, which she did. Y used a digital dictionary and found the character, 晒, using its *pīnyīn* (*shài*) on her own. Dictionaries were especially helpful when Y learned to read and write in all of her three languages. It appeared easy and enjoyable for her to look up words in a dictionary, which in turn supported her to read and write independently. It is her parents who initially taught her to use paper and electronic dictionaries and who also frequently modelled this practice by referring to a dictionary while doing their own research. However, using a dictionary quickly became part of Y's own learning experience. This might help explain the development of her high level of writing skills and her strong interests in keeping writing as a daily routine. Having realized Y's learning abilities, her parents came to consider her more and more as a language expert and an equal partner in many aspects of their family activities.

Dyson (1997) proposes that children are active consumers and interpreters of the media. In Japan, books written in English, music and movies featuring English soundtracks, and other English TV programs were available online or at shops. Y listened to nursery rhymes, stories, and chapter books using a CD or DVD player, a reading pen, or an iPad. She also watched BBC and NHK news with her parents every day. The benefit of exposure to the multilingual media in terms of the acquisition of pronunciation is evident in Example 15.

Example 15 is from an observation note (3;5).
MOT: Why do you speak English with a British accent?
CHI: Because I watch BBC and listen to *Oxford Reading Tree*. (*Oxford Reading Tree* is a series of audio books published by Oxford University Press.)

In this example, Y explained how she learned to speak good English through reading and access to the English media. Y had started to watch YouTube cartoons from one year old, particularly those dubbed in her three languages. She often picked up new expressions beyond her parents' knowledge or usage from cartoons. For example, the Mandarin term, 平板电脑 [tablet], was a new term which had rapidly spread and come to be used with the invention of iPad in 2010. Her mother rarely heard the translated Mandarin word (in Japan) and simply referred to the item as tablet or iPad. However, Y learned the Mandarin equivalent from Chinese cartoons and actually used it in some situations. The media also provided Y with information and knowledge useful for daily conversations, as seen in Example 16.

Example 16 is from an observation note (5;6).
Situation: Y and her mother were talking about the meaning of the words "north" and "south".
MOT: How should I describe "north"?
CHI: North Korea.
MOT: That's right and the opposite is "south".
CHI: South Korea.

In the above, Y employed the knowledge that she acquired from news to help explain "north" and "south" to her mother. The examples Y provided nevertheless indicated her knowledge of the two words.

5.3.2 Code-mixing and code-switching: from unintentional to intentional

In the earlier research on FLP, the issues of child language development relating to psycholinguistic questions such as language differentiation in bilingual and monolingual children were addressed (De Houwer 1990). Researchers indicated that no scientific evidence had shown that language confusion or language delay is caused by rearing children bilingually regardless of whether or not any specific languages policies are adopted (King and Fogle 2006; Lanza 1992). Language differentiation and language mixing are therefore regarded as natural behavior of multilingual speakers and these are important topics in the research on FLP. Taking a study of two French and English siblings as an example, Swain (1972: xiv) viewed bilingualism as a first language of infant bilinguals and bilingual first language acquisition as "a general human capacity to learn linguistic codes and switch between them".

Mixed codes were observed in different stages of Y's language development. She was able to speak simple English and Mandarin sentences from one year and a half. She spoke predominantly in Mandarin in a Mandarin context and in English in an English context. Generally, there was no code-mixing behavior observed when Y played with her monolingual Japanese friends. However, on some occasions she used two languages in the same context. This is illustrated in examples below.

Example 17 is from a diary entry (1;8).
CHI: Mama carry bike. Y だっこ helmet.
[Y carries the helmet.]
MOT: Y carries the helmet.

Example 18 is from a diary entry (1;9).
Situation: There was a strawberry and a slice of pineapple on Y's plate.
CHI: 我喜欢吃那个草莓，不喜欢吃那个 pineapple。
[I like the strawberry. I don't like the pineapple.]
MOT: 菠萝。
[Pineapple.]

Example 19 is from a diary entry (2;0).
CHI: 谁把花ぽい在那里了?
[Who threw the flowers there?]
MOT: ぽい, 扔。
[Throw.]
(Y's mother provided the Mandarin equivalent word, 扔, of the Japanese term, ぽい.)

Mixing words as seen in the above examples was thought to mainly relate to language input environment, lack of equivalents, or language availability. In this stage of language development, Y's parents normally provided the correct form and repeated her speech. Her mother noticed that frequent code-mixing gradually disappeared after Y turned 2;6. She had an adequate vocabulary in each of her three languages by that age, such that borrowing items by virtue of their availability was no longer a typical cause of language mixing. However, there were other reasons for her to mix codes, such as language preference and language learning experience, as shown in Examples 20 and 21 respectively.

Example 20 is from an observation note (2;10).
MOT: 星期天叫爸爸带你去公园看小鹿。
[Let daddy take you to the park to see deer.]
CHI: 我要给小鹿吃 biscuits。
[I want to give deer biscuits.]
MOT: Biscuits 叫什么?
[How do you say "biscuits" (in Mandarin)?]
CHI: 饼干。
[Biscuit.]

The English word, biscuit, was frequently used in Y's daily life. Although its Mandarin form, 饼干, was sometimes referred to in a Mandarin context, Y had certainly

5.3 From participant to child leader in family language practices

heard and used its English equivalent form more often, either when talking to her parents, or reading and watching cartoons by herself. Example 21 in the following also involves English items mixed into her Mandarin utterances.

Example 21 is from a diary entry (4;11).
今天我在 forest 做 woodwork, 我把 nail 放到 rock 上, 然后用 hammer 把 nail 打进去. [I did some woodwork in the forest today. I put nails on a rock and then hammered the nails into the rock.]

The above example quotes part of a recording of Y talking about her new experience in Scotland. Some Mandarin equivalents of the English words in the example were not commonly used in her daily conversations, such as 铁钉 [nail] and 锤子 [hammer]. However, doing woodwork was her weekly activity in the Scottish preschool and thus she preferred to use the English items.

While borrowing available vocabulary would gradually disappear as her development in each of her three languages progressed, syntactic mixing started to emerge around the age of two. The following examples illustrate code-switching of this nature.

Example 22 is from a diary entry (1;9).
CHI: Daddy, 起床して。
　　　 [Get up.]
　　　 (Y mixed the Mandarin verb, 起床, and the Japanese suffix, して.)
Correct wording in Mandarin: 起床了。 [Get up.]
Correct wording in Japanese: おきて。 [Get up.]

Example 23 is from a diary entry (2;0).
CHI: 我要吃 sand 明治。
　　　 [I want to eat a sandwich.]
　　　 (The Mandarin word, 三明治, is a phonetic translation of its English equivalent, sandwich.)
Correct form in Mandarin: 我要吃三明治。 [I want to eat a sandwich.]

Example 24 is from a diary entry (2;10).
CHI: Y 要 be 三岁了。
　　　 [Y will be three years old.]
Correct wording in Mandarin: Y 要三岁了。 [Y will be three years old.]

Example 25 is from a diary entry (2;11).
CHI: 我不会的もん。
　　　[I can't.]
　　　(In Japanese, もん is used at the end of a sentence for emphasis.)
Correct wording in Mandarin: 我不会。[I can't.]
Correct wording in Japanese: できないんだもん。[I can't.]

This type of mixing behavior shown in the examples above involves the grammatical arrangement of two sets of lexicon and syntax within a single utterance, which requires a high level of trilingual competence.

Although Y sometimes mixed or switched among her three codes, she held a hostile attitude to her mother's code-switching from Mandarin to English or borrowing non-Mandarin words in Mandarin conversations. For example, Y and her mother had about one hour of Mandarin breakfast time every morning before her father got up. They would watch BBC news while eating breakfast and chat about the news. It was often difficult for the mother to explain the news accurately only in Mandarin without borrowing any English words from the news. However, Y stopped her mother every time and told her, "要讲中文, 不要讲英文, 不要把中文和英文混在一起讲。" [Speak Mandarin. Don't speak English. Don't mix Mandarin and English when you speak.] (5;0). This attitude could be explained by Y's preference for speaking only one language in one situation. It could also be seen as reflecting Y's desire to prove that her Mandarin ability was as good as that of English and thus she wanted to stop her mother from borrowing and mixing English words in Mandarin conversations.

Studies reporting grammatical features, functions, and patterns of children's use of different languages in interaction suggest that children are capable of using more than one language flexibly and strategically for various purposes, in diverse contexts and to distinct audiences (Shin 2010). Children, for example, may switch codes to get attention from adults, emphasize and clarify meanings, change topics and discourse styles, accommodate contexts, express linguistic and cultural identities, change and establish stance, and mitigate uncomfortable situations (Iannacci 2008, Reyes 2004, Shin 2010).

In the present study, Y had a good mastery of equivalents in her three languages by the second birthday. She could switch languages naturally and effectively in different contexts. It also seemed that when she used a borrowed term, it was intentional, because she already knew the equivalent of the borrowed item in the language she was speaking. Moreover, she displayed good fluency with the hybrid speech. Examples 26 through 31 illustrate Y's developing awareness of the complex contextual factors conductive to code-switching.

Example 26 is from a diary entry (1;8). (Emphasizing)
MOT: 睡觉了。
[Sleep (now).]
CHI: 要玩。Play.
[(I) want to play.]

Example 27 is from a diary entry (2;6). (Learning new words)
CHI: Chestnut 中文是什么?
[How to say "chestnut" in Mandarin?]
MOT: 板栗。
[Chestnut.]
CHI: 你吃板栗吗?
[Do you want some chestnuts?]
(Y asked her Chinese grandmother.)

Example 28 is from a diary entry (3;5). (Quoting directly)
MOT: 叫爸爸起床。
[Go and ask daddy to get up.]
CHI: Daddy, get up!
MOT: 他说什么?
[What did he say?]
CHI: 爸爸说: "I'm going to get up now."
[Daddy said, "I'm going to get up now."]

Example 29 is from a diary entry (3;5). (Quoting indirectly)
Situation: Y made a phone call to her father.
MOT: What did he say?
CHI: 他说他在办公室,马上回来。
[He said he was in the office and would be back soon.]

Example 30 is from a diary entry (2;3). (Including a speaker)
Situation: Y and her mother were talking about going out.
MOT: 问问爸爸要去吗?
[Ask daddy whether he wants to go or not.]
CHI: Daddy, do you want to go?
(Y's father was working in the same area but was not involved in the conversation.)

Example 31 is from a diary entry (5;2). (Excluding an interlocutor)
Situation: Y's family was waiting for a train on the platform in Scotland.
CHI: あのひとママとおなじかさをもってる。
[That person's umbrella was the same as mama's.]

The above examples show Y using code-switching as a means of communication for the purposes of emphasizing, quoting others' utterances, mimicking their tones of voice, and including or excluding a speaker. Y's parents considered that it was common for competent multilingual speakers to employ multiple languages and switch codes in a contextually appropriate manner. Likewise, Fotos (1995) addresses how Japanese-English bilinguals use code-switching as a device for different conversational functions, such as to indicate topics, to emphasize and clarify, to attract and hold attention, and to report the speech of others.

Y would also switch to her preferred language or use code-switching as a discourse strategy to avoid borrowing or mixing with a different code. She would request her parents to provide an equivalent word by asking them "How to say it in English, Japanese, or Mandarin?" These are reflected in the following example.

Example 32 is from a mother-child conversation (5;6).
Situation: Y met a Scottish classmate, A, in a park.
1 MOT: 我没认出是 A, 我以为是 B。
[I didn't recognize A. I thought it was B.]
(B was also Y's classmate.)
2 CHI: B 要在 Australia (. . .) for four weeks.
[B will be in Australia for four weeks.]
(Y thought for a few seconds after saying "Australia".)
(After ten seconds)
3 CHI: Four weeks 用中文怎么说?
[How do you say "four weeks" in Mandarin?]
4 MOT: 四个星期。
[Four weeks.]
5 CHI: 噢! 四个星期。
[Oh! Four weeks.]
(After five minutes)
6 MOT: 你怎么不问我 Australia 用中文怎么说?
[Why don't you ask me how to say "Australia" in Mandarin?]
7 CHI: 澳大利亚。
[Y gave the Mandarin equivalent of the word "Australia".]

In the above example, Y mixed the English name of the country in her Mandarin speech even though she knew its Mandarin equivalent item (Turn 7). This type of code-mixing seemed not to be an issue of language proficiency but her language preference. However, Y borrowed the English expression, four weeks, because it seems she did not recall the correct Mandarin form at that moment (Turn 2). She was aware of her language deficiency and asked for help from her mother (Turn 3).

More interestingly, in order to move on without breaking down an ongoing conversation, Y would switch completely from the language in which she lacked the term to the one in which she had all the necessary terms. Through this type of code-switching, she protested against the language choice of her parents. Examples 33 and 34 show code-switching of this nature.

Example 33 is from a video recording (5;4).
1 CHI: 我要吃 cupboard 里的那个。
        [I want to eat the one in the cupboard.]
2 MOT: Cupboard 是什么?
        [What do you call "cupboard" (in Mandarin)?]
3 CHI: I want to eat something in the cupboard.

Example 34 is from a video recording (5;4).
1 CHI: 你可以给我 icing sugar 吗?
         [Can you give me icing sugar?]
2 MOT: 什么?
         [Pardon?]
3 CHI: Can you give me icing sugar?
4 MOT: 你为什么突然说英文?
         [Why do you suddenly speak English?]
5 CHI: 因为我不知道 icing sugar 的中文。It's quicker to say everything in English.
         [Because I do not know how to say icing sugar in Mandarin.]

In Example 33, instead of asking for an equivalent in the middle of a conversation, Y switched the whole utterance from Mandarin to English (Turn 3). In order to get her mother's response quickly, Y even refused the mother's language correction request. In Example 34, Y suddenly switched from Mandarin to English (Turn 3). This seemed to be because she believed code-switching was "easier" and "quicker" for making a smooth conversation (Turn 5).

Observing and assessing these actual language practices of Y shows how code-switching behavior attests to children's metalinguistic knowledge and metacognitive ability[20] (e.g. their awareness of audience and environment). Researchers

---

20 Metalinguistic knowledge refers to the knowledge about "abstract structure of language that organizes sets of linguistic rules", such as the phonetic, semantic, and syntactic features of languages; metacognitive ability is the ability to use metalinguistic knowledge (Bialystock 2001: 123).

acknowledge that children are very sensitive to the language views and behavior of their parents; they are likely to adopt a more bilingual mode with those who mix or accept mixing words, whereas they are more monolingual with someone who does not do so (Genesee, Boivin, and Nicoladis 1995). Influenced by her parents' positive attitudes toward code-switching, as well as many instances of such modelling, when an unknown expression was needed in her utterances, Y would naturally switch the code of the whole utterance.

5.3.3 Socializing in dual-lingual conversations

Saville-Troike (1987) argues that *dual-lingual* conversations are qualitatively different from truly bilingual conversations. In a dual-lingual conversation, speech partners mutually understand each other's codes, but where one partner consistently uses one code while the other partner another (Smith-Christmas 2014). However, in a bilingual conversation, both speakers are competent at both languages and capable of switching between the two (Saville-Troike 1987).

From two years old, Y sometimes replied to her father in Japanese when the father addressed her in English. Her code-switching sometimes led to dual-lingual conversations between herself and her father in which she spoke in Japanese and he responded in English. Following the OPOL approach, Y's parents would normally refuse to carry on dual-lingual conversations with her and they would try to correct her language choice. Similarly, dual-lingual conversations have also been reported by Smith-Christmas (2014) in her study of a Gaelic-English family, where the mother and the grandmother persistently used Gaelic while the children normally replied in English. The Gaelic-dominant grandmother occasionally felt it difficult to continue in Gaelic, maintaining a dual-lingual conversation with the grandchildren who constantly replied to her in English; the grandmother said this was demoralizing (Smith-Christmas 2014).

However, a different type of dual-lingual conversation was observed after Y turned three; that is, she code-switched to Mandarin purposefully when talking to her father, as shown in Example 35.

Example 35 is from an observation note (3;8).
1 CHI: 爸爸, 我要吃饼干。
         [Daddy, I want to eat cookies.]
         (Y had a package of cookies in her hand.)
2 FAT: Ok. I'll give you cookies after lunch.

As shown in the above example, Y's father sometimes decoded a few simple Mandarin words in a specific context and he attempted to interact with Y assisted by her body language (Turn 2). However, most of the times her father did not quite understand her. One example of this nature is shown in Example 36.

Example 36 is from a video recording (5;1).
CHI: It's Chinese time. 你想读什么?
[What do you want to read?]
(It was Japanese reading time but Y wanted to read Mandarin books.)
FAT: 今日何を読む?
[What shall we read today?]
(Her father had a Japanese book in his hand.)
CHI: 你喜欢这个吗?
[Do you like this (book)?]
FAT: このページをよむ?
[Shall we read this page?]
(Her father didn't understand Y's Mandarin.)

In the above example, Y and her father were not successful in maintaining a dual-lingual conversation, which hence turned out to be *dilingual* – a conversation in which two languages are used by two speakers but neither one understands the other's code (Smith-Christmas 2016).

Despite many challenges, Y believed that dual-lingual conversations helped her father learn Mandarin and thus purposefully chose Mandarin in situations such as those above. Dual-lingual and dilingual conversations were also observed in the conversations between Y and her monolingual Chinese grandparents. It is found that despite the fact that her grandparents knew only Mandarin, they tried hard to strengthen their bonds with Y through their language use. This expectation was shared by Y's father and seen in the efforts that he made in constructing the above dual-lingual conversations. The bi-directional nature of language socialization thus became apparent as Y changed the adults' language briefs and language practices using a variety of unique agencies.

5.3.4 Collaborative translating

In studies of bilinguals' flexible use of the totality of their linguistic repertoires, it is found that children learn unfamiliar items in a different language by making potential meaning connections between the target language and their stronger or more familiar language (Song 2016). Translating is a collaborative operation in the process of acquisition of multiple languages, and it can be either child-directed or parent-directed. Parents can use translating as an explicit pedagogical practice to mediate understanding in interaction with children, whereas children are also provided with opportunities to engage in translating or paraphrasing to negotiate and construct meaning with parents (Song 2016).

Using translation equivalents

Translation is a temporary device to learn and practice a second language by making use of a speaker's total linguistic resources (Song 2016). An important element in the development of multilingualism is the acquisition of translation equivalents—lexical items that refer to the same thing in each of a multilingual's languages. Y's parents considered it vital for her to have a mastery of the equivalents in her three languages. It was therefore only natural for them to help her overcome gaps in this aspect of her linguistic knowledge. Indexing occurred when Y's parents said a word unfamiliar to her and then immediately offered its translation in her more familiar language. Y's mother also purposefully included more than one language in conversation, to teach functions such as emphasizing and clarifying meaning. Example 37 illustrates this.

Example 37 is from a diary entry (2;5).
Situation: Y wore a new headband and was admiring herself in the mirror.
CHI: かわいい。
 [Cute.]
MOT: Can I have it?
CHI: Yかわいい、あげない。
 [Y is cute. (I'll) not give it to you.]
MOT: Y is very cute. 很可爱。
 [Very cute.]
 (Her mother provided the Mandarin equivalent of the expression, very cute.)

As seen in the above example, Y's mother considered the simultaneous acquisition of translation equivalents through parental modelling to be the best way to achieve this goal. Her mother also expected her to reply using equivalents, and it was observed that chanting a word and its equivalent expressions in two or all of her three languages become a feature of Y's speech. She used this particular way of "translation" to index the same object or clarify meaning. For example, when her mother stopped her from jumping, saying, "No jumping. Bump your head", Y patted her head and replied, "いたい、いたい、好痛, 好痛 [painful]", first in Japanese and then in Mandarin (1;9). When her mother said, "We don't have any ice creams", she continued with "Shopping, shopping. ちりんちりんはやい [Cycling will be fast]. Mummyはやい [fast], daddyはやい [fast], Yはやい [fast]. Mummy fast, daddy fast, Y fast." (1;9). She used these equivalents for such purposes as telling, emphasizing, or clarifying. Seeing that Y understood everything that parents said in each of her three languages and that Y displayed a good use of the equivalents in different contexts, her mother gradually stopped offering equivalents after she turned three. Instead, the mother created more opportunities for Y to employ a specific code or its equivalent as expected by parents by asking questions such as "How do you say this in English, Japanese, or Mandarin?"

During the early stages of this process, a translation equivalent tended to be referenced according to who spoke it. Announcements such as "Mummy or Daddy says . . ." would be made when Y offered the translation of a word that she said in a parent's language. As evident in two other studies, conducted by Cruz-Ferreira (2006) and De Houwer (1990), by a child's second birthday, he or she may be able to provide a real translation from one language to another spontaneously or when prompted. Y was able to do what was described as word definition translations such as 客厅就是 [Living room is] living room (2;0). After two, children may also start to use the actual name of a language to make explicit comments about what forms in what language they and others use (Cruz-Ferreira 2006; De Houwer 1990). Y was able to treat languages in this way, as seen in Example 38.

Example 38 is from a video (2;4).
MOT: Just now I asked her, "If you visit China, which language do you speak, English, にほんご [Japanese], or 中文 [Mandarin]?" She said, "中文 [Mandarin]."
(Her mother was talking to her father.)
MOT: Daddy can't speak Chinese. Can you help him?
(Y nodded.)
MOT: How do you say "It's yummy." in Chinese?
CHI: 好吃。
[Yummy.]
MOT: How do you say "I'm tired." in Chinese?
CHI: 睡着了。
[Fall asleep.]
MOT: 睡着了? 好累好累。
[Fall asleep? Very tired.]
(Her mother corrected her Mandarin translation of the word "tired".)
FAT: How do you say "Let's go shopping." in Chinese?
CHI: 买超市。
[Buy the supermarket.]
MOT: 买超市? 去超市。
[Buy the supermarket? Go to the supermarket.]
(Her mother corrected her Mandarin translation of the expression "go to the supermarket".)

The above shows how translation is a useful tool in communication for clarifying and making meaning in multilingual families. Y's parents provided translations in a language that she did not frequently use in daily conversations. Moreover, translating, as an integral part of translanguaging, was also used as a pedagogical strategy by Y to draw her parents into the meaning-making process. The following two examples represent such a pedagogical translation practice initiated by Y.

Example 39 is from an observation note (2;6).
1 MOT: 你生病了，就不要出去了。
[You are sick. Don't go outside.]
2 CHI: 会把小细菌 (xiǎo xì jūn) 给别人。
[Will pass little bacteria to others.]
3 MOT: 小飞机 (xiǎo fēi jī)?
[Little airplane?]
(Her mother didn't catch her pronunciation of the word 细菌 (xì jūn) but heard 飞机 (fēi jī) instead.)
4 CHI: 小细菌。Bacteria.
(Y said the word "bacteria" first in Mandarin and then in English.)

Example 40 is from an observation note (4;7).
1 CHI: What's this fish?
2 FAT: I don't know.
3 CHI: What's the Japanese name?
4 FAT: アユ。
[*Ayu* or sweetfish.]

In Example 39, Y offered the English equivalent word when the original Mandarin item was not understood by her mother (Turn 4). Similarly, in Example 40, Y led in the meaning negotiation and checked her father's understanding of a type of fish in both English and Japanese. She requested a Japanese translation of the name of fish (Turn 3) after realizing that a lack of a common English equivalent impeded her father from giving information (Turn 2). Translation, through comprehension checks, is thus helpful for both children and adults to relearn forgotten expressions while elucidating meanings in different languages.

Baker and Wright (2017) believe that bilinguals rarely show equal ability in each of their languages and that they use them in different contexts. Some terms in one language either have no exact equivalents in a different language or appear unfamiliar to children in that language. Translating or paraphrasing these types of items seems challenging and unneeded. Example 41 shows the meaninglessness of literal translations of this type of lexical item. Y translated the names of foods served at lunch time in her Scottish school.

5.3 From participant to child leader in family language practices

Example 41 is from a mother-child conversation (5;3).

1 MOT:	今天午饭吃了什么?
	[What did you eat for lunch today?]
2 CHI:	意面, 香肠, 小鱼指头, 西红柿。
	[Pasta, sausage, fish finger, (and) tomato.]
3 MOT:	意面是什么?
	[What is 意面?]
4 CHI:	意大利面条。
	[Italian noodle.]
5 MOT:	小鱼指头是什么?
	[What is 小鱼指头?]
6 CHI:	Fish fingers.

In this example, Y's mother was confused by her Mandarin translation of "fish fingers" (Turn 5). The English translation of 小鱼指头 [fish finger] did not have a context-based meaning in Mandarin, because such food did not exist in the Chinese culture. When translating a culture-related lexical item which lacks its natural equivalent in a different language, Y sometimes provided a description of the coined term. For example, in a later conversation, she explained a "fish finger" as follows, "It is made of fish and it looks like a finger." (5;3).

In spite of Y's best endeavors, her mother considered it needless to translate food names and other proper nouns if they were attached to a language and its culture whose equivalents were not available in other languages. There were other reasons why her parents maintained some terms in the original English (when residing in Scotland) or Japanese (when residing in Japan). For instance, Y's mother admitted that translating or rephrasing some terms into Mandarin often resulted in miscommunication or confusion, while maintaining them in the original form tended to convey meanings clearly, avoiding confusion.

5.3.5 Translanguaging

As discussed in 5.2.3, translanguaging is a relatively new way to look at a language practice that involves an integrated use of two languages and, more importantly, a process of knowledge construction (Li 2018). In Y's family, translanguaging was an invaluable strategic practice in multiple contexts (e.g. a bilingual or trilingual context) and in different language modes (e.g. speaking, reading, writing, or playing). Using translanguaging as a methodological tool and family as a space for multilingual repertoires, language practices were successfully established in her home. Translanguaging also enhanced parent-child intimacy, owing to which Y's overall development became possible. Figure 1 is an example of Y and her mother working on place value and big numbers through translanguaging.

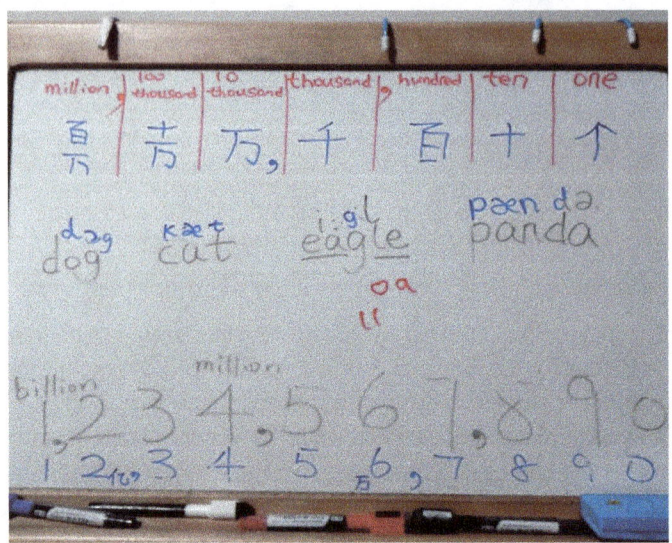

Figure 1: Learning place value (4;11).

As noted by Li (2018), translanguaging is a characteristic of multilingual language performance which treats languages as multilingual and multimodal resources for meaning-making. In the above example, Y's mother felt it would be ineffective for transferring knowledge and rather confusing if she explained in each of the child's three languages separately, because many words of place value in English do not have equivalent terms in Japanese or Mandarin. In order to help Y understand place value of a number in three different ways, her mother thus looked at all three languages in the same setting. She also used English words and Chinese characters which helped Y compare and understand them.

A similar use of translanguaging can be found during a writing task. That is, writing is completed in the academic language, or less commonly, the heritage language, while code-switching is employed for discussions. Translanguaging and code-switching are two different theoretical and analytical concepts. Code-switching refers to the grammatical and interactional rule-governed alternation between languages at specific points in a discourse. Translanguaging is a practice that involves an integrated use of different languages and language varieties, and "more importantly, a process of knowledge construction that goes beyond language(s)" (Li 2018: 15). By using translanguaging in writing activities, a multilingual's whole linguistic repertoire can be flexibly employed in the cognitive processes of thinking, judging, negotiating, and problem-solving. This is shown in Example 42.

Example 42 is from a video recording (5;7).

Situation:	Y was writing an English story.
CHI:	"The bird was very beautiful." Comma.
MOT:	这个不是 comma, 这个是 full stop。小蝌蚪叫 comma。
	[This is not a comma. This is a full stop. The one similar to a tadpole is a comma.]
CHI:	/f/-/l/-/u:/? Small case "w" 怎么写?
	[How do you write the lower case "w"?]
	(Y spelt the word "f-l-ew" using IPA.)
MOT:	Lower case?
CHI:	怎么写 lower case?
	[How do you write the lower case "w"?]
MOT:	写小一点。小 "w"。
	[Write it smaller. Small "w".]
CHI:	跟 big case 一样?
	[Same as the big case?]
MOT:	是。Upper case.
	[Yes. Upper case.]
CHI:	大 W。
	[Big W.]

Pedagogical strategies were used in Y's family to help her learn in an accessible and collaborative environment. In the above example, Y and her mother went back and forth between English and Mandarin in order to make sure that she had understood how to write the upper case and the lower case of some alphabet letters. It is clearly shown that translanguaging goes beyond the concept of code-switching, which is based on the monoglossic view that bilinguals have two separate named languages (Gort and Sembiante 2015).

From age three, Y became a Mandarin teacher to her parents. Teaching Mandarin greatly strengthened the family bonds while also involving her three languages. Translanguaging was employed as a multilingual practice and a pedagogical strategy by Y in interaction with her parents. In the following example, she gave her father a test on Chinese characters after teaching him to read a Mandarin text. She was fluent in both languages at the time.

Example 43 is from a video recording (5;10).
CHI: Ok, let me do you a quiz. Which is 鸟 [bird]? Which is it?
(Y asked her father to find the Chinese character "bird".)
(Her father pointed at the Chinese character 鸟 [bird].)
CHI: How about 儿 [son]? 花 [flower]? Where is it? Just point to where. Anywhere it is. I say 花 [flower]. Ok. 开 [open]. Good. 不 [no]. Good. 捉 [catch], 鸟 [bird], 们 [everyone]. Good. Where is the other?
(Y required her father to find more Chinese characters and he did as she told.)
CHI: 爱 [love]. Where is it now? I will get you to the difficult one.

In this example, Y taught a foreign language (Mandarin) to her father in his stronger foreign language (English). Her ability to go back and forth between the two languages was not simply a shift from one to the other, but a reorganization of the two in the process of language use. Translanguaging thus helped Y construct meanings during literacy activities.

Other dispositions and attitudes can also be developed in translanguaging, such as being tolerant of differences and being patient (Canagarajah 2013). In this way, translanguaging was regarded as a positive experience in Y's language learning. What she did with languages was similar to the translanguaging practice commonly found in a bilingual classroom context. It encompasses a range of communicative and cultural practices, through which multilinguals perform their identities that are shaped and constrained by social norms, expectations, and language ideologies (Sayer 2013).

To conclude, this chapter demonstrated new patterns in Y's family's language socialization. Language is a natural object while language choice is not (Armstrong 2014). Language practices are negotiable and can be parent-led or child-led. In order to enhance the quality of family communication, her parents were willing to take Y's desires and attitudes into consideration and adjust their own attitudes and make decisions accordingly. As her parents gradually switched their role from language facilitators to language supporters, Y gradually became the leader in different contexts who established new rules and supervised familial activities. The sharing of responsibilities among the three family members in intergenerational interactions strengthened their family bonds and ensured the child's sustainable language development. Family language policy is thus a collaborative achievement of both parents and children.

6 From parent facilitators to child manager

Although parents and children using the same language does not absolutely guarantee conflict-free intergenerational communication, parent-child intimacy may be at risk if they exercise different language choices (De Houwer 2020). For children whose home language is also their mother tongue, it most likely does not serve the family relationship well when children speak only the societal language and parents speak only the home language (De Houwer 2020). Language policies do not guarantee every member's language choice without effective management (Spolsky 2009). Language management manipulates and modifies language use in everyday practices. It functions as the "manifestation of values, attitudes and understandings of those who use them" (Cross 2009: 30). Like most other parents, Y's parents were the managers in their family events when she was young, especially before her third birthday. They attempted to maintain the two non-societal languages and develop the child's multilingual skills. Y also tended to meet her parents' expectations. However, her language and literacy abilities dramatically progressed after three years old. Y exercised her unique agency to position herself as "leader" and "teacher" in family language practices; accordingly, her parents switched their role from learning facilitators to child supporters.

6.1 Parents as language facilitators

Childhood acquisition of a non-societal language may be undermined by different pressures from the dominant society and thus requires great efforts, such as instructing on what and how to speak and monitoring unsatisfactory performance (King et al. 2008; Spolsky 2009). In the family context, such efforts are traditionally derived from parents' beliefs about "language correctness" and their aims to persuade children to speak in "what parents believe to be the standard or correct form of the language" (Spolsky 2009: 14). It is parents who normally act as managers in language practices, attempting to maintain the heritage language and develop the child multilingualism. Family language management is often attributed to the strategies that parents use to supply input in the languages that they want their children to acquire and the strategies that parents use to deal with the mixed codes in children's discourse. However, parents' visible efforts sometimes show incongruence between their claimed ideologies and actual actions (Kopeliovich 2010).

6.1.1 Adopting a flexible one-parent-one-language policy

Three major input strategies have been distinguished in a variety of settings of simultaneous bilingual acquisition: one-parent-one-language (OPOL), one-location-one-language, and mixed-languages-at-home (Grosjean 2010; Piller 2001; Romaine 1995). Among the three, the OPOL strategy is the most widely used in families whose parents have different language backgrounds or speak different dominant languages. The OPOL approach was initially postulated by a French linguist, Maurice Grammont (1902), as *une personnne; une language* [one person one language] and involves each parent typically speaking in his/her native tongue to their child (as cited in Barron-Hauwaert 2004). Lanza (1997) discovered cases of the contextual use of the OPOL approach; that is, the minority language speaking parent spoke only in that language with the child, whilst the majority language speaking parent used the minority language in certain situations. Lanza (1997) considers the application of this approach in family conversations to represent true bilingual practices. Lanza (1997) further points out that even when some parents purposely use a language other than their first language in an attempt to achieve additive child bilingualism, the OPOL strategy can work naturally. This is evidenced in the case of Y, whose parents used English, a language non-native to both of them, between themselves and with their child.

Parents' attitudes concerning the particular type of interaction that they choose reflect their language beliefs. Those who employ the OPOL policy may hold a negative attitude toward mixed codes. They monitor their children's language production and tend to establish a "pure" linguistic environment – that is, communicating in only one language at a time. The child's use of a language other than the parents' will normally lead to a language choice correction. Döpke (1992) argues that applying the OPOL policy and using an interactional strategy to elicit a target language are significant for the acquisition of the minority language.

The OPOL policy used in Y's family required an appropriate choice of a named language to be used with a specific interlocutor. This practice was seen as helpful for her to develop a good knowledge and usage of each of her three languages in the early stages of trilingual acquisition. Before the age of three, Y mainly followed her parents' language choices, selecting the language that a parent spoke. In addition to her parents, Y's appropriate language use with her monolingual Mandarin-speaking grandparents was discussed in a different study that reported on her language choices in conversations with them. The study shows that Y's Mandarin utterances outnumbered any other single type of language when she addressed her grandparents (Zhan 2021). Meanwhile, her mixing behavior was also observed. It was noticed that when her grandparents spoke predominantly in Mandarin, she used few non-Mandarin terms; however, when her grandparents mixed languages, her non-Mandarin forms also increased (Zhan 2021). This parallels the observation data from two separate studies, those of De Houwer (2009) and Lanza (1997), which show how children tend to monitor and adjust to their parents' modelling behavior.

Researchers have noticed that families which have adopted the OPOL strategy in a similar way may produce very different outcomes in terms of children's language proficiency (Fogle and King 2018; Spolsky 2004, 2009). It is common for children whose parents employ the OPOL approach to be able to understand both languages but speak only the dominant language of the society (Döpke 1992; Romaine 1995; Yamamoto 2001). In other words, the adoption of the OPOL policy does not guarantee the fluent use of two languages. Researchers have also found that strictly and consistently using the OPOL strategy is not necessarily the reality. The data from two separate surveys on bilingual families, one in Flanders (De Houwer 2007) and the other in Japan (Yamamoto 2001), revealed that parents who self-reported using this strategy actually mixed or switched languages. In fact, the most common input patterns adopted by the families in these two studies were: one parent spoke a non-community language while the other spoke the non-community as well as the community language, and both parents addressed children in the same two languages (De Houwer 2007). De Houwer (2009) advises that the OPOL strategy is best seen and followed as a main but not the only principle in daily practices. Studies on the OPOL strategy thus gradually began to focus more on its pragmatic aspect when looking at actual parent-child interactions.

The OPOL policy was practiced flexibly in Y's family. Considering learning three languages from childhood could be undermined by different pressures from the dominant society, OPOL was a major but not the sole policy that Y's parents used to supply input in the languages that they wanted her to acquire. OPOL was also recognized as an important strategy in their family's language management. However, inconsistencies between Y's parents' language ideologies and their language practices were occasionally identified. For instance, her parents, while claiming to have strictly followed the OPOL strategy, sometimes mixed languages in their parental modelling.

Flexibility in family language policies is indicated by the parental reports implying that their language use and language strategies had changed over time depending on where they lived, the language proficiency of family members, and the language environment. Moreover, her parents' perception of the minority language's status in the host society played an important role in their language use. Living in Japan, Y's parents saw themselves as locally based, but contributed a significant time and effort to practicing the two non-community languages (English and Mandarin) at home. While living in Scotland, they saw themselves as foreigners and negotiated to create more home time for Japanese. For example, her father changed the way he read in Japanese with her from father modelling to father-child turn-taking. Y and her father also used Japanese while cooking and doing artwork. In addition, her mother referred to Chinese characters in both Mandarin and Japanese forms during reading. Nevertheless, realizing that the one-year sojourn in Scotland would be temporary, her parents decided to continue with English as the family's lingua franca, although this decision made it even more difficult to promote the acquisition of the two minority languages (Japanese and Mandarin). In the following note from a diary entry, Y's mother reported why Japanese was not selected as the language for the OPOL approach in Scotland.

> We didn't change our home language environment from English plus Mandarin to Japanese plus Mandarin, because the parents' beliefs in and their expectations for the three languages remain unchanged regardless of the change of the social speech community. Besides, it takes time and efforts for both the parents and the child to become accustomed to the new rules, especially when the old rules have already become our daily routines. (Recorded when Y was 5;0)

Y's mother's hidden hopes for her child surrounding the academic and career values of English thus contradicted her stated OPOL policy. The mother also reported in the diary entries to have adopted a combination of the OPOL strategy and the one-situation-one-language strategy, which she used as the source of the English, Japanese and Mandarin input during a period when the father was away for several weeks. For example, Mandarin was used for the home communication and English for playing outside, and Mandarin was used in the morning and English in the afternoon, but all three languages were employed for reading, writing, and learning. These practices were successfully carried out by Y's mother alone, and though she was not a single parent per se, they may provide some suggestions for how the OPOL strategy may be adapted to non-mainstream families. Despite the fact that most family language policies are made based on two residential parents, a single parent raising multilingual and multiliterate children is not completely out of the question when the parent is actively involved in the child's learning (Obied 2010).

Y's father also adjusted his language choices on two occasions. One was just before she entered the Japanese nursery (1;10). According to the family's reading policy, the father was advised to speak only in Japanese when reading Japanese books. This attempt eventually failed because both Y and her father preferred to interact with each other in English. The other occasion was during the one-year stay in Scotland (4;10). There, Y and her father successfully employed Japanese in some specific home situations, such as cooking and playing games.

Y's mother reported that although the general OPOL policy remained unchanged at home, language choices outside the home came to be mostly negotiated after Y turned three years old, by which time she had become a competent trilingual speaker. While her mother had spoken in English outside with the one- and two-year-old child, she started to leave the language choice up to the three-year-old. Y's mother also followed the child's lead, using Mandarin when they were outside in both Japan and Scotland. The child's agency appeared to have become even more significant when Y turned five, at which age she surpassed her parents in many aspects of language skills, such as the pronunciation of Mandarin *pīnyīn*, the pronunciation, vocabulary and syntax of spoken English, and multilingual and multicultural awareness. Her parents thus changed from language managers to positive participants.

Overall, Y's degree of trilingualism was related to her parents' child-centered policy such as using a flexible OPOL strategy. Her parents focused on meaning-making with her rather than on controlling her language choice. Nevertheless, language input patterns alone will not result in a child's use of their parents' languages; discourse strategies related to the child's mixed codes will also affect the child's language choice.

6.1.2 From monolingual-like discourse strategies to bilingual-like discourse strategies

Parental language policies are not static or unidirectional but subject to negotiations among family members (Barron-Hauwaert 2004; Fogle and King 2013). While randomly mixing codes from different languages is regarded as a natural process in child language development by some parents, it seems unacceptable to many others who try to keep every language separate (Lanza 1997). When parents' attempts to control the family language environment are rejected, they may make some explicit decisions, such as restricting a language to specific time slots or in conversations with certain individuals (Caldas 2012). Studies on FLP have explored how families negotiate and modify their language policies in face-to-face interaction and highlight the role of parental discourse strategies (Döpke 1992; Lanza 1997).

In her study, Lanza (1997) identified five discourse strategies of bilingual parents in dealing with the mixed codes of their English-Norwegian children in different situations, based on the degree of flexibility in socializing children into specific language practices. These strategies are: (1) Minimal Grasp, where the adult pretends not to comprehend the child's language and requests clarification from the child by using prompting words, such as "What?" and "Pardon?", (2) Expressed Guess, which means the adult seeks confirmation from the child through a "Yes" or "No" reply to the adult's guess as to the child's meaning, (3) Adult Repetition, in which the adult uses the appropriate language to repeat the content of the child's utterances, (4) Move On, in which the adult continues a parallel mode of communication with the child after noticing the "inappropriate" language used by the child, and (5) Code-Switches, which involve the adult switching to the child's preferred language (Lanza, 1997). Following Lanza, Y's parents adopted all of these discourse strategies but in a more flexible way.

Focusing on monolingual-like strategies before 3;0

Children can be socialized into different interaction patterns by their parents. It is commonly assumed that the more the minority parent proposes a monolingual context using explicit discourse strategies, the more likely it is that the minority language will be maintained. Before Y turned three years old, an elicitation of the desired code would be made by her parents when she selected a language other than the one used by her parents. Such a monolingual-like discourse strategy, similar to Lanza's first one – Minimal Grasp – was commonly adopted. For example, her mother feigned to be a monolingual Mandarin speaker and insisted on a correction in the English-bound "calendar activity", as shown in Example 44.

Example 44 is from a video recording (2;7).
1 MOT:	现在是什么季节?	
	[What season is it now?]	
2 CHI:	It's winter.	
3 MOT:	现在是冬......?	
	[It's win...]	
4 CHI:	冬天。	
	[Winter.]	
5 MOT:	对了,冬季。现在是什么季节?	
	[Right. Winter. What season is it now?]	
6 CHI:	冬季。	
	[Winter.]	

In this example, her mother pretended not to comprehend Y's English answer to the Mandarin question. The mother first repeated the beginning of the same question in Mandarin (Turn 3), which would be a hint to Y that she was expected to reply in the mother's language. The mother then prompted Y to produce the key word, winter, in Mandarin (Turn 4), modelled the language, and then repeated the same practice (Turn 5). Y eventually expressed herself in the mother's language (Turn 6). Similarly, in Lanza's (1997) study, Siri's bilingual mother successfully feigned the role of a monolingual in English and insisted on a rephrasing of her child's Norwegian utterances.

One reason that Y's parents favored a strict approach was probably that they expected her to acquire equivalent terms in all of her three languages and to use them in a contextually-appropriate manner. Lanza (1997) considers Minimal

Grasp the most successful strategy for drawing a language spoken by a parent out of a child when that language differs from the one used in the larger social context. However, this highly-constrained practice did not always function well in the father-child practices in Y's case. In Example 45, Y did not conform to her father's code choice (Turns 2 and 4) and provided no appropriate responses to her father's request for code correction (Turns 3 and 5).

Example 45 is from a video recording (2;4).
Situation: Y was playing cooking house with her father.
1 CHI: これYちゃんの。
[This is Y's.]
2 FAT: What?
3 CHI: おいしそう。くるくる。
[Yummy. Round and round]
4 FAT: くるくるかきごおり。You need to put something in. What's in it?
[Round and round shaved ice.]
5 CHI: くるくる。
[Round and round.]

Y's responses in the above example, however, suggested that using a parent-centered policy might not in fact result in her use of that language. Smith-Christmas (2014) in her study of an extended bilingual Gaelic-English family also discovered that the reification of a strong pro-minority language policy is not necessarily correlated with a high degree of minority language use.

One possible explanation for why a strict elicitation strategy may result in divergent language production in children is that, as described by De Houwer (2009), child caretakers vary in the strength of their impact beliefs – that is, the degree to which they see themselves as duty-bound and skillful in shaping a child's language choices. Taking two separate studies of trilingual families as examples, Barnes (2011) and Chevalier (2012) have found that children tend to be more active in each parent's language when they are required to speak the language of each parent with that parent, whereas children are less active when they are not required to do so.

Another possible explanation for the ineffectiveness of a strict elicitation strategy may be related to the adults' use of interactional techniques as a part of their language practices, including whether or not they are consistent. Kasuya (1998), for instance, looked at the dyadic interactions of English-Japanese preschool children living in the US and found that children whose parents explicitly demonstrated their preference for Japanese and consistently used Japanese at home became good Japanese users with higher potential, compared with those whose parents contributed less to the Japanese maintenance. Similarly, Takeuchi (2006), in an examination of Japanese-English bilingual children in Melbourne,

Australia, suggested that parental consistency and commitment in parent-child interactions were related to their children's level of Japanese proficiency. Those children whose mothers consistently spoke in Japanese with them at home appeared to accept the role of this language in their daily lives and the expectations placed on them to use it (Takeuchi, 2006).

The above two explanations were evidenced in Y's family, where her mother was seen as more influential and responsible, as well as more persistent and determined in monitoring Y's language choice, than her father was. For that reason, Y appeared to have paid more attention to her language choice in mother-child conversations, and showed lower awareness when talking to her father.

In addition to the reasons discussed previously, children's abilities to understand the intentions of interlocutors in communication vary. Some children may not understand a parent's language choice correction question such as "What?" and either mistakenly respond to it or ignore it (De Houwer 1990). To sort out this issue, Y's mother labelled the relevant language from an early stage in her lexical acquisition and this also served as a discourse strategy. Instead of saying "How do you say it in mummy's language?" Y's mother more commonly instructed her to "Say it in Chinese." This is seen in Example 46.

Example 46 is from a diary entry (2;5).

1 CHI:	I want (to) play /ʌp'tɛː/.
	(/ʌp'tɛː/ is the IPA representation of the word "upstairs" as Y said it. Neither the voiceless nor voiced sound of "s" was clearly pronounced as it would be in /ʌp'stɛːz/.)
2 MOT:	What do you want to do?
	(Her mother did not catch her words.)
3 CHI:	/ʌp'tɛː/.
4 MOT:	Sorry. Are you speaking English or Chinese?
5 CHI:	English. /ʌp'tɛː/.
6 MOT:	中文是什么?
	[How do you say it in Mandarin?]
7 CHI:	楼梯。
	[Stairs.]
8 MOT:	No, you can't play on the stairs. It's dangerous.
9 CHI:	Not dangerous. /ʌp'tɛː/.
10 MOT:	How do you say it in Japanese?
11 CHI:	わからない。I want (to) kick the ball /ʌp'tɛː/.
	[I don't know.]
12 MOT:	Ah, /ʌp'stɛːz/!
	(Her mother understood when Y pointed at the second floor.)
13 CHI:	Yes.

In the above example, a correction was successfully elicited in Y's response to her mother by labelling the actual name of each language. She labelled the form, upstairs, as English (Turn 5) and the equivalent, 楼梯, as Mandarin (Turn 7), and expressed through the Japanese term, わからない (Turn 11), that she did not know the Japanese equivalent. Even though the equivalent word in Mandarin that Y offered was incorrect and she could not produce an equivalent item in Japanese, one can clearly say that Y was aware there were equivalents of the word "upstairs" in her three languages.

Although the Minimal Grasp discourse strategy tends to be successful in socializing children into the using of home language, this insistent strategy may not suit every family's parenting style and may result in tension within the family. The strategy may also go against the well-being of parents who speak only the societal language. In such a situation, encouraging children to do translations or use translanguaging can help them take pride in speaking the home language while involving every family member and spending quality family time together. Parental couple relationship can also benefit from such strategic translation practice.

Adopting bilingual-like strategies after 3;0
Lanza's (1997) five strategies provide a framework to understand how children make language choices in relation to the parents' instructions and their observable efforts in parent-child interactions. These strategies also indicate how parental efforts and language choices are challenged by the child's mixed codes, and how parents may be socialized into the child's language practices. Following Lanza, researchers more and more explored language policies within the family context emphasizing parenting as a critical part of the FLP formation. For example, Curdt-Christiansen (2014b) reported that in Singaporean-Chinese bilingual families, both highly organized and overt policies and unreflective, laissez-faire attitudes were established and enacted through parental discourse strategies.

It should be pointed out that from her second birthday, Y had been experiencing rapid language development, particularly in the aspects of pronunciation and vocabulary. Although Y's mother consistently believed that knowing the equivalents in three languages was a precondition of appropriate language use, she also realized that a strict monolingual-like strategy, insisting on eliciting a correct form from Y, sometimes broke down the natural flow of an ongoing conversation. With that in mind, the mother gradually became less strict with Y's "wrong" word choices. She occasionally accepted Y's use of an equivalent in a different language and provided its translation as appropriate.

Even though Y had become a fluent trilingual speaker by two and a half years old, inappropriate forms were still found in her speech from time to time, either due to the unavailability of equivalents or her language using habits. In such cases, Y's mother would not use strict elicitation questions but mostly moved on in the conversation by providing the equivalents in the expected language. Y's father seemed less sensitive to her language behavior and often continued the conversation without addressing her language. In addition, the code-switching strategy was also intentionally employed by Y's parents at times. As a result, the parent-child communication shifted toward a more bilingual-like mode in Y's family.

Lanza (1997) claims that adults who use the last two strategies, Move On and Code-Switches, seem to have followed the lead of the child and allowed communication to shift toward bilingual-like patterns. However, Y's parents took her multilingual development into consideration when they decided to move on or switch their codes; they also adopted more bilingual-like discourse strategies in an attempt to ensure smooth intergenerational communication. This is shown in Example 47.

Example 47 is from a diary entry (2;0).
Situation: Y showed her drawing to her mother.
1 CHI: So many banana.
2 MOT: So many bananaS.
(The mother emphasized the plural suffix "-s" by saying it loudly.)
(After a while, Y showed her drawing to her mother again.)
3 CHI: みせて。
[Show it to me.]
4 MOT: みて。Look!
[Look.]
5 CHI: Look.
6 MOT: Red bananaS.
(Y's mother emphasized the plural suffix "-s" by saying it loudly.)

In the above example, her mother corrected Y's wording and language choice without breaking down their conversation. Her mother first switched to the child's language (Japanese) and then immediately switched back to her original language (English) (Turn 4). Meanwhile, Y followed and switched to her mother's language (Turn 5). This kind of double code-switching can be seen as a language negotiation between Y and her mother based on both parties' awareness of the FLP. As a whole, Y's parents considered the primary goal of interaction to be to encourage language behavior irrespective of its form. In monolingual families, this motivation is shown by "parents' tolerance of a variety of linguistic errors" (Kasuya 1998: 342).

6.2 Child as language manager

Up to now, this chapter has given a detailed account of the strategies used by Y's parents to monitor her language choice and language use. As her linguistic and cognitive abilities continued to develop, Y had a growing influence on her parents' language policies. This bottom-up impact is clearly shown in instances where Y shaped her family's language practices or where she developed new language activity, such as teaching her father to speaker Mandarin and monitoring different aspects of her parents' linguistic mistakes in English, Mandarin, and Japanese. She also used strategies, such as "asking metalinguistic questions" and "mock teaching", to position herself as "teacher" and "manager" while directing her own learning processes. This is precisely what is meant by child agency.

6.2.1 Redefining the one-parent-one-language policy

Y had a good awareness of the OPOL policy and the one-situation-one-language policy, which was reflected in her appropriate language choice in daily conversations. Her understanding of the policies was also evidenced in the connection that she made between a language's written form and its speakers. For example, when she passed the books to each parent to read, she said, "中文 [Mandarin] mama, にほんご [Japanese] daddy, English mummy daddy." (Mum reads Mandarin books, daddy reads Japanese books, mum and daddy read English books.) (1;11). Moreover, Y was aware of her mother's multilingual competence and flexible language choice during reading, as seen in Example 48.

Example 48 is from an observation note (2;1).
Situation: Y found the Japanese version of the book *Brown bear, brown bear, what do you see?* in the library.
1 CHI: Mama read.
2 MOT: Brown bear . . .
3 CHI: No, くまさん.
 [No, (Brown) bear.]

Y's mother "read" the Japanese version of the story in English even while looking at the Chinese characters (Turn 2). However, Y observed her mother reading both the English and Japanese versions at home and thus asked the mother to read the Japanese book in Japanese (Turn 3).

Among her three languages, Mandarin was Y's favorite one due to a close bond with her Chinese mother and a fondness for the Chinese culture, as well as her having a sense of identity as Chinese. Although Y ranked English and Japanese as her best and second best languages in reading and writing, she was proud of her fluency in spoken Mandarin. Her preference for using the mother's tongue was seen in a variety of situations in which she intentionally created a Mandarin context at home. This is illustrated in the examples below from her mother's observation notes.

Example 49: Redefining the OPOL policy (2;7)
Situation: Y's father wanted to get up, but she pushed him back to the bedroom.
1 CHI: Don't get up now. I want to speak Chinese with mummy.
(Y said it to her father.)
2 CHI: 我就要讲中文。爸爸起床,我就和爸爸点点头。
[I'll only speak Mandarin. If daddy gets up, I'll only nod to him.]
(Y said it to her mother.)

Example 50: Redefining the one-situation-one-language policy (4;1)
Situation: Y's father was in the open kitchen while she started to talk in Mandarin with her mother in the living room.
1 MOT: Daddy is here.
(The mother reminded Y of her incorrect language choice.)
2 CHI: But he is in the kitchen!
(Y considered the kitchen and the living room to be two separate locations, despite the fact that the kitchen was an open one, which means the father could see and hear them well from the kitchen.)

Example 51: Making a temporary code-switching (3;4)
Situation: As soon as her father left the living room for a short moment, Y wanted to switch her language from English to Mandarin.
CHI: 现在一起讲一下中文吧。
[Let's quickly speak Mandarin for a while.]

In the above examples, in order not to cause any conflicts between her desires for using Mandarin and her family's language policies, Y increased mother-child time by changing the language used toward her father from English to body language (Example 49, Turn 2), re-defining the one-situation-one-language policy (Example 50, Turn 2), and temporarily code-switching (Example 51). Moreover, she strictly monitored her mother's language choice using an "insisting" strategy. This is shown in Example 52.

Example 52: Insisting (3;4)
Situation: Y and her mother were watching BBC news at breakfast.
1 CHI: 什么?
[What's the news today?]
2 MOT: 英国要离开EU了。Brexit.
[Britain is leaving the EU.]
3 CHI: 说中文!
[Speak Mandarin!]

Her mother felt it would be easier for Y to understand the English terms "EU" and "Brexit" in English, but she insisted on her mother using their Mandarin equivalents (Example 52, Turn 3). In this way, Y negotiated language choices with her mother in the child-designed practices.

6.2.2 Reshaping adults' discourse strategies

It was mentioned in Section 1.1 that Y's Chinese grandparents visited her family in Japan for about three months (2;6–2;9). When investigating Y's language choices in interaction with her Mandarin-speaking grandparents, it was found that she had a good awareness of her grandparents' monolingualism and generally respected their language by responding mainly in Mandarin. However, in actual communication she nevertheless used all of her three languages flexibly rather than passively following the adults' lead. Y demonstrated four specific behaviors in response to her grandparents' monolingual or bilingual-like discourse strategies for dealing with her mixed codes. They were: (1) resisting through no response, (2) moving on in a dual-lingual conversation, (3) assisting her grandparents to decode her non-Mandarin speech, and (4) modifying the language choices of herself and others. Examples of each of these strategies are presented in the following sections.

Resisting through no response
The first agentic action taken by Y was resisting by failing to respond when language clarification was required by her grandparents. In the following excerpt, her grandmother tried to negotiate a Mandarin context and insisted that Y's reply be clarified in Mandarin. However, it seemed that the grandmother was unsuccessful in her attempt to draw Mandarin out of Y, as shown in Example 53.

Example 53 is from a video recording (2;6).
1 CHI: What's the weather like today?
2 GrM: 听不懂。
 [I don't understand (English).]
3 CHI: What's the weather like today?
4 GrM: 用中文说一遍。
 [Say it in Mandarin.]
5 CHI: (0).
 (No response.)

In the above exchange, Y refused to make a language correction from English to Mandarin and moved on in English (Turn 3) even when her grandmother asked for either a content repair (Turn 2) or a language choice repair (Turn 4). When asked more than once, Y simply ignored the adult's request (Turn 5). Her grandmother's approach to eliciting Mandarin was similar to the most monolingual-like strategy, Minimal Grasp, employed by Y's mother as well as the bilingual mothers in Lanza's (1997) study. In Y's family, her mother could always successfully feign the role of a monolingual speaker in Mandarin and insist on Y rephrasing her mixed utterances in their conversations. However, it seemed impossible to achieve alignment in conversations between Y and her grandparents as she would not switch to their language despite the efforts that they had made.

How much adults see themselves as duty-bound when supporting their children's language development is thought to be closely related to their attitudes toward a language and the expectations about its social value. Curdt-Christiansen (2009), for instance, described how Chinese parents in Canada showed approval toward the heritage Chinese language and the value of multilingualism, and therefore consistently invested in their children's multilingual development. Children are sensitive to the adults' hidden attitudes by observing their actions such as whether or not an adult insists on a correction of the child's language choice. Y might detect her grandparents' laissez-faire attitude to using Mandarin in a Mandarin context and therefore refused their efforts related to the use of this language.

Moving on in a dual-lingual conversation
Y's grandparents sometimes guessed the meaning of her non-Mandarin utterances and responded appropriately to the content. This was positive evidence of their comprehension of Y's speech even if they responded in Mandarin. Y thus perceived that she was permitted to move on in a different code in parallel to her grandparents, who attempted to decode her non-Mandarin utterances but continued in Mandarin. Her grandparents' behavior coincided with the parental strategy, Move On, described in Lanza's (1997) study. Through this practice, a multilingual context is

negotiated and a dual-lingual paradigm is adopted. A dual-lingual conversation between Y and her grandparents is shown in Example 54.

Example 54 is from a video recording (2;6).
Situation: Y was showing her pictures to her grandmother.
1 CHI: おえかき。おえかき。
[Draw pictures. Draw pictures.]
2 GrM: おえかき是什么?
[What is おえかき?]
3 CHI: アンパンマン。
(アンパンマン is a Japanese cartoon character.)
4 GrM: 啊! アンパンマン。
[Ah! It's *Anpanman*.]
(The grandmother knew the cartoon character.)
5 CHI: みて。
[Look!]
6 GrM: みて。看一看。
[Look. Look.]
(The grandmother translated the Japanese term into its Mandarin equivalent assisted by Y's body language.)
7 CHI: おやま。
[A mountain.]
(Y drew a mountain.)
8 GrM: 在上面。
[(*Anpanman* is) on the top of the mountain.]

In the above exchange, the grandmother first asked Y the meaning of the Japanese word, おえかき [draw pictures] (Turn 2). As mentioned earlier, this insisting strategy did not work well. Once the grandmother recognized the cartoon character, *Anpanman*, she immediately showed her understanding using a Mandarin exclamation, 啊 [ah], and said the cartoon character's name (Turn 4). Interestingly, Y accepted her grandmother's Mandarin expression, 在上面 [on the top] (Turn 8), as an appropriate reply to her Japanese word, おやま [a mountain] (Turn 7). Thus, a language negotiation began with a disagreement between the two participants about which language to use, and it ended with the grandmother giving in to Y's preferred language.

Holding the same expectation as her father of establishing an intimate family tie, although her grandmother had noticed Y using another language, she still responded to Y by attending to the content of the conversation. The desire to continue a conversation, regardless of the language form, may be enough of a reason to move on. Whether or not a code-switch into Y's language takes place, a bilingual context is created and a parallel conversation in the two languages ensues. As discussed in 5.3.3, Y also had some purposeful dual-lingual conversations with her father because she believed this type of interaction could help parents learn a new language. Seeing how much initiative Y took and how organized she was in teaching her parents different language skill including Spanish at a somewhat later age (see 8.5), it might be reasonable to presume that Y used these "dual-lingual" conversation as a special context of socialization in which she could exercise her role as a language teacher.

Assisting grandparents to decode her non-Mandarin speech

Being aware of her grandparents' attempts to guess the meaning of her non-Mandarin speech, Y sometimes assisted them in decoding her English or Japanese message. In Example 55, with the aid of Y's nonverbal cues her grandparents successfully guessed the meaning of an English expression and modelled its Mandarin equivalent.

Example 55 is from a video recording (2;7).
1 CHI: Pee-pee.
          (Y pointed to the toilet.)
2 GrF: Pee-pee 是什么?
          [What is pee-pee?]
3 GrM: Pee-pee 就是小便。
          [It is pee.]
          (The grandmother translated the English word, pee, into Mandarin.)
4 CHI: Pee-pee.
          (Y nodded.)

Y told her grandparents, in English, that she wanted to pee and explained the meaning of the word by pointing to the toilet (Turn 1). Her grandmother confidently translated the English term "pee" into its Mandarin equivalent (Turn 3). Y might have thought a switch into Mandarin was no longer necessary since her English message had been successfully transmitted, so she confirmed the grandmother's translation in English (Turn 4). Providing translation equivalents was originally an input strategy used by her parents to help her acquire different linguistic forms. Y, in turn, adopted it as a strategy to fulfil different conversational functions in parent-child interactions. What is more, Y might have seen the process of decoding or meaning-making as a pattern in multilingual practices, as well as an opportunity for the monolingual Chinese grandparents to learn new languages from her.

Modifying her own and others' language choices

Aspirations for smooth communication across generations even prompted her grandparents to imitate Y's utterances and deliberately "switch" to her language.

6.2 Child as language manager

Y continually monitored her grandparents' "code-switching" behavior and her own and others' language choices. Unlike the code-switching strategy used by the bilingual parents in Lanza's (1997) study, two languages were not available as alternatives in this bilingual-like context, as shown in Example 56.

Example 56 is from a video recording (2;6).
Situation: Y and her grandmother were playing LEGO games.
1 CHI: これ。
[This one.]
(Y picked a LEGO piece and gave it to her grandmother.)
2 GrM: これ。
[This one.]
(The grandmother did not accept Y's help, found one by herself, and imitated Y's pronunciation of the Japanese word これ.)
3 CHI: いやだ。
[I don't like it.]
(Y moved her hands back and forth seeing the grandmother putting the piece in the wrong place.)
4 GrM: いえじゃ。
(The grandmother insisted on putting the piece in the place she wanted and tried to imitate Y's pronunciation of the Japanese word いやだ.)
5 CHI: だめ。
[Don't do it.]
(Y tried to grab another piece from her grandmother but failed.)
6 GrM: たま。
(The grandmother continued to put the piece in the wrong place while trying to imitate Y's pronunciation of the Japanese word だめ.)
7 CHI: 不是, 不是这里。
[No, not here.]
(Y switched to Mandarin and told her grandmother that she was wrong.)

In the above exchange, Y tried twice to stop her grandmother from putting the LEGO pieces in the wrong place while speaking in Japanese accompanied by body language (Turns 3 and 5). However, the grandmother repeatedly refused her help (Turns 2, 4, and 6). Y eventually switched to Mandarin after her protest in Japanese had failed once again. She did not continue in Japanese after her grandmother switched to Japanese. Thus, Y's response to the adult's code-switching act was different from what is usually seen in bilingual (Döpke 1992; Lanza 1997) and trilingual children (Chevalier 2012; Quay 2001). For example, the trilingual child Freddy, in Quay's (2001) case study, recognized his parents' attempts to use the community language, Japanese, and indirectly socialized them into using it by responding in Japanese to their Japanese utterances. However, when the communication was hindered by her grandmother's feigned code-switching behavior, Y corrected her language choice and switched back to Mandarin.

These four discourse strategies demonstrated how Y resisted, negotiated, and modified her monolingual grandparents' language choices. It highlighted Y's bottom-up agency in response to the explicit decisions and efforts made by her grandparents. With regard to their "bilingual" strategies, Y demonstrated a general awareness of their monolingualism ("They can only speak Mandarin.") (2;3) and tended not to associate their "bilingual" behavior with their real language abilities. Resisting, making dual-lingual conversations, decoding, and code-switching can be seen as distinctive behavior of multilingual speakers and reflect the communicative competence of proficient multilinguals. More and more, these should be considered as multifaceted practices where a multilingual's entire linguistic repertoire is used. These strategies show how sociocultural roles and values, relationships, and cultural identities are established through language choices (Zhu 2008).

6.2.3 Becoming a language teacher to parents

As noted previously, Luykx (2003) argues that language socialization involves mutual influence between parents and children. While adults teach children languages, children also affect adults' language use (Gafaranga 2010). Correcting the other speakers requires a child to reflect on language as a system and monitor others' language use (De Houwer 2017). This can be seen in the present study. Example 57 shows Y could differentiate her three languages when she was one. Here, she made a request for her parents to sing a song called きらきらばし [Twinkle, twinkle, little star] by refusing to accept its Mandarin or English version.

Example 57 is from a video clip (1;1).
Situation:	The family were playing and singing.
CHI:	Mama, *guja*.
	(*Guja* probably meant "go". Y wanted her mother to sing.)
MOT:	*Twinkle, twinkle, little star?*
	(Y's mother was confirming the English name of the song with her.)
CHI:	Uh.
	(It meant "No". Y moved her index finger left and right.)
MOT:	一闪一闪亮晶晶?
	[Twinkle, twinkle, little star?]
	(Y's mother was confirming the Mandarin name of the song with her. The first character of its Mandarin name was 一 [one] and the mother thought Y's index finger meant "one".)
CHI:	Uh.

	(It meant "No".)
MOT:	きらきらぼし。
	[Twinkle, twinkle, little star.]
	(Y's mother was confirming the Japanese name of the song with her. She was looking at the mother and trying to imitate the intonation.)

Although Y could not talk clearly at this stage (1;1), the judgments she made based on early metalinguistic awareness nevertheless challenged her parents' language choices. The responses that she gave through body language were a hint to her mother that neither English nor Mandarin was acceptable to her. Y prompted her mother to change language repeatedly until the mother switched to her expected code.

From two years old, Y used the real name of a language to refer to the language, such as "In English?" "にほんご。" [In Japanese?], or "中文?" [In Mandarin?], when requesting an equivalent, as illustrated in Example 58.

Example 58 is from a diary entry (2;5).

Situation:	The family were having lunch at McDonald's.
1 CHI:	Mummy, hamburger, 中文?
	[How do you say hamburger in Chinese?]
2 MOT:	汉堡包。
	[Hamburger.]
3 CHI:	にほんご。
	[How about in Japanese?]
4 MOT:	ハンブーグー。
	[Y's mother's Japanese pronunciation of the word was similar to its English pronunciation.]
5 CHI:	No, it's English. Daddy, hamburger, にほんご?
	[How do you say hamburger in Japanese?]
6 FAT:	ハンバーガー。
	[Hamburger.]
7 CHI:	ハンバーガー。
	[Y looked at her mother and repeated the word.]

Thus, Y accepted the Mandarin equivalent of the word, hamburger, modelled by the mother (Turn 2) but commented that the Japanese form was wrong (Turn 5). Phonological awareness aided Y in making a judgement about her mother's pronunciation of the loanword borrowed from English. She repaired her mother's Japanese by modelling the correct sound provided by her father (Turn 7). The simultaneous activation of three languages when monitoring her mother's language use showed that Y had similar levels of phonological awareness in her three languages. Similarly, Silva-Corvalán (2014) describes how a three-year-old bilingual boy made fun of his grandfather's English-style pronunciation of a Spanish word.

From three years old, being confident with her own language skills, Y started to act as a language teacher at home, as shown in Example 59.

Example 59 is from a video recording (3;10).
Situation: Y was teaching her father Mandarin.
CHI: 谢谢。What do you say?
　　　[Thank you.]
FAT: 不用谢。
　　　[You're welcome.]
CHI: 请进。What do you say?
　　　[Come in.]
FAT: What do I need to say?
CHI: I don't know.
CHI: 晚安。What do you say?
　　　[Good night.]
FAT: 晚安。
　　　[Good night.]
CHI: So good Chinese.
　　　(Y made a comment on the father's Mandarin speaking skill.)

In addition to teaching her father some basic conversations in Mandarin as shown in the above, Y also made a teaching plan for him based on her own learning experience. That is, "First, teach him '*a, o, e*' (*pīnyīn*), then ask him to sing a lot of Chinese songs, then let him read a lot Chinese books, then he can speak Chinese." (3;10). Y also acted as a Japanese teacher for her mother, mostly when the mother was writing in れんらくちょう [nursery-home communication book] and sought help from her. This is shown in Example 60.

Example 60 is from a mother's diary note (4;2).
MOT: How do you say "I played cooking house" in Japanese?
CHI: ままごとであそんだ。
　　　[Played cooking house.]
MOT: がっこうで—マンをたべさせてください。
　　　[Please ask her to eat green peppers at school (lunch).]
CHI: 不是这么说的。
　　　[You are wrong.]
MOT: 怎么说?
　　　[How shall I say this (in Japanese)?]
CHI: 你自己想。
　　　[You have to think about it by yourself.]

Children may refuse parents' requests that are seen as against their will and offer no language help. This is clearly shown in the above example, which can be understood as an exercise of Y's agency to challenge her mother's authority. Y didn't like green peppers and didn't want her mother to write that, thus she refused to help her mother with this task.

In an analysis of the children's narratives on their experiences as language brokers, Antonini (2016) shows the impact of language brokering on children's lives and the big contribution children made to help their immigrant parents to deal with various social issues. Language brokering is one of many translanguaging practices that bilingual and multilingual children and teenagers engage in every day. Despite concerns about whether it is appropriate for children to do this work, or whether they are competent to do it, this practice is normative in new immigrant families (Antonini 2016). Relying on children's language abilities and their mobility will empower children, no matter whether they are guiding the parents' choices or not (Antonini 2016).

According to Clark (1978), from the age of four, children normally begin to exhibit a higher level of skills and monitor their own and others' utterances. This was true of Y, who was attentive to specific aspects of a language and to the mistakes that her parents made when speaking that language. What's more, with rich and cheerful learning and practicing experiences and a consuming passion for teaching, Y replaced her parents as the source of English input in the family from four years old. She became an important English source of vocabulary and a model of more standard pronunciation and a more natural way of speaking. Thus, her parents' modelling was replaced by Y's teaching.

6.2.3.1 Pronunciation

Y had a good phonetic awareness and started to monitor her parents' pronunciation as young as two years old. She sometimes corrected her parents' pronunciation of English letters, modelled the word stress, and clapped the word syllables. In Example 61, Y pointed out a mistake in her father's pronunciation; that is, the sound of "v" in the word "Sven" was not correctly pronounced.

Example 61 is from a diary entry (4;1).
CHI: I don't want daddy to read (English) anymore. He is not good.
MOT: What is not good? For example?
CHI: He said /sbɛn/ (Sven).
 (The father's pronunciation of /svɛn/ sounds like /sbɛn/.)

Mandarin Chinese and dialect Chinese
Y also demonstrated an exceptional language sense for Mandarin *pīnyīn*. The retroflex and flat tongues as well as the front nasal and back nasal finals were

common pronunciation issues for the Mandarin speakers from the southern part of the country, including Y's mother, since they were affected by the phonetic systems of their dialects. Although her mother was conscious of trying to use a standard variety of Mandarin, she nevertheless made mistakes when speaking fast or carelessly. Y was able to pick out the nonstandard sounds, even when her mother's utterances were long and fast. Y also reported pronunciation errors made by a couple of British born Chinese schoolmates in Scotland. She told her mother, "他说: '你是 (sì replaced shì) 中 (zōng replaced zhōng) 国人吗? 你要吃 (cī replaced chī) 点心吗?' 他没有翘舌音。" [He said, "Are you Chinese? Do you want some snacks?" He didn't use the retroflex consonants."] (4;11). Although Y never corrected others' variant Mandarin pronunciations, she told her mother, "They are from your area." or "Their parents are from your dialect place." (4;11).

Scottish accent and Scots

The English variety spoken in Scotland differed greatly from the English varieties that Y had experienced from her parents, in audio and video materials based on standard varieties of English, and in TV news and radio programs. In the first week after Y entered a school in Scotland, she picked up on the variations used by a few local teachers and children. She summarized some variant sounds, such as /s/ in "classroom" turning to /ʃ/ in /kla:ʃru:m/, /r/ in "rabbit" turning to /w/ in /wæbɪt/, or the silent /d/ in "Wednesday" that was slightly enunciated in Scottish English. Y used these "phonetic rules" when listening to others' talking. She seemed to understand that these were different varieties of English language and referred to these variations as "Scottish accent". She realized that a classmate who said /wug/ (rug) and /wous/ (rose) "can't say /r/" rather than thinking the girl's English was wrong (4;11). Using the sound /w/ for the tapped /r/ seems common at this year among Scottish children. Although Scottish English is often cited as a typical example of a rhotic accent of English, no case of rhotacization was reported by Y, indicating that the postvocalic /r/ in words, such as "car" or "card", was not articulated. This somehow supports the result of a sociophonetic investigation of derhoticisation (a completely loss or weakening) in postvocalic /r/ in Scottish English (Stuart-Smith, Lawson, and Scobbie 2014).

It was also found that Y was able to decode the phonetic rules of the Scots language, but it was not very clear how she became able to do so. For instance, she could read through a library book called *The Gruffalo in Scots* fairly fluently on the first try. An excerpt from the book is shown in Example 62.

Example 62 is from a diary entry (5;3).
A moose took a dauner through the deep, mirk widd. A tod saw the moose and the moose looked guid. (Donaldson and Scheffler 2012: 2)
[A mouse took a stroll through the deep, dark wood. A fox saw the mouse and the mouse looked good.]

About the time she read this book, she had been living in Scotland for around six months. Y listed some variant sounds in Scots and compared them with those in the standard English (5;5). For example, "oo" in Scots was "ou" in English (mouse →*moose*), "a" in Scots was "y" in English (my→*ma*), "ui" in Scots was "oo" in English (good→*guid*) and "th" was omitted in Scots (with→*wi*). It took a rather longer time for her parents to transfer the equivalents from Scots to standard English when reading the same book.

British English and non-British Englishes

Having already understood the differences between Mandarin and other Chinese dialects, and between Scottish English and the standard British English, it did not seem difficult for Y to distinguish British English from other varieties of English. Pronunciation and vocabulary are the two most noticeable features of spoken language. Y's audio books bought in the UK were mainly read in British English, while many of her other books such as Disney-related products were in American English. There were also some that included both varieties. Y preferred to listen to the British English tracks, saying, "Y British, mummy American." (3;10). She seemed to have trouble getting used to some American English pronunciations, such as the low front vowel "a" in "apple" (/'æpəl/) and the rhotic consonant "r". Y's opinion of the pronunciation of "r" in British and American Englishes can be seen in Example 63.

Example 63 is from a mother and child conversation. (5;2).

Situation:	Y was reading a novel while listening to its CD modelled reading.
1 CHI:	我读了英国的和美国的。
	[I read in both British and American English.]
2 MOT:	你喜欢哪个?
	[Which one do you like?]
3 CHI:	英国的。
	[British English.]
4 MOT:	为什么?
	[Why?]
5 CHI:	因为美国的那个r太重了。
	[Because American English has a strong "r".]
6 MOT:	那英国的呢?

	[How about the British one?]
7 CHI:	英国的刚刚好。
	[The pronunciation of "r" in British English is just all right.]

The linking "r" in word-final position is normally silent before a following consonant and is pronounced before a following vowel in British English. However, it is always pronounced in both situations in American English. In this example, Y described the American way of pronouncing "r" as "roll up the tongue at all times" (5;2) and thus it was "too strong" (Turn 5).

Watching cartoons was another important means for Y to get familiar with different English varieties. Through this activity, Y was largely exposed to the standard varieties of British and American English. A third opportunity of getting in touch with world Englishes was watching and listening to BBC, CNN, and NHK's English and Japanese bilingual news with her parents every day. Y started to pay attention to the news and the language of news from four years old. For example, her awareness of Australian English was shown once, "Do you know 'G'day' means 'Hello'. It's Australian." (5;4). In addition, when she heard a Japanese speaker speaking in English in a BBC interview, she said, "That people's Japanese accent is too strong" (4;3). Thus, Y's language learning environments and experiences helped her understand the varieties of languages and enabled her to be adaptable to changes.

6.2.3.2 Vocabulary

After the family moved to Scotland, the biggest change in Y's English was the increasing number and variety of her vocabulary items. Expressions used by the native speakers living in this environment and the colloquial speech that would be hard to acquire solely through reading literature were quickly picked up by Y in the Scottish schools and in her neighborhood. This is shown in Examples 64 and 65.

Example 64 is from an observation note (5;0).
1 MOT:	Will you and your friend wear the same type of underpants tomorrow?
2 CHI:	Knickers. They are called knickers.
3 MOT:	Are "underpants" called "knickers" in the UK?
4 CHI:	Yes.

Y brought back the word "knickers" (Turn 2) from school and taught it to her parents. In addition, Y was also able to explain the usage of a vocabulary item with easy-to-understand examples, as seen in Example 65.

Example 65 is from a mother-child conversation (5;4).
1 CHI: Somebody told on S and she cried.
2 MOT: Told what?
3 CHI: Told on.
4 MOT: What's the meaning of "told on"?
5 CHI: It means somebody told teacher she did something bad.
6 MOT: Where did you learn the expression? Did the teacher say it?
7 CHI: No. I thought about it by myself.

Although it was not clear where Y picked up the expression "told on" (Turn 2), the mother assumed that Y had seen or heard it somewhere in her daily life environment. A similar pattern had been observed earlier in Y's life as well, when she was developing her own understanding of Mandarin through independent learning and reading. This is shown in Examples 66 and 67.

Example 66 is from a diary entry (2;8).
MOT: 吃饭了。
[Mealtime.]
CHI: 不是"吃饭",是"早饭"。
[Not "mealtime". It's "breakfast time".]

Example 67 is from a diary entry (3;8).
MOT: 你浪费了吃的东西。
[You wasted things for eating.]
CHI: 吃的东西还有一个名字, 食物。
[There is another name for "things for eating". Food.]

Y's attitude toward speaking correctly was reflected in her monitoring of her mother's careless use of Mandarin words as shown in the above examples.

6.2.3.3 Grammar

Psychologists have long distinguished stages of children developing their use of grammatical speech in their language (Vygotsky 2004). According to Brown (1973), cited in Lightbown and Spada (2013), there is a specific order in which young children acquire grammatical morphemes, although they do not acquire all morphemes at the same age or rate. By five years old, Y had acquired all of the basic morphological aspects of her three languages. This is more or less evidenced in Examples 68 through 71, which were recorded in the mother's diary entries.

Example 68: Pronouns (3;2)
Situation: Y's mother was telling a story in Mandarin.
MOT: 从前有一个小女孩和小男孩, 他对着山下大声喊。
[Once upon a time, there was a girl and a boy. He yelled at the foot of the mountain.]
CHI: 不是"他", "他们"。
[Not "He", but "They".]

Example 69: Plural "-s" (5;0)
MOT: Give me a books.
(The mother did not realize that she said "a books".)
CHI: How many books?
MOT: One.
CHI: Why you say "bookS" if only one?
(Y emphasized "S" by saying it slowly and loudly.)

Example 70: Third-person singular present (5;7)
Situation: Y sent a text message to her friend's mother, "Hello, Santa give me this LEGO. I played with this LEGO." Y read it again before the message was sent.
CHI: "-s" is missing, "gives". Grammar mistake?
MOT: Yes.

Generally speaking, Y was able to use correct word forms in her own speech in a natural way and she was very sensitive to her own and others' grammar mistakes, as seen in the examples above. Through reading English stories, Y also learned the usage of the past suffix "-ed" which is shown in Example 71.

Example 71: Past tense (5;3)
Situation: Y was reading her mother's text message to a Japanese friend, "Tokyo Handsで カードを かいました". [I bought cards in Tokyo Hands.]
CHI: 不是 かいました。ました 是 did something, かいます。
[Not *kai-mashita*. *mashita* means "did something". (You should write) *kai-masu*.]
(A verb + *masu* shows the present tense of the verb; a verb + *mashita* shows the past tense of the verb. Y thought her mother would go to buy cards after she wrote the message.)

Y applied the English grammatical rule (past tense marker) cross-linguistically, which prompted her to correct a mistake of this nature when reading her mother's Japanese text message. The topic of grammar checking was more frequently brought up when the mother needed to have her doctoral dissertation proofread. Y demonstrated a strong interest in the mother's research on her learning of three languages and liked to read the mother's writing. She would often say, "Mummy, you have grammar mistakes. I'll correct your grammar mistakes." (5;2).

To conclude, although the parents and other input sources acted as main language models before her third birthday, Y gradually took the lead in some family activities after that age. From five years old, she developed into a manager in the family's language practices. Included in her agency were strategies that her parents once used to socialize her into their language practices, such as inviting them to participate in her own practices, redefining the parents' OPOL policy, and choosing monolingual-like strategies to deal with the adults' mixed codes. Furthermore, Y took control over her family's language activity as a teacher, monitoring the parents' choice of linguistic micro units (sounds, lexical items, or syntactic structures) or macro variety (a language or dialect). The facts that Y had come to judge her parents' decisions and make new language rules were a visible manifestation of her values, attitudes, and understanding of her three languages and the family's language policies.

7 Metalinguistic, cultural awareness, and evolving identity

Decisions about what languages to use and what strategies to employ to control language behavior are inevitably related to a speaker's language ideologies. A significant part of the research on family language policies thus highlights the importance of the family members' language ideologies. Every member has his/her own beliefs about language choice in light of their varying commitments to acquiring the dominant language on the one hand and to maintaining the heritage variety on the other (Spolsky 2012). They may also attempt to influence or manage the language practices and beliefs of others (Spolsky 2012). Traditionally, parents are the real decision-makers; thus, parents' perspectives and influence on children's language development must be taken into account. Parents' ideas about which language should be used for what purposes play a pivotal part in a family's language policies. However, children start to think about and reflect upon the nature and functions of language from an early age; such abilities, as a component of their agency, are complex but critical in explaining their language choices in the family network (Pratt and Grieve 1984).

In the present study, Y's growing metalinguistic awareness and evolving concepts of language competency and identity reflected her dynamic orientation toward the different languages in her total linguistic repertoire. She modified the language, literacy and cultural practices that were specific to her parents, but which they had originally absorbed from the dominant society. She also interpreted cultural meanings in terms of her own perceptions and explained different cultural practices to her parents. Such evaluation of meaning, as conveyed in communicative, ideological, cultural and emotional dimensions, has been considered as having a significant effect on language production (Said and Zhu 2019). Insights into Y's and her parents' perspectives on these issues, as recorded in the mother's diaries and seen in family conversations, are discussed in detail in this chapter.

7.1 Parents' flexible language ideologies

While some parents have clear goals in raising multilingual children, others do not (De Houwer 1999). However, the natural aspiration of being good parents will surely reflect on every family's child rearing practices (King and Fogle 2006). Depending on the levels of commitment to helping children acquire the societal language and maintain the heritage language or language variety, parents have different opinions and make different decisions about language choice (Spolsky 2012). De Houwer (1999) points out that three kinds of parental ideologies may impact linguistic practices in bilingual families: parents' ideas about which language should be used for what purpose with children, parents' views toward bilingualism, and parents' attitudes to code-switching.

Y's parents believed that all of her three languages were important but they had different expectations for her achievements in each of them. These beliefs were influential in the decisions that they made and practices they implemented. Similar to the majority of other parents, her parents acted as decision makers, especially before her third birthday. However, after that age they either subconsciously or deliberately modified their behavior and were willing to share power and responsibilities with Y in their family's activities. The changing of her parents' ideas and its effect on the family's language policies was realized in their language practices.

7.1.1 Parents' attitudes to trilingualism

Home is a place for acquisition and learning. Rearing children multilingually is not a privilege that only traditional, middle-class families have; it belongs to a wide range of multilingual and transnational families, including those of ethnic minority, adoptive, and other non-traditional backgrounds (Curdt-Christiansen 2015; Fogle 2012). Multilingual families' cultural and linguistic capital is a valuable resource for their children's learning experience. Parents should positively view childhood multilingualism as a means of enrichment in child education. However, Ferguson (2015) indicates that a lack of knowledge and information about the nature of multilingual acquisition can negatively affect the language practices in the family. Some parents consider that using both the heritage and societal languages is valuable; others think speaking two languages to their child is confusing and that may become a problem for the child's language development such as by causing a delay in the acquisition of the societal language. These parents may abandon their heritage language because of lack of knowledge about bilingual language learning (Ferguson 2015; Pérez-Báez 2013). Moreover, others assume multilingualism adversely affects family relationships and disapprove of their children being raised with more than one language (Braun and Cline 2010; Said and Zhu 2019).

A critical factor in deciding on a trilingual policy in Y's family was her parents' good knowledge about childhood language development, which was closely linked to their own educational and life experiences. These provided them with positive, flexible attitudes toward language. This is similar to a study by King and Fogle

(2006), which described how parents of middle-class families in the United States who themselves had valuable experience of learning an additional language helped their children achieve additive Spanish-English bilingualism through an online Montessori bilingual curriculum. The impact of parents' own multilingual experience on families' language practices and management is also seen in Kirsch's (2012) interview-based study of Luxembourgish mothers living in the UK. Those mothers showed positive attitudes toward bilingualism owing to their own multilingual experience and wished for their children to acquire similar multilingual skills (Kirsch 2012).

Similarly, the decision of Y's mother to invest in Y's trilingualism was attributed to her mother's own childhood trilingual experience (in Mandarin, a dialectal variety of Chinese, and English). Her mother was thus keen on practicing language and literacy skills with Y in three different languages since her birth. Her parents did not consider the simultaneous acquisition of Mandarin and English a hindrance to the development of the societal language, Japanese, but the opposite. They thought Y's overall language and cognitive abilities would benefit greatly from early trilingual practices. Her parents' positive attitude toward trilingualism was also evident in their providing Y with new vocabulary in the three languages and acting as bilingual and bicultural models for her.

It is said that parents' ideologies mostly originate from a common belief that "good" and "successful" parents are responsible for their children's linguistic competence (King and Fogle 2006). Undoubtedly, Y's mother saw it as her obligation to practice Mandarin as a responsible Chinese mother for maintaining the child's ethnic and cultural background. Moreover, her parents considered that trilingualism could contribute to her overall well-being including academic and career success. Balanced bilingual speakers are said to be in an even better position than their monolingual counterparts who only know the societal language (De Houwer 2020). Although early multilingual acquisition is desirable, frequent and quality language input from birth is not available to everyone. Y's parents viewed themselves as good parents who offered their child the gift of early trilingualism and triliteracy. Although English was non-native to both parents, they had a fondness for this language and its literature. Needless to say, English as a world language is appealing with regard to its socioeconomic influence and is greatly supported by school education. For these reasons, English was used as a lingua franca in Y's family.

However, Y's parents did not believe that achieving "ideal" trilingualism with a perfect balance of skills in each of the three languages would be a symbol of "good" parenting. Raising Y trilingually was merely one aspect of overall parenting and child development. To her parents, being multilingual was more a consequential by-product than a pre-sought-after goal (Doyle 2013) and they simply saw the value of trilingualism as a part of Y's life experience. The perception of the value of multilingualism across generations has also been discussed by Curdt-Christiansen (2009) in her study of FLP in ten Chinese immigrant families in Montréal, Canada. The author emphasizes the role of parents' beliefs and aspirations in their children's language and literacy education in Chinese, English, and French, finding that parents who held positive attitudes towards trilingualism most commonly translated their beliefs into practices (Curdt-Christiansen 2009).

Rather than expecting her to be a perfect trilingual speaker, Y's parents desired her to be a harmonious trilingual. When family members in a multilingual setting do not generally experience any problems because of that setting, or when their subjective well-being is not negatively affected by factors related to the setting, one may speak of *harmonious multilingualism* (De Houwer 2020). The notion of harmonious multilingualism goes beyond the scope of family after early childhood development; such experience is particularly important for children in developing a more balanced language proficiency in both the societal and home languages (De Houwer 2020). Y had been growing up in a harmonious family environment and had developed a well-balanced proficiency in all of her three languages. These balanced skills allowed her to continue developing smooth communication within the family and in the community.

7.1.2 Parents' invisible ideologies and factors affecting them

Developing family language policies can be complex. Even though family activities are governed by home rules, they are nevertheless influenced by external forces. In most situations, decisions are not strategically plotted but made naturally in consideration of circumstances beyond the control of parents (Caldas 2012). In this way, parents should be aware that government policies and the social situation in the community are likely to affect the families' choices when those policies contradict the families' interests (Spolsky and Shohamy 1999). Challenges and conflicts tend to arise in the interplay between the values of the wider society and the values of the family. Such tensions may also cause ideological conflicts within a family; for example, parents' ideologies and their policies may be congruent at some times but diverge at others (Curdt-Christiansen 2016; Kirsch 2012).

Home is a physical location which has a social interpretation that is relevant to language choice (Armstrong 2014). The influence of social, political, cultural, and economic contexts of the three languages on Y's parents' expectations was notable. It contributed to her parents' attitudes towards language and their opinions on the value of multilingualism, which in turn underpinned the parents' invisible ideologies and translated their beliefs into unplanned practices in family language education. Of Y's three languages, English is most widely used in world politics, economy, business, and technology. Mandarin is also one of the most influential languages in the world. Moreover, it is the only tool to access her mother's heritage, tradition, and culture. Japanese is the community language in Japan where Y's family resided during most of the present study. Y's mother showed an appreciation of the educational value of Japanese and English, and the cultural functions of Mandarin. She valued both the family's bilingual policy, which recognized English and Mandarin as home languages for daily communication, and the family's educational policy, which established all of the three languages as the medium of reading, writing, and instruction.

However, the data showed that the efforts made by Y's parents in learning activities were sometimes incongruent with what they professed to believe. Parental language background and learning experience are influential on any decisions about language use (King and Fogle 2006). Y's parents had a deep affection for English; they also firmly acknowledged the significance of developing high level English skills to ensure Y's success in academic studies and in her future career. This is shown in her mother's subconscious code-switching from Mandarin to English in mother-child conversations in a Mandarin context, or in her redundant use of English to clarify meaning in a Mandarin or Japanese learning context. Moreover, her parents' recognition of the academic and career values of English and Japanese were convincingly confirmed through the family's reading and writing practices, while this was not true of their treatment of Mandarin. For example, from two years old, Y spent over an hour every day reading English books and spent about one hour in total reading Japanese and Mandarin books. From four years old, Y's English and Japanese reading abilities greatly improved. Consequently, the level of her English and Japanese reading materials and the time she spent reading in these two languages both increased. However, seeing the difficulties in reading in Chinese characters only (without *pīnyīn* symbols written above Chinese characters), the level of her Mandarin reading materials and the time spent reading in Mandarin remained more or less the same as those from a younger age.

Y's mother had an awareness of these issues, but she did not consider it particularly urgent for Y to raise her Mandarin ability to levels similar to that of her English or Japanese. Rather, the mother gave priority to the acquisition of English and Japanese. She also felt that academic abilities across languages were linked and could be transferred, particularly in the case of reading and writing skills. The overall lack of time and opportunity also impeded the mother, in supervising Y, from allotting a relatively equal amount of time for each of her three languages, or from reading to Y as a part of her Mandarin time. In fact, her mother tended to not have much free time when Y was in the mood for reading and Y also preferred to read independently.

The influence of the host culture and identity on parental emotions as regards the minority language maintenance cannot be ignored. Y's mother admitted that maintaining the Chinese language and culture was strongly desired. She regarded Mandarin as having a particularly important emotional value for herself, and saw that it served as an appropriate medium for conveying intimate emotions and rich affective repertoires in her family. As such although English was the lingua franca when the whole family were together, her mother sometimes moved on in Mandarin in an ongoing conversation even when Y's father was within hearing distance but was not an active participant. In this situation, the mother probably regarded Mandarin as a means of passing on her culture and creating a sense of Chinese identity.

Language maintenance in multilingual families is a complex and emotionally charged matter. Whereas a considerable number of studies have been focused on social, cultural, and economic aspects as important factors affecting parents' decisions, few studies thus far have considered the emotional and relational perspectives (Pavlenko 2004; Tannenbaum 2012). These aspects are invisible and cannot be planned but are nevertheless fundamental to the success of FLP. Y's parents took them into serious consideration and adjusted decisions while acting.

Language choice in family social life is associated with its members' positive emotions and family intimacy. Studies show that parental ideology of raising children bilingually may sometimes cause tensions in families; that is, even though young children may adapt to parents' language choices to show affective feelings for their parents, older children who experience peer influence in the majority language in educational contexts tend to move toward the societal language (Caldas 2006). Then, when children resist the parents' language, parents may accommodate the children's choices (Fogle 2012). Tannenbaum (2012) argues that parents accommodating children's choices may be emotionally motivated. The flexible OPOL strategy (see 6.1.1) and the bilingual-like discourse strategies (see 6.1.2) adopted by Y's parents were evidence of parents' efforts at promoting family ties. Fogle (2012) points out that parents who refrain from forcing children to use the parental language act against their own language ideologies.

Y's parents also realized that in spite of family members' "loyalties" to their heritage language and their consistent practices using that language, which may prevent a language shift at home, schools are likely to take over the responsibility for child language development as soon as a child starts formal schooling (Spolsky 2009). Thus the school language may come to undermine the family support that is given to the home language (Spolsky 2009). With this in mind, family members' beliefs about the importance of acquiring the societal language on the one hand

and about the maintenance of the home language on the other hand are vital to the family policies and practices. Y's parents had been thinking about these questions since she entered a local preschool: to what extent should they continue to hold positive attitudes toward multilingualism and multiliteracy? Should they consistently translate their beliefs into particular actions? Should they adjust home policies and practices to fit those of schools in order to foster their child's academic success in the societal language? These and similar questions are undeniably demanding for the parents of any multilingual children, but they are certainly worth considering. Such questions should also be considered by school teachers who wish to better support their students who have a multilingual background.

7.2 Y's emerging agency: from birth to 8;1

The above section described Y's parents' flexible ideologies and how they successfully practiced and managed home language activities guided by their ideologies. This section will focus on Y's metalinguistic sense, her cultural awareness, and her emerging identity, which contributed to her agency. It attempts to show that although her behavior was subconsciously influenced by her parents' ideologies, she nevertheless had her own unique ideas and opinions. The perspectives that she developed were the result of her cognitive development and her understanding of the social, cultural, and linguistic environments surrounding her across time and space, which were very different than those of her parents.

Being an independent thinker, Y came to influence the language ideologies of her parents and to negotiate their decisions. She assessed their language abilities and built a monolingual Mandarin or English context with each parent in routine communication, a bilingual context in topic-related conversations, and a trilingual context primarily during the reading, writing and other learning times. Moreover, Y also made planned decisions and gave deliberate performances with regard to an overall consideration of more than one situational factor, and either resisted, negotiated, or modified the parents' OPOL rule. How Y took into account the adults' policies and practices with respect to certain linguistic and contextual factors can be seen as evidence of the assertion of her agency.

7.2.1 Assessing general language proficiency

Children's growing sense of agency is closely related to their age-appropriate underlying metacognitive development and life experience. It is difficult for very young children to provide an explicit account of their awareness of language, and so indirectly studying what they are aware of is a helpful way to uncover their conceptions of language (Pratt and Grieve 1984). Evidence that can be considered as indicative of language awareness has to be deduced from what they may say and do, such as monitoring an ongoing utterance, commenting on the utterance, and predicting the consequences of using inflections, words, phrases, or sentences (Clark 1978; Pratt and Grieve 1984).

Y's awareness of being a trilingual speaker emerged as early as two years old. From this age, she was able to use the actual names of languages to make explicit comments about what language forms her parents and others used. For example, she said, "I speak three languages. I am trilingual." (2;5). However, the levels of her competence in each language were differently self-evaluated, which is as shown in Example 72.

Example 72 is from a mother-child conversation (3;3).
MOT: Which is your best language? Chinese, English, or Japanese?
CHI: Chinese.
MOT: And the second best is . . . .?
CHI: English
MOT: The third best is . . . ?
CHI: Japanese.

In the above example, although Y was aware of her trilingual abilities, the perceived proficiency seemed different from the real proficiency in each of her three languages. This was probably influenced by the perception of her cultural identity, which will be illustrated later in Example 82. The level of home language proficiency also appears to have positive associations with the quality of family relationships; that is, the more fluent children are in their home language, the more they respect their parents (Boutakidis, Chao, and Rodríguez 2011).

By the time Y was four, she demonstrated a high level of oral proficiency in each of her three languages. She was good at extensive reading and general writing in English and Japanese. In Example 73, she displayed an early awareness of the Japanese language proficiency of herself and her mother.

Example 73 is from a mother-child conversation (4;1).
MOT: 别人问我: "你会日文吗?", 我都说: "できない"。
[When people ask me, "Can you speak Japanese?", I always say, "I can't."]
CHI: ちょっとだけ。
[A little bit.]
(Y corrected her mother's answer.)
MOT: 如果别人问你: "你会日文吗?", 你怎么说?

[If people ask you, "Can you speak Japanese?", what do you say?]
CHI: いっぱい。
[Very well.]

Similar positive comments on Y's Japanese competence were made by two kindergarten classroom teachers who supervised her in the year before she left for Scotland (3;10–4;10) and the year after she returned to Japan (5;10–6;10). Neither of the teachers was aware that Japanese was not Y's daily conversational language at home. When Y's mother asked them, "Yのにほんごはほかのこどもとちがいますか?" [Is Y different from the other children in terms of her Japanese speaking?], both teachers affirmed that they noticed no differences and that they both considered Y's Japanese to be fluent and appropriate. When Y was a P1 student in Scotland, at a parent-teacher meeting the classroom teacher commented that Y's (academic) language skills were much higher than the others. This assessment was somehow confirmed in Y's self-evaluation, as seen in Example 74.

Example 74 is from a mother-child conversation (5;5).
MOT: Whose English is good in P1?
CHI: Y.
(Y thought for a few seconds.)
MOT: Do you feel your English is a little different from that of others?
CHI: No.
(Y answered without thinking.)

In this example, Y was not hesitant to evaluate her own English skills when she was educated together with children who had been growing up in native English countries and with native English-speaking parents. Moreover, Y demonstrated an awareness of the language abilities of people around her. Her perception of each parent's language abilities was reflected in her choice of a language that a parent knew when talking with that parent. For example, when she addressed her father, either English, Japanese, or a combination of the two was selected. She never heard any Mandarin utterances naturally from the father, and consequently no Mandarin statement was directed toward him in routine conversations. In many situations, Y observed her mother speaking in both Mandarin and English at home and communicating in Japanese with Japanese monolingual speakers outside. Realizing the mother's trilingual ability, any one of the three languages or a mixture of the languages was adopted by Y in interaction with her mother.

Y also noticed language mistakes made by monolingual speakers. For instance, she found in her Scottish school that "老师的英文很好, 小朋友的英文很好。小朋

友的英文讲错了，老师教他们。" [Teachers' English is very good. Children's English is very good. When children make mistakes, teachers help them.] (4;10). She also found in her Japanese kindergarten that "有些小朋友的日文很好，有些小朋友的日文不好。" [Some children's Japanese is good while others' is not.] (4;2). She noticed that some Japanese children could not "say some ひらがな [*hiragana*] clearly." (3;11). Talking about her own language weakness, she admitted that reading Mandarin books was challenging since "I don't know all Chinese characters." (4;10). She also made frequent spelling mistakes in English writing of which she was not aware. However, in the speaking context, mistakes were always spotted and spontaneously self-corrected. For example, she said, "I draw, I drew this picture this morning." (4;1).

7.2.2 Distinguishing relative language proficiency

McClure (1977) has noticed that young children appear to make binary judgements about linguistic competence; that is, one either knows a language very well or does not know it at all. Y seemed to lack the ability to judge others' relative language proficiency levels at two years old but this ability emerged over time and was well developed by the time she reached three, as illustrated by Example 75.

Example 75 is from a diary entry (2;4).
1 MOT: Whose Japanese is better, mummy or daddy?
2 CHI: Mummy and daddy.
3 MOT: Whose Chinese is better, mummy or daddy?
4 CHI: Mummy. Daddy can't speak Chinese.
5 MOT: How about Y? Whose Chinese is better, mummy or Y?
6 CHI: Mummy is good. Y is good. Mummy and Y can speak Chinese.

As shown in the above conversation, Y assumed her mother's Japanese was as good as that of her father (Turn 2). She did not make a clear distinction between her own Mandarin proficiency and that of her mother (Turn 6). When asked about her father's Mandarin ability, Y simply defined him as a person who had no knowledge of that language (Turn 4). In fact, her father understood some Mandarin expressions that Y used in context and responded with body language such as passing food to her following her request to the mother.

However, at the age of three, Y had clearly come to show her awareness of her parents' different levels of language abilities. Two diary entries recorded similar comments made by Y when observing her mother reading Japanese books, "Mummy, your English is good, your Chinese is good, your Japanese is different"

(3;0) and "Your Japanese is not as good as daddy." (3;0). After her fourth birthday, Y could evaluate her parents' language abilities even more specifically. She said, for example, "Daddy's Chinese like one-year-old children. Mummy's Japanese like three-year-old children." (4;2). In other words, she considered that her father's Mandarin ability resembled that of a one-year-old Mandarin speaker and that her mother's Japanese ability was similar to that of a three-year-old Japanese speaker. At age five, when her mother was reading a Dickens chapter book in English, Y said, "Mummy, your reading . . . sounds not right." (5;0). She compared her mother's reading with the model from the book's attached CD and became very critical of the mothers' reading skills.

Y's assessment of her parents' language abilities was also shown in their daily practices. For instance, it sometimes took many seconds for her mother to read a sentence in a Japanese storybook. Being excited to know what would happen next in the story, Y decided to read it by herself and thus told the mother, "算了算了，我自己读吧，你太慢了。" [Forget about it. I'll read it by myself. You are too slow.] (4;1). Having thus come to understand her parents' language deficiencies, Y started to correct their mistakes and teach the father Mandarin and mother Japanese from four years old. This has been discussed in 6.2.3.

7.2.3 Distinguishing literacy skills from language skills

In general, literacy skills are not directly related to a speaker's spoken language skills. However, language and literacy skills were not separately developed in the process of Y's language acquisition. As a result, Y was not able to distinguish her parents' speaking skill from their reading skill when she was four years old, as shown in Examples 76 and 77.

Example 76 is from a diary entry (2;4).
Situation: Y was holding a book.
FAT: I'll read it to you.
CHI: It's Chinese. You can't read, daddy.

Example 77 is from an observation note (4;2).
Situation: Y took out a delivered book from the letterbox.
MOT: 妈妈的书。
 [Mummy's book.]
CHI: 我觉得是爸爸的书。
 [I think it's daddy's book.]

MOT:	为什么? [Why?]
CHI:	因为爸爸会讲日文。我觉得是爸爸的书和Y的书。 [Because daddy can speak Japanese. I think it's daddy and Y's book.]

In Example 76, Y's awareness of her father's deficiency in speaking Mandarin and her lack of awareness of his certain level of comprehension of Mandarin text were evidenced by her refusing to give him a Mandarin book. In Example 77, Y did not distinguish between her parents' speaking and listening skills and their reading and writing skills. However, she was able to do this at five years old, as shown in Example 78.

Example 78 is from a mother-child conversation (5;4).
MOT:	Which language do you speak the best?
CHI:	Chinese and English and Japanese.
MOT:	Which language do you read and write the best?
CHI:	English.

In the above example, Y accurately described her trilingual and triliterate skills. Her confidence in her English ability was also shown in a self-assessment of reading Usborne Young Reading Series. She said, "你知道吗, 我已经和CD读的一样快了。CD读这么快, 我的眼睛也可以看得一样快。" [Do you know I can read as fast as the CD player. I scan with my eyes at the same pace as CD reading.] (4;1). To her, the speed of reading or speaking was a sign of linguistic competence. In addition, Y recognized knowledge of vocabulary to be another sign related to language proficiency. She considered her English to be good because she knew and could use a variety of words. Her P1 classroom teacher in Scotland was amazed to find that Y knew a lot of difficult words that children of the same age (5;1) normally didn't know. In the final report, the teacher assessed Y's "Literacy & English Language" by writing, "Y started in Primary One knowing all her single sounds, some digraphs and being able to read quite complex text. A confident writer . . . Y builds her story logically." (The report was made when Y was 5;9).

7.2.4 Associating language ability with language practices

Y's parents always emphasized the importance of daily practices in language acquisition. They adopted a combination of the OPOL policy and the one-situation-one-language policy to make sure that all the three languages were practiced every day. Y's mother often told her, "Practice makes perfect." She seemed to agree with the mother's opinion and often said, "没有讲中文就不会讲中文, 没有

讲英文就不会讲英文, 没有讲日文就不会讲日文。" [You can't speak Mandarin if you don't use it, you can't speak English if you don't use it, and you can't speak Japanese if you don't use it.] (3;10). Her perception of the importance of practice in childhood is illustrated in Example 79.

Example 79 is from a mother-child conversation (3;7).
CHI: Mama, why your English is so good?
MOT: Because I practice every day.
CHI: Why your Chinese is so good?
MOT: Because I have been using it since I was a child.
CHI: Why your Japanese is so bad? Because you didn't speak when you are a child?

In this example, Y made a connection between her mother speaking good English and Mandarin and language practice, and between her mother speaking poor Japanese and lack of practice. Moreover, she appeared to notice different contexts in language input, as seen in Example 80.

Example 80 is from a mother-child conversation (4;6).
MOT: Which language do you like the most?
CHI: English and Chinese.
MOT: How about Japanese?
CHI: I speak Japanese at school.

In the above conversation, Y considered that both home practice and school practice were important. After her family relocated to Scotland when she was 4;10, the way she spoke English changed as regards vocabulary, sentence structure, and speech style. Her parents said to her, "You are speaking like a native speaker." and her response was that "Because I listen to their talking and I read books." (5;3). To Y, communicating with other English speakers and learning from books were the two main sources of her English input.

7.2.5 The development of linguistic and ethnic identity

Language provides access to cultural wealth from one generation to the next. A heritage language provides a strong sense of ethnic belonging, whereas the loss of it is a potential loss of cultural identity (Curdt-Christiansen 2009). Caldas (2002) points out that ideologies and discourses associated with a specific place or a specific person help with constructing identities in that place or through the socialization with that person. In the present study, the close bond between Y and her mother strongly motivated her to identify herself as Chinese. For example, she said, "妈妈是中国人, Y

也是中国人。" [Mummy is Chinese. Y is also Chinese.] (2;10). Y saw important connections between language ability and ethnic identity. She confidently said, "我会讲中文, 我是中国人。" [I can speak Mandarin. I am Chinese.] (3;2). She expressed doubts about other aspects of her identity such as "为什么我是日本人, 我也会讲中文?" [Why I am Japanese even though I can speak Mandarin?] (3;9). Although language is just one feature of culture and linguistic identity is just one aspect of a person's multiple identities, Y's desire to be Chinese supported her Mandarin use enormously, as shown in Example 81.

Example 81 is from a mother-child conversation (3;10).
MOT: 为什么你喜欢讲中文?
 [Why do you like speaking Mandarin?]
CHI: 因为我讲好多中文, 我就会变成中国人。
 [Because if I speak a lot of Mandarin, I'll become Chinese people.]

In this way, Y generalized about different language skills of a speaker. She also made simple judgments about a multilingual's language ability according to their cultural identity. Although Y's English reading, writing, and other academic language skills were at a much higher level than those in Japanese or Mandarin, and she excelled in English literature and history knowledge, her opinions about her own language abilities nevertheless seemed to be influenced by her Chinese ethnic aspirations, as indicated by her assertions below.

Example 82 is from a mother-child conversation (3;10).
MOT: Which is better, mama's English or Chinese?
CHI: (. . .) Chinese.
 (Y thought for a few seconds. She used to say her mother's English was as good as her Mandarin.)
MOT: Why?
CHI: Because mama is Chinese people.
MOT: How about daddy? Which is better? His English or Japanese?
CHI: Japanese
MOT: Why?
CHI: Because daddy is Japanese people.
MOT: How about you? Which is the best? Chinese, English, or Japanese?
CHI: Chinese
MOT: Why?
CHI: Because Y want to be Chinese people.

Spolsky (2004) notes that a speaker's real proficiency may not be as influential as their perceived proficiency in terms of its impact on the speaker's willingness to speak a language. In the above conversation, Y's belief that a person's perceived language proficiency is the key to their cultural identity led her to ignore her real language proficiency as demonstrated in language practices.

However, as her cognitive competence developed, Y learned to think critically about the relationship between language and ethnic identity. She started to consider different possibilities and affecting factors when looking at the connection, or lack thereof, between the two concepts. By the time she turned four, Y had developed an awareness of her English language ability and non-English identity, as demonstrated in statements such as "I can speak English, but I am not English people." (4;0). In fact, Y and her mother were often thought to be Americans by monolingual Japanese children and adults when they spoke English fluently outside, regardless of their Asian appearance. Y was also recognized as a locally born child in Scotland by her school teachers and parents who thought that they did not see any difference between Y's English and behavior and those of other children.

Holding a strong desire to become a real Chinese person ("我想变成真正的中国人。" [I want to be a real Chinese person.]) (5;1), Y made greater efforts to learn Chinese characters and learn to read and write in Mandarin from the time she turned two years old. These endeavors notably supported her language practices and Mandarin development, as seen in Example 83.

Example 83 is from a mother-child conversation (5;1).
CHI: I am Chinese. I want to change to a Chinese passport.
MOT: You are not Chinese like me even you have a Chinese passport. You need to read and write Chinese well.
CHI. I can read Chinese books.
(Y took out a book called 冰雪奇缘 [Frozen] and started to read.)

Thus, to Y, the ability to read and write in Chinese was a characteristic of being Chinese. This is also shown in Example 84.

Example 84 is from a mother-child conversation (5;4).
MOT: 铅笔借我一下。
[Can I borrow your pencil?]
CHI: 这个中国的给你。你是中国人，Y也是中国人，可以写汉字。
[I'll give you this Chinese one. You are Chinese. Y is also Chinese. You can use it to write Chinese characters.]

In the above conversation with her mother, a strong association can be found in Y's mind among a pencil made in China (with a label printed in Chinese characters), Chinese characters, and Chinese people

While Y's perceptions of self-identity were directly influenced by her language abilities, her growing cognitive competence enabled her to eventually distinguish a linguistic identity from an ethnic identity. She started to think that a person's identity was connected with various culture-related factors in addition to their language ability. Thus, Chinese speakers did not equal Chinese people, and Chinese children born and raised overseas were not equal to their counterparts in China. Due to a strong bond with her mother, Y had a persistent preference for Mandarin and a self-identification of Chinese ethnicity from one year old. However, since the family lived in Japan, Y started to refer to herself as "Chinese and Japanese", as seen in Example 85.

Example 85 is from a mother-child conversation (2;7).
MOT: Are you Chinese?
CHI: Yes.
MOT: Are you Japanese?
CHI: Yes.
MOT: Which one?
CHI: Chinese and Japanese.

Y's sense of Japanese origin shown above was further strengthened after the family relocated to Scotland. There, she showed a willingness to be identified as Japanese. She said, "I am Japanese. Mrs T (a school teacher) knows I am Japanese." (5;0). Living in the unfamiliar Scotland, strong feelings about home country triggered her emotional attachment to Japan. While she often said, "I miss my home in Japan", she rarely said, "I miss China". To Y China meant more about her Chinese mother while Japan was the home country.

Moreover, both Y herself and her Scottish teachers reported that she actively carried out Mandarin conversations with a couple of British-born Chinese children. It appeared that Y was able to realize her trilingual identity in her Scottish schools, because she regarded children born to bicultural, although "monolingual" families (e.g. English-Scottish, Australian-English, etc.), as the norm. However, her trilingual competence and tricultural sense were not recognized in the Japanese kindergarten that she attended.

Studies of the relationship between parents' attitudes and parents' beliefs about the social acceptability or unacceptability of using non-English languages in the UK give different clues. Okita (2002) revealed that practices among Japanese families raising bilingual children in England appeared not to be recognized or supported by the English-speaking society. The Japanese mothers had to delay or abandon their Japanese education plans under the pressure of the English community. Likewise, the impact of the sociolinguistic environment on the mothers' efforts to raise bilingual children is also reported by Kirsch (2012) in her study of seven Luxembourgish-English families living in England. Under the pressure of English-only attitude, the mothers' strong ideologies about learning the heritage language were at odds with their actual language practices, which were reflected in their constant accommodation to the children's English requests (Kirsch 2012).

The explanation for the diverse reactions from Y and the Japanese and Luxembourgish bilingual mothers to the British sociolinguistic environment is complex and cannot be generalized. Nevertheless, Y's positive response enormously supported her language and cultural learning in a new and challenging situation.

7.3 Y's consistent agency: from Japan to Scotland

Harris (1995) points out that a child's socialization is a highly context-dependent form of learning. In bilingual and bicultural situations, decisions on when to use the home language are connected to "behavioral, cognitive, and emotional responses that occurred at home" (Harris 1995: 462). However, language behavior and family language policies may vary in response to the change of external contexts, such as the relocation to a new country, a visit to the monolingual relatives in their country of origin, the birth of a sibling, and the start of schooling (Luykx 2005; Tuominen 1999). Caldas (2012) points out that it is commonplace for even the best parental efforts to be defeated by the external environment. Although language policies in Y's family remained relatively stable, they were nevertheless dynamic and fluctuated subject to negotiations between Y and her parents due to their different life experiences. This section focuses on a particular change in Y's living environment – the family's move from Japan to Scotland two months before Y turned five – and on Y's agentic responses to these sociolinguistic and cultural changes.

7.3.1 Language preferences

One of the explicit language practices was the family's metalinguistic conversations regarding their opinions about language and language use. Since Y was two years old, her mother had many conversations with her to find out about her feelings and language preferences. Examples of such conversations are seen in Examples 86 through 88.

Example 86 is from a mother-child conversation (2;2).
MOT: Which language do you like the best?
CHI: Chinese.
MOT: Which do you like No. 2?
CHI: English.
MOT: Which is No. 3?
CHI: Japanese.

Example 87 is from a mother-child conversation (3;5).
MOT: 你喜欢和我说什么语言？
[Which language do you like to use with me?]
CHI: 中文。
[Mandarin.]

Example 88 is from a mother-child conversation (5;5).
Situation: Y and her mother were choosing bedtime books.
MOT: Time to read.
CHI: C for Chinese, E for English, J for Japanese. Chinese first, then English, then Japanese.

As shown in the above three examples, Y demonstrated a consistent preference for the mother's tongue, Mandarin, at different ages and in different sociocultural environments. Y's emotional dimension attached to her mother's L1 is an aspect of her "internalization" (Curdt-Christiansen and Huang 2020). Research shows that children who speak the same home languages as their parents feel emotionally closer to them and are more likely to engage in parent-child conversations compared with those who speak a different language from their parents (Tseng and Fuligni 2000). The close relationship between Y and her parents enabled her to overcome the external pressures and be consistent in using the non-societal languages both at home and outside and thereby maintain harmonious multilingualism. FLP is thus not just about rules for language use but also a means to develop a strong family bond. Maintaining a home language in the second generation is a key element of a harmonious family relationship (De Houwer 2009).

Moreover, Y's affection for Mandarin was also shown in her social network. When studying in Scotland, although her best playmates were some British children from the same P1 class, she often invited a preschooler, who was a British born Chinese, to play together during lunch break. This is shown in the following example.

Example 89 is from a mother-child conversation (5;11).
1 CHI: 明天还要和那个中国小男孩玩。
         [I want to play with that Chinese boy again tomorrow.]
2 MOT: 为什么?
         [Why?]
3 CHI: 因为他会讲中文。
         [Because he can speak Mandarin.]

In the above example, although Y pointed out that the boy was Chinese, it seemed that the social network was constructed based on the boy's Mandarin ability rather than his Chinese identity (Turn 3).

It is found that children's linguistic skills in the school language (normally the community language) are consistently developing through mainstream schooling. It is common for children to start to value speaking the school language over their home language when they begin to socialize in a society in which the former variety is the most valued linguistic form (Fillmore 1991), which, however, is not true in Y's situation. Although she knew Japanese well and used it in her Japanese nursery school, it did not appear to be her favorite language with either of her parents even when the family was outside in the Japanese society. She stuck to Mandarin with the mother and English with the father in libraries, supermarkets, and parks. Regarding Japanese, she said, "I speak にほんご [Japanese] at school." (4;2). Y's language choice of mainly using Mandarin with her mother and mainly using English with her father in daily communication remained unchanged even after she entered a local Japanese primary school.

It has been found that children's preferences for a language tend to reflect their sensitivity to the language environment (Caldas 2002). Caldas (2002) notes that the varied experiences outside the home will have a strong influence on a child's language values and language practices. In particular, the impact of social networks cannot be neglected. Harris (1995) describes how Russian-speaking children in Israel acquired the societal linguistic codes of their peers, in addition to their parents' language, and used these codes in their Russian immigrant families. Although these families had been motivated to maintain their heritage language and had implemented what should have been a successful policy to preserve Russian at home, only moderate success was achieved (Harris 1995).

However, Y's case shows an opposite result. Although she commonly favored the behavioral norms of her peers when playing together with them at school or in the neighborhood, the outside norms did not override the practices that she had acquired at home. Y did not copy the language of her playmates nor did she tend to shift from the home language to the community language in family conversations. Instead, Y always favored Mandarin and English at home.

7.3.2 Consistency between beliefs and actions in the non-societal languages

Doyle (2013) recognizes that raising multilingual children successfully does not exclusively rely on the FLP; the multilingual nature of the place – or lack therefore – is a regular contributor to be considered. Some places are assumed to be more multilingual while others are more monolingual. If a family speaking a heritage language resides in a neighborhood of diverse linguistic and ethnic backgrounds, where signs written in different languages can be seen and speakers of different languages can be found, the family members most likely will not be considered to be completely different from the local residents (Doyle 2013). However, if the majority of neighbors are monolingual in the societal language and there are no signs in other languages in the neighborhood, children from the family may experience peer pressure to conform to the majority language and culture (Doyle 2013).

In the present study, the linguistic landscape in the two communities in which Y's family resided (Japan and Scotland) created some difficulties for the family members' language choices outside the home, despite the efforts made by her parents to maintain a stable FLP. Although signboards containing Chinese characters and English words are seen everywhere in Japan, these do not change the fact that Japan is by nature monolingual and monocultural. Taking into consideration the attitudes of the majority language speakers toward the minority language speakers in Japan, as well as the greater acceptance and intelligibility of some minority languages over others, Y's mother decided to speak English with Y in the Japanese community on most occasions. She also code-switched to Japanese when Japanese speakers were nearby. Similarly, the Scottish city in which Y's family temporarily resided was also a highly monolingual society despite its reputation as a tourist attraction. After the family moved there, her parents mainly used English with her outside.

However, after Y turned two, by which time she had become a good trilingual speaker and an independent thinker, a conflict in the language choice outside home arose between Y and her parents. For instance, in Example 90, when her mother suggested code switching to Japanese when monolingual Japanese speakers were in earshot, Y said she did not mind being different and preferred to continue speaking in English or Mandarin with her mother.

Example 90 is from a mother-child conversation (2;5).
MOT: Everyone speaks Japanese outside and they may think you are strange if you speak English or Chinese.
CHI: I don't mind.

From studying language practices of a Chinese immigrant family on the west coast of the United States, Liu (2018) found that after children started to play in the neighborhood, there were pressures from the neighbors who spoke the dominant community language and had adopted its dominant values, which worked against the immigrant parents' authority as language managers. This is also true in Y's mother's attitude. Even though she strongly recognized her role as the main source of the input of Mandarin and English, she had come to compromise her belief in recognizing Japanese as beneficial to a wider social context, as illustrated by the above example. Nevertheless, having thus learned about Y's language attitude and preference, her mother always negotiated language choice with her in different social contexts. The two examples below describe this.

Example 91 is from a mother-child conversation in Japan (3;1).
MOT: Many Japanese children go to English じゅく [cram school] and know some English, but not many Japanese people speak Chinese.
CHI: No, I like Chinese. I want to speak Chinese outside.

Example 92 is from a mother-child conversation in Scotland (5;0).
CHI: I want mummy to take me to school and pick me up every day.
MOT: Why?
CHI: Because I want to speak Chinese.
(Y wanted to speak Mandarin with her mother on the way to and back from school.)

In these two examples, although Y had a good awareness of the dominant status of Japanese in Japan or English in Scotland, and was aware of the high level of popularity of English in Japan, she was nevertheless determined to use Mandarin outside in both societies. Y's preference for the mother's tongue is somehow similar to the situation that is reported by Fishman (2006) in a Yiddish immigrant family, in which English was limited to schoolwork and receiving visitors while Yiddish was the main language used for daily communication within the family, even though speaking Yiddish did not bring any economic benefit in the English dominant society. Again, it was presumed that Y's fondness for Mandarin was related to her attachment to her mother.

How speakers practice a language reveals their real attitudes to that language. A contextually-inappropriate or disparaging type of practice may devaluate that language and lead to a language shift (Smagulova 2014). Looking at the language shift from Kazakh to Russian in ethnic Kazakh families, Smagulova (2014) has reported that Kazakh was used by adults in a baby talk register while Russian was adopted in formal discussions. The practice in Russian had raised children's self-esteem as "autonomous social agents" while the practice in Kazakh inadvertently devalued this language (Smagulova 2014: 370).

The inconsistency between a speaker's language attitude and language practice was also found in Y's mother. Regardless of her strong beliefs in the value of Mandarin or the great efforts she made to promote its domestic use, the mother was always conscious of her behavior when speaking Mandarin (or even English) in Japanese society. Most of the time, she would communicate with Y using body language, or intentionally lower her voice and choose short non-Japanese words. However, Y seemed not to be influenced by her mother's "awareness" of speaking Mandarin outside, and decided to use Mandarin in both the Japanese and Scottish communities, acting out her decisions in a natural manner.

Armstrong (2014) points out that parents may understand their own and their children's agency in very different ways. Parents who attempt to implement divergent language norms that include the use of a low-status language need to acquire a "critical awareness" of their own agency (Armstrong 2014). In the process of language socialization outside the home context, Y's parents were aware that using a non-societal language as a social practice in critical informal domains, not just as an abstracted code, was the key to sustainable language development. Nevertheless, they admitted that implementing a minority-language-outside policy would not feel natural, at least not all the time, to many people who only spoke the societal language. However, Y's modelling in using Mandarin and English outside helped her parents develop a natural attitude toward the use of a "special" language in a broader social context.

7.3.3 Learning language and culture in native and non-native environments

Doyle (2013) argues that multilingualism is linked to places and constructed in places. It was surprising to notice how much some aspects of Y's English had changed after residing in a place where English was the native language of most people, such as her use of a melodic English-like voice in speech and the habit of using tag questions. Y was also sensitive to the signposts in the surroundings, which illustrated her understanding of the sociolinguistic and sociocultural aspects of the community in which she lived. For example, she put a "Staff only" and a "Keep out" signpost on the door of her bedroom in Scotland because these signboards were "everywhere in Scotland" (4;10). New English expressions were brought back home from school every day, after the family move to Scotland. They included "snip", a replacement for "cut", "rumbling tummy" for "hungry", "soggy" for "wet", "stiff" for "hard" or "difficult", and "crunchy" for "crispy".

New English language cultural customs were also acquired as Y was immersed in this English environment. For example, she soon began to add "xxx" at the end of a message ("xxx means love, love, love.") (5;0). Curdt-Christiansen (2009) considers that the symbolic value of a languages includes prestige, access to equality and cultural identity. Fillmore (2000) points out that language maintenance should not only be considered from a purely linguistic perspective; the links between the cultural values of the ethnolinguistic group also need to be considered.

Even though Y picked up many linguistic aspects from being in a native English environment, the home input from parents, books and the media were still evaluated by both herself and her parents as the main input of general linguistic and cultural knowledge. This brings to mind Noguchi's (1996b) observation that parents can act as bicultural models for their children, allowing themselves to be seen dealing with two cultures. In fact, Y's knowledge of her three cultures had developed through her acquisition of the three languages at home in Japan and Scotland. Her parents considered that language and culture were closely related and that learning a language necessarily entailed the learning of its culture, and vice versa.

Despite a lack of opportunities for learning the Mandarin and English languages and cultures in Japanese schools, or those of Mandarin and Japanese in Scottish schools, there were other possible ways to learn and practice at home, such as reading literature and history or being involved in culture-related topics and activities. A typical practice with English language and culture would involve texts by Shakespeare, Dickens, and other authors as well as texts about English history; a typical practice with Chinese language and culture would include texts about old Chinese expressions and Chinese classics; and a typical practice with Japanese language and culture would connect with Japanese literature and customs. Cultural awareness, in turn, was reflected in Y's language behavior. In the example below, Y adopted 成语 [four-character idioms] in her speech.

Example 93 is from a mother's diary note (4;1).
CHI: 我会用成语了,大头儿子,小头爸爸,白雪公主。
[I can use four-character idioms. Big-head son, small-head father, Princess Snow White.]

The three underlined examples that Y gave were four-character words but not recognized Chinese idioms. However, she believed that being able to use four-character idioms was a symbol of being Chinese people and knowing Chinese culture and this belief inspired her to practice this type of special expression. Making more and more attempts at this, she exhibited her strong sense of identity as belonging to Chinese culture. Bilingualism and biculturalism do not necessarily coexist, however. People who grow up in a monocultural society may become bilingual through language practice, and those who were born from a mixed marriage and grew up with two different cultures may speak only one language (Grosjean 2008). Only those who take part in the life of two cultures, who adapt their languages and behaviors to these two cultures, and who blend aspects of the two cultures are described as bicultural (Grosjean 2008). Heritage culture can be acquired and ethnic identity can be established and reinforced through specific language practices; and new languages can be mastered while being socialized into a new cultural context. Thus, learning language and culture simultaneously is one important issue in transnational families.

7.4 Cross-linguistic influence and child agency

Cross-linguistic influence (CLI) is a well-known phenomenon in second and third language learning and has received considerable attention in early bilingual and trilingual acquisition studies (Barnes 2006; Genesee, Nicoladis, and Paradis 1995; Hoffmann and Stavans 2007; Hulk and Müller 2000). The data from the present research demonstrate that Y's languages were influenced by one another to some extent in the areas of vocabulary, speech style, and particularly sentence grammar. The possible causes for this, related to Y's exercise of her agency, will be analyzed from the perspectives of both the language-internal and language-external influences, such as language dominance, developmental errors, parental modelling, and home language mode.

7.4.1 Language dominance

Y's parents often translated their languages and asked Y to do the same practice. While this helped develop her abilities in her three languages, it involved literal translations that sounded awkward and stiff in the target language. This can be seen in Examples 94 through 96.

Example 94 is from a diary note (2;6).
CHI: 好重的雨! (How heavy the rain is!)
MOT: 好大的雨! (How big the rain is!)
 (A "heavy" rain is described as a "big" rain in Mandarin.)

Example 95 is from a video recording (3;6).
CHI: Y 的房子好壮, 大灰狼吹不倒。
[Y's house is very strong. The big bad wolf can't blow it down.]
MOT: 房子很牢固。
[The house is solid.]
("Strong" can be used to describe "a strong house" or "a strong body" in English. 壮 [strong] is considered appropriate to describe one's body, but it is incorrect to describe a house in Mandarin.)

Example 96 is from an observation note (4;4).
CHI: 我不小心画在桌子上了, 画得很严重。
[I painted on the table accidently. It looks serious.]
(Y was worried about the damage that she made to the table. While the English word "serious" was an appropriate choice to describe the above situation, its translated Mandarin equivalent, 严重, was not. 严重 commonly described more serious situations or consequences.)

The above examples show that the influence from English was especially common in Y's Mandarin acquisition. The influence of English on Mandarin grammatical elements, such as "Wh-" interrogatives, was also observed in her Mandarin speech. In a Mandarin "Wh-" clause, Y put a "Wh-" interrogative word at the beginning of a sentence, which was the correct order in English but a grammatical mistake in Mandarin. Examples 97 through 99 illustrate this tendency.

Example 97 is from the observation notes (3;0).
CHI: 哪个甜甜圈你要? [Which doughnut do you like?]
MOT: 你要哪个甜甜圈? [Do you like which doughnut?]

Example 98 is from the observation notes (3;1).
CHI: 什么我要看? [What shall I watch?]
MOT: 我要看什么? [I shall watch what?]

Example 99 is from the observation notes (3;2).
CHI: 在哪里 Y 的家? [Where is Y's home?]
MOT: Y 的家在哪里? [Y's home is where?]

The above types of CLI appeared when Y was about three years old. They occurred much less frequently but had not completely disappeared by the age of six. The same type of CLI was also reported by Yip and Matthews (2007) in the bilingual Cantonese-English children who were dominant in Cantonese, although the directionality of influence was opposite. In early multilingualism, language dominance is considered a relevant factor in relation to CLI. The dominant language is the language that a speaker knows the best or uses the most (De Houwer 2009). Language preference is another indication of language dominance, but a lesser and more indirect one (Saunders, 1988). The data from the present study and the author's other studies investigating Y's trilingual competence at two and three years old showed that she made appropriate language choices in different contexts (Zhan 2018, 2019, 2021). These studies also showed that Y had an extensive knowledge of both Mandarin and English.

However, Baker and Wright (2017) believe that bilinguals rarely show equal ability in each of their languages and that they use different languages in different contexts. By and large, one language is always dominant in a given context. Although Y was more or less equally proficient in her three spoken codes, the level of the language acquired through English reading and writing was probably higher than that gained in Japanese or Mandarin. For this reason, English tended to prevail in some situations and related to certain topics.

7.4.2 Developmental errors

CLI from Mandarin on English relative clauses emerged when Y was three years old. In a noun or noun phrase clause, Y did not know how to use the relative pronoun in English, as shown in "This is me and daddy cooked" (3;5). Although the relative clause in this sentence syntactically conformed to the order of its Mandarin equivalent, it is difficult to attribute this error to CLI from Mandarin. Instead, it would seem to have been due to other causes such as language development.

Native English speakers normally begin to acquire more complex linguistic structures, such as relative clauses, in the preschool years (Lightbown and Spada 2013), so it may have been simply too early for Y to have learned how to construct them in English. At five years old, Y was able to produce long and complex speech including utterances using different relative pronouns for subjects and objects in clauses. Two examples of this ability were recorded in the mother's diary: "I don't like the food which has no taste." (5;1) and "This is what I said just now." (5;3). Thus, the data might suggest that some apparent CLI was actually a de facto developmental issue which would disappear with Y's evolving ability to use complex language.

7.4.3 Parental modelling

Quay (2001) believes the directionality of influence tends to be from the community language, which is often a speaker's dominant language, to the home language. However, Yip and Matthews (2007) argue that directionality of influence can also come from the relatively weaker language to the relatively stronger language. In Y's case, although the direction of influence on vocabulary was largely from English to Mandarin, the opposite direction was also noticed. For example, instead of saying "turn on/switch on the light", she sometimes used "open the light" (a literal translation of its Mandarin expression) (3;0). However, Y consistently adopted the correct form, "turn off the light", rather than saying "close the light".

Seeing that Y knew the correct forms of "turn on" and "turn off" in English, a cause other than language dominance or developmental errors might explain language deviation such as the mother's modelling. Y's mother believed she had rarely said "close the light", whereas she sometimes subconsciously said "open the light". Although in these cases, the mother would immediately become aware of her mistakes and corrected herself by adding the correct form "turn on the light", her incorrect modelling may have affected Y's language use nevertheless. Thus, the effect of a parent's role as a language model, in either a positive or negative sense, on children's language development should not be ignored.

7.4.4 Home language mode

Children take contextual factors into account when they evaluate the meaning conveyed in communication, such as the interlocutors (e.g. their language beliefs, language abilities, language preferences, and discourse strategies) and situational factors (e.g. topics, activities, and conversational situations). According to Grosjean (2001: 3), these sociolinguistic factors are influential in defining a bilingual's language mode – "the state of activation of the bilinguals' languages and language processing mechanisms at a given point in time." Grosjean (2001) explains that a bilingual's two languages are always switched on but at different levels; when one language is activated, the other is temporarily deactivated to some extent rather than being totally switched off. Hoffmann (2001) extends the notion of language mode to trilingualism.

CLI is related to the language mode in a specific context in which communication takes place (Grosjean 1998). Depending on the variables concerning the quantity and, more importantly, quality of language input, a conversation may take place closer to a monolingual or a bilingual mode. With the speaker's desire

7.4 Cross-linguistic influence and child agency

to use a target language in a particular mode, lexical items associated with that language will be selected over non-target language items (Finkbeiner, Gollan, and Caramazza 2006). The language decision made in a specific language mode is considered to be part of a child's sense of agency.

Looking at Y's production of verb (V) and prepositional phrase (PP) constructions in Mandarin,[21] the data reveals that she was dominant in the VPP order – a constant feature of English – even when PPV was the correct form (Zhan 2019). This is despite the fact that the community language, Japanese, shares the PPV feature. In this case, CLI is considered to be determined by both linguistic and cognitive factors. While the overlapped VPP structure in English and Mandarin suggests that the PPV Mandarin order is vulnerable to the invariable VPP English ordering, Y's cognitive tendency toward the home language mode seems to explain her acceptance of the word order in English or avoidance of the order in Japanese (Zhan 2019).

In the Mandarin context, the English VPP pattern being chosen in preference to the Japanese PPV, one could be perceived as a result of Y's desire to use the home languages in the home language mode. In her family, English and Mandarin were employed for home communication while Japanese was for outside socializing. These language practices therefore encouraged Y to choose either Mandarin or English in the family environment. She may be more likely to activate the grammatical structures of English, which was tagged as a "home language", and exclude the structures of Japanese, which was tagged as a "non-home language" (Zhan 2019). The presence of the English-Mandarin bilingual mother and her interactional strategies may have further caused the Mandarin processing to occur in an English-Mandarin mode. For example, using Japanese in conversations with the mother often resulted in a request for a language change. In that event, even in a Mandarin context, English was probably assumed to be a default supplier language, the language used to supply material for word production (Williams and Hammarberg 1998).

---

[21] The word order of verbs (V) and prepositional phrases (PP) in Mandarin is variable and is linked to the pragmatics or syntax interface of grammar. In Mandarin, depending on the pragmatic function of a verb or a sentence, a PP may appear in either the preverbal (PPV) or postverbal (VPP) position. For example, with a verb, such as 坐 [sit], either order is possible, as shown in (1) "我 [I] (NP)在这里 [at here] (PP) 坐 [sit] (V)." and (2) "我 [I] (NP) 坐 [sit] (V) 在这里 [at here] (PP)." However, when an action verb, such as 吃 [eat], is involved, only the PPV form is grammatically acceptable, as shown in (3) "我 [I] (NP) 在这里 [at here] (PP) 吃 [eat](V)." In English, a PP invariably follows a verb (V) and that corresponds with the VPP ordering in Mandarin shown in (2) "I (NP) sit (V) at here (PP)". The Japanese ordering of these elements is constant PPV and that corresponds to the Mandarin order in (1) "わたしは [I] (NP) ここに [at here] (PP) すわる [sit] (V)."

In this chapter, the family members' language ideologies were discussed in detail. Y's mother reported that she had no initial desire to develop Y's academic abilities in Mandarin. As a Japanese citizen living in Japan, academic Japanese and English skills are highly respected, while Mandarin skills are unnecessary. However, Y's deep connection with the Chinese language, culture, and identity, as well as her native-level mastery of its spoken and written form, persuaded her mother to take on higher expectations for her Mandarin development. As a result, her mother began to teach her *pīnyīn* before her second birthday and helped her learn to read and write academic text in Mandarin, which had not been originally planned. The changing of her mother's ideologies and language policies evidences that family language policy is a collaborative, "polycentric" (Blommaert 2010) achievement by both children and adults.

Child agency is discussed again with reference to Y's opinions about language and language use. Y's agentive sense emerged long before she started to talk. Although she absorbed and was influenced by some aspects of the adults' ideologies, she developed her own perspectives about language and society and made unique rules as a part of family socialization, which notably challenged the beliefs and policies established by her parents. She exercised her agency in ways specifically suited to the diversified sociolinguistic environments that she encountered from birth to eight years and in Japan and Scotland as her metalinguistic awareness and cognitive skills emerged. Child agency is indeed critical in childhood development and family language socialization. It is a developing notion and that needs to be further understood.

8 Creativity and literacy-driven language socialization

An important area of child studies and developmental psychology is the issue of creativity in children (Vygotsky 2004). Creative activities somehow depend directly on the richness and variety of a child's life experience from which the material of imagination is constructed (Vygotsky 2004). It is found that "of all the types of creative activity, literary, or verbal, creativity is the most characteristic of school-age children" (Vygotsky 2004: 42). Olszewski-Kubilius (2008) points out that voracious reading in childhood builds the rich background of cross-disciplinary knowledge and that habitual writing is a hallmark of creative producers. Caldas (2012) specifies that reading and working on activities in a language that parents try to advocate seem an easier way of creating practice than organizing rigid home language lessons. Early literacy has been little explored in the studies of very young bilingual and multilingual speakers. However, the child's language learning in the present study was mostly literacy-driven. She was very focused on written language which seemed to be largely self-directed and was a key to her language development. This chapter thus discusses the bi-directional nature of language socialization but from a new perspective, that is, looking at the child's precocious literacy and the ways it influenced her language development and agency.

8.1 Creativity in childhood

Many people have commented on Y's language development and said that she must be gifted, but her parents did not consider her particularly exceptional and had not had her tested. Gallagher (2008) considers the answer to the question, "Who are the gifted?", to be those who score 130 or better in the Stanford-Binet IQ. Other psychologists argue that if multiple dimensions of intelligence were included in the existing measures of intelligence, this would change people's ideas and definitions about who is gifted and who is not (Gallagher 2008). Moreover, others argue that decision-making ability as an essential component central to the productive thinking of the individual has been left out of the measure of intelligence (Gallagher 2008). So, the constraints of the instruments need to be taken into consideration when addressing questions of who the gifted are and what they are like; in other words, there are no clear definitions of "giftedness" and one always needs to keep in mind the criteria for giftedness in individuals that are being used to answer these questions (Gallagher 2008).

Since the term "giftedness" is not very precise, one cannot say that Y is definitely gifted; however, the characteristic of emotional closeness found in Y's family does appear to be similar to that in families said to be bringing up gifted children. According to Silverman and Golon (2008), gifted families tend to be child-centered ones who are generally responsive rather than controlling, and parents in such families consider the relationship between a child's creativity and their developmental psychology. Y's parents believed that learning, especially the child's self-learning, would not easily take place separate from her emotional and cognitive development, or without a harmonious family environment. Children's creative processes can be identified at a very early age in both their play and their verbal and literacy activities, through which they present examples of the most authentic, truest creativity (Vygotsky 2004).

8.1.1 Play

Although play is not the predominant form of activity from the point of view of intellectual development, it is, in a certain sense, the leading line of development in the preschool years (Vygotsky 2016). The fact that children satisfy special needs and incentives in play is very important for the whole of the child's development and should not be ignored (Vygotsky 2016).

Children are great actors in a self-organized way when playing with interests (Vygotsky 2016). Multilingual competence was just one of Y's lived experiences, the development of which was closely associated with her other growing talents such as being creative in play and artistic and musical activities. Cooking together and playing chess with father built up her reasoning skills; skip counting on the way to school provided an excellent foundation for her mathematics and critical thinking skills; an introductory knowledge of maps of the local community, home country, and the world helped her understand the foundations for the subject of geography.

Y's desires to play with language, draw, and practice music are typical examples of her interests and passions. Many elements of Japanese culture originated in China (e.g. たなばた [Chinese Valentine's Day]) and developed in Japan. Some aspects of western cultures are also appreciated and celebrated in Japan (e.g. Mother's Day and Father's Day). Comparative learning provides enrichment to a better understanding of general customs and beliefs in different ways. Cultures can also be jointly learned through cross-linguistic activities. Y developed English and Mandarin しりとり [word chain game] based on the Japanese game rules. This is shown in Examples 100 through 102 recorded in her mother's observation notes.

Example 100: Japanese しりとり **[word chain game] (4;3)**
や<u>ま</u>-<u>ま</u>ほ<u>う</u>-<u>う</u>ま
(ya*ma*-*ma*ho*u*-*u*ma)

Example 101: English しりとり **[word chain game] (4;11)**
g<u>o</u> /gəʊ/-<u>o</u>pe<u>n</u> /'əʊpən/- <u>n</u>ote /nəʊt/

Example 102: Mandarin しりとり **[word chain game] (4;11)**
早<u>上</u>-<u>上</u>午-午饭
(zǎo **shàng**-***shàng* wǔ**-***wǔ* fàn)

In the above word chain games, the final sound of the first word is the same as the initial sound of the second word, and the final sound of the second word is the same as the initial sound of the third word. In this way, Y gained further interest and motivation in learning new languages through these natural practices during play. As noted by Vygotsky (2016), it is at the preschool age that a child learns to consciously recognize his/her own actions and becomes aware that every object has a meaning, while beginning to distinguish the meaning field of a word from its visual field. In play, children separate their thoughts from objects and their actions are guided by thoughts rather than objects (Vygotsky 2016). In the above word games, Y enjoyed an illusory freedom within which she apparently determined her own actions but in fact acted according to the grammar of the languages.

Play in the early years involves an imaginary situation which contains rules and behavior guidelines from a person's real life experience (Vygotsky 2016). One can imagine instances of play in which Y adopted a mother rabbit's voice when talking to a baby rabbit, as if talking vicariously through her own mother. The shared set of practices co-creating a shared family culture may contain elements of various languages (Van Mensel 2018). In multilingual families, for instance, this third voice could be spoken in different languages. Y imitated the OPOL policy practiced in her family when speaking to toy "children". This gives rise to a multilingual *familylect* – multilingual family repertoire, which characterizes specific linguistic features of a family (Van Mensel 2018: 236).

Imitation plays an enormous role in a child's play and learning activities as an echo of what they saw and heard (Vygotsky 2004). However, this is not a simple reproduction of a child's previous experience, but an agentive reworking combining the impressions they have acquired and using them to construct a new reality conforming to their own needs and desires (Vygotsky 2004). Every child is unique and creative in their own way. The notion of child agency therefore needs to be critically analyzed in relation to research into language policy and multilingual repertoires.

8.1.2 Artistic and musical creativity

The influence of family is critical with regard to what children attain and to what level children's abilities are developed. A nurturing family environment provides an opportunity to accomplish creativity and achieve psychological wellness in children. In childhood, children's play serves as the preparatory stage for their artistic and musical creation (Vygotsky 2004). Y's parents created favorable circumstances at home, such as a quiet reading corner, an art desk, and a music space, and encouraged her to practice her artistic and musical skills.

Drawing is the primary form of creative activity, especially in a child's preschool period (Vygotsky 2004). As Y learned to hold a pencil, she started to illustrate what she saw, heard, read, and imagined in her pictures. She loved expressing her feelings and emotions through drawing, such as the two shown below, in addition to what she expressed verbally and through writing.

Figure 2: A drawing of a classic Chinese novel (4;9).

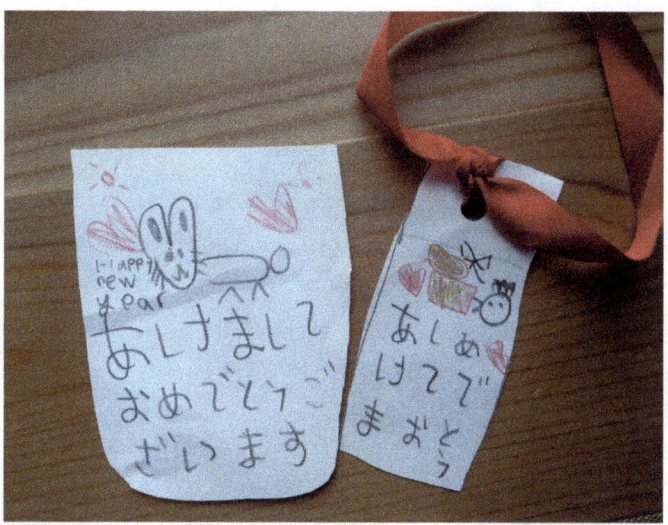

Figure 3: A piece of artwork (5;7).

Drawing requires a person's imagination and social experience. The characters from the classic Chinese novel, *The Journey to the West*, that Y drew (Figure 2) represent her imaginary journey to ancient China inspired by the books she read and the TV programs she watched. The artwork, おまもり [Amulet] **(**Figure 3), is a reflection of Japanese New Year celebrations that she experienced.

Musical talents often show up early in life. When a family has a musical instrument, the child may be able to pick out tunes at a young age. Like many other parents, Y's parents simply shared their music interests with their child and this became the most meaningful experience of Y's childhood. Her parents singing to her was one of the most often used practices since she was born. From as early as a half year old, she spontaneously responded to rhythm and music. She learned the names of alphabet letters from singing ABC songs and learned to count in English from singing number rhymes. Many popular children's songs were dubbed into her three languages. By the time she was three, Y was able to read English song lyrics (looking at the letters and processing them) which helped her acquire vocabulary and grammatical structures. She had also been learning to play the keyboard from one, and could practice independently from two by referring to Japanese music books when living in Japan and to English music books when living in Scotland. Singing was crucial in Y's well-being development, as well as a good means for her to communicate with speakers from different language backgrounds. For example, when Y played the piano and sang children's songs in Mandarin, her father would hum a tune, or sing in Japanese or English.

With a highly developed ear and a good memory for the music she heard, Y liked composing music to express her feelings. Figure 4 includes two pieces of music that Y created on two separate occasions, the top one named うたごえの しいな [Happy singing voice] and the bottom one called "fight".

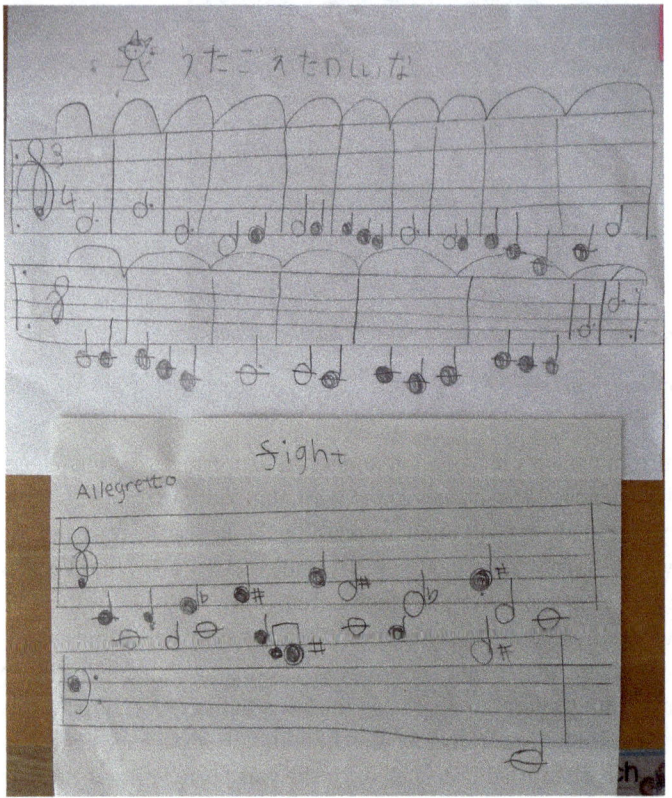

Figure 4: Composing music (7;1).

Although Y created this music completely on her own, she tried to socialize her parents into her hobby by sharing with them and teaching them the music. She would either play a melody on the piano and guide them to sing or help them read sheet music. Example 103 shows an instance where Y was teaching her father to play a piece of music that she created.

Example 103 is from a video recording (4;8).
Situation: Y was teaching her father to play the piano.
CHI: Pass. Next song.
MOT: Show daddy こうおん... 高音符号 [treble clef].
(Her mother did not know how to pronounce "treble clef" in Japanese and used the Mandarin word instead.)
CHI: This is こうおんきごう.
[Treble clef.]
(Y talked to her parents.)
CHI: Do you know how to play *do do re re mi mi fa fa mi re do*?
(Y asked her father. He then played.)
CHI: はなまる。
[*Hanamaru* means "perfect" in Japanese.]

The above illustrates Y's ability to associate music knowledge with visual symbols. In this conversation, translanguaging was performed as a joint practice, through which Y and her parents worked together to clarify meaning and Y taught them new language and information. They interacted with each other using an integrated linguistic system that included elements from different languages. Activating the whole multilingual repertoire while playing and discussing music helped Y develop her metalinguistic awareness and multilingual competence.

Y was undoubtedly the music teacher in her family who organized her parents to sing and perform in various occasions. In addition to playing the piano, she learned to play the recorder, guitar, and violin by herself at three, six and seven years old respectively. She practiced these instruments every day at home by referring to music books published in one of her three languages. She also assessed herself by comparing her own playing with online videos showing other players playing an instrument. The online players included both children and adults from different linguistic and cultural backgrounds. Musical talent thus became part of Y's life experience and that significantly supported her language, literacy, and cognitive development.

8.2 Creativity in literacy

When play is the dominant creative activity in preschool years, verbal and literary creativities become more important characteristics of school-age children (Olszewski-Kubilius 2008). Living in the monolingual Japanese society where English is neither a community nor a heritage language, using English is often limited to learning grammar and vocabulary in classroom-based reading or writing lessons. However, communicative and literacy skills cannot be easily developed without practice at frequent intervals in a natural environment. Extra efforts need to be made, including increasing the time, space, and usage of the target language outside the school venue. Y's parents adopted various strategies to support her learning of English and Mandarin at home, for example, using these two languages for routine conversations, adopting language and culture related resources including songs, books and movies, learning to read and write in the different language systems, and encouraging her to take other opportunities that may be beneficial for her to gain a better understanding of different languages and cultures.

Vygotsky (2016) indicates that literary creation as a form of play is fundamentally tied to the child's personal interests and experience. Y acquired her multiple languages at home, including English, Spanish, and Japanese sign language which were not among her parents' heritage languages. She practiced all languages inclusive of their spoken and written forms through a great variety of literacy-driven activities. While some activities were introduced by her parents before three, she was self-motivated and self-directed to practice others after that age. For instance, she learned new forms and words through reading and writing even on the street in Japan. Her agentive action formed the basis for her sustainable linguistic development.

8.2.1 Acquiring three linguistic systems

Y learned to read independently in three languages before her second birthday and became an effective writer from five years old. Influenced by her parents' daily writing habits, she started to trace letters and numbers using fingers and

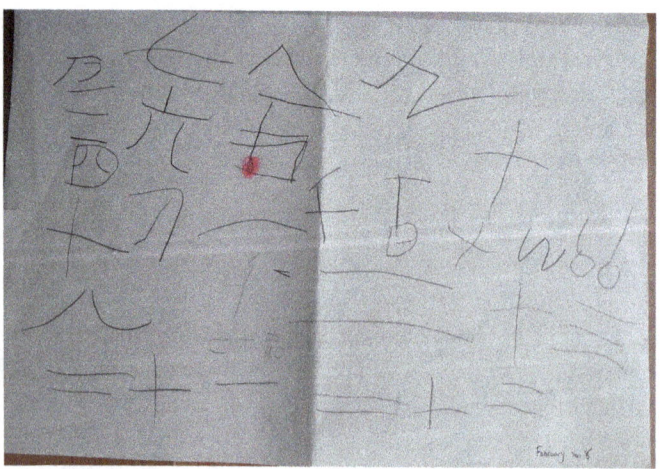

Figure 5: Handwriting (3;7).

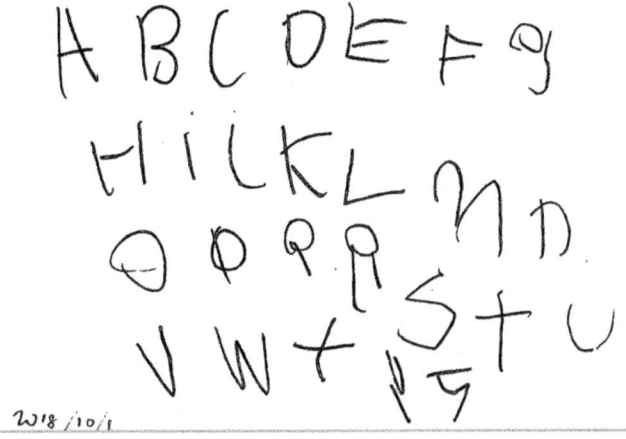

Figure 6: Handwriting (4;4).

pencils from as early as one year old. Although her parents did not think it necessary to practice copying alphabet letters or Chinese characters, she consistently showed a strong interest in doing this. The work shown in Figures 5 and 6 were made when she was a bit older.

It is interesting that even though Y had learned to write all the lower case and upper-case alphabet letters while she was in Japan, she was still fond of letter tracing homework after starting P1 in Scotland, as seen in Figure 7.

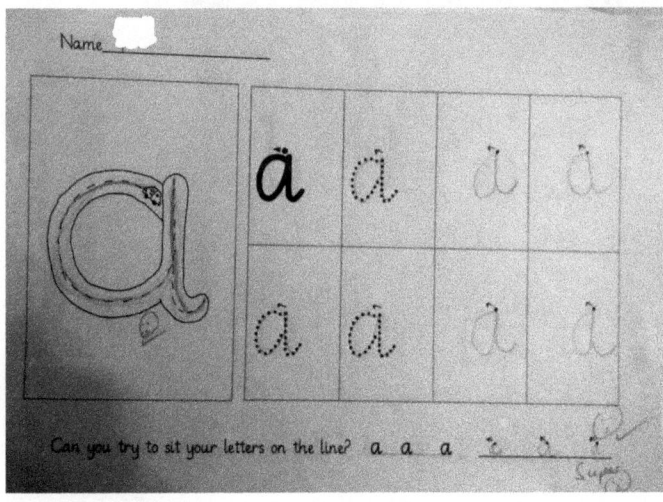

Figure 7: P1 homework in the Scottish school (5;2).

Y told her parents how her British teacher taught students to write the 26 alphabet letters; she said, "Mrs T said we need to write a flick here" (the exit flick) (5;3). Practicing the curly end when tracing the lower-case letter "a" (Figure 7) was an interesting point for her in doing this work. In general, Y found a great deal of pleasure from what she was doing and could engage in most activities cheerfully. Her exceptional character and these attitudes were genuinely considered as Y's "gifts" by her parents, and these could explain her agentive, unusual behavior in play, learning, and other aspects of her daily life.

Y liked writing about what she saw and read; the development of her reading and writing skills were not separated. She developed a good pencil grasp through drawing, writing stories, and making picture books from two years old. She normally wrote on paper or typed on her laptop, and when going to parks she scribbled on the ground using twigs. Moreover, the home whiteboard was effective for modelling and correcting writing. Figures 8 and 9, respectively, show how her mother corrected Y's Mandarin phonetic sounds and English IPA. The circled part of *pīnyīn* in Figure 8 and the blue IPA symbols above the words in Figure 9 were written by Y.

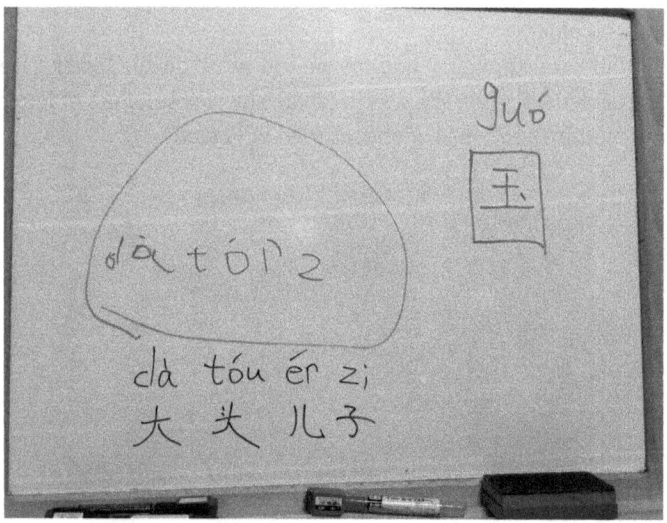

Figure 8: Practicing *pīnyīn* (4;3).

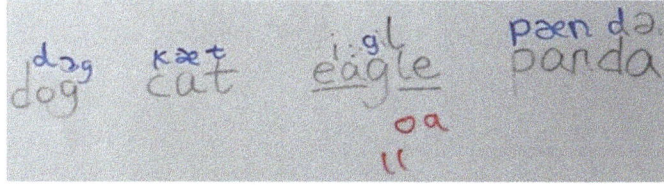

Figure 9: Practicing IPA (4;11).

Using a whiteboard created a new multilingual and multiliterate space for child language development and family socialization. It offers an effective means to promote literacy-driven practices, which normally occur in the classroom context, in the home setting. While Y's parents would teach her about the three scripts, she taught them other aspects of the three languages, as well as two new languages (Spanish and Japanese sign language), on the whiteboard. She showed them how the generational order could be challenged when a child took on a teaching job through this medium. Y also expanded the usage of the whiteboard from a learning tool to a socialization tool. In the rest of this chapter, many instances will be shown where the whiteboard was used for family events other than literacy activities.

Among the three scripts that Y learned, Chinese characters are the most complex system and the most difficult to master. The teaching and learning of Mandarin in the home has been reported in FLP studies conducted in Singapore, Scotland, England, Netherlands, Norway, Russia, Australia, and Canada (Curdt-Christiansen 2014; Kopeliovich 2010). These studies have found that establishing intergenerational rapport through the teaching of Chinese literacy, in addition to oral skills, also reflects the value of Chinese culture. In addition, Saunders (1988: 198) notes that "it is psychologically important for children to be aware that their parents' language is also, like the majority language, a fully-fledged medium of communication, with its own literature, its own writing conventions, etc." In order to help Y learn to read and write Chinese characters, her mother introduced the character strokes and radicals. This is shown in the following example.

Example 104 is from a mother-child conversation (4;1).
Situation: Y and her mother were on their way to the supermarket.
CHI: 妈妈, 你说笔画, 我说字。
[Mum, you say a Chinese character's strokes in order and I guess the Chinese character.]
MOT: 撇, 捺。
[Falling leftwards stroke, falling rightwards stroke.]
CHI: 八。
[Eight.]

MOT:	还有呢?
	[Any other Chinese characters (written in this order using these two strokes)?]
CHI:	入。
	[Enter.]
MOT:	还有呢?
	[Any other Chinese characters?]
CHI:	人。
	[People.]

As mentioned in Section 1.3, although Chinese characters have long been used in the Japanese writing system, the pronunciation of a Chinese character is different in Mandarin and Japanese and its form has been simplified to different degrees in the two languages. For this reason, identifying the different sounds, forms, and meanings of a Chinese character or a word tends to be a challenging task for bilinguals in these two languages. Y's mother taught her to type Chinese characters using *pīnyīn* and *romaji* (using roman alphabet to read and write the Japanese language) before she turned three. Through a daily practice of typing the names of cartoons that she wanted to watch on YouTube, Y learned a good number of Chinese characters. In addition, picking up Chinese characters from printouts, house name plates,

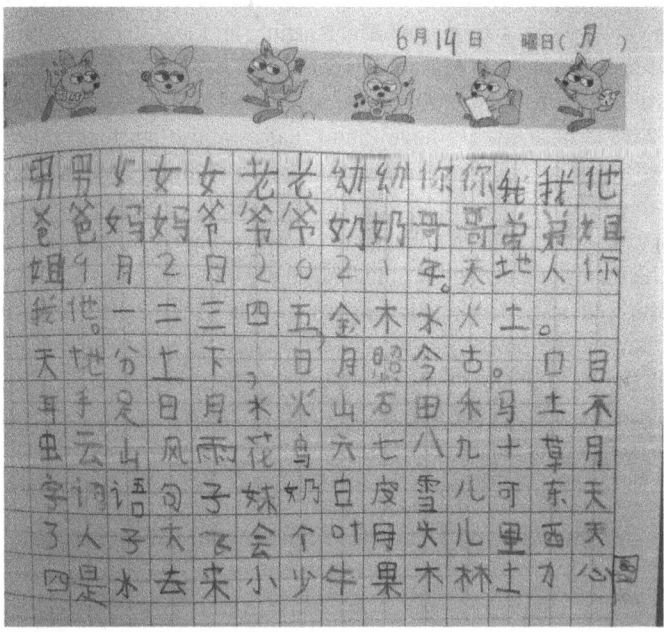

Figure 10: Practicing Chinese characters (7;0).

or signboards was an effective way for her to learn them. Y therefore came to make consistent progress in her understanding of the Chinese writing system.

As Y grew older, the academic development of her Mandarin seemed to be slower than that of her English or Japanese. While she would write at length using a variety of styles in English and Japanese, her creative writing in Mandarin was confined to a short story or a simple diary. Nevertheless, Y was fond of learning new Chinese characters and always found joy in practicing them. She could do this job independently by referring to books or an electronic dictionary. One page of this practice is shown in Figure 10 (7;0).

Literacy is generally associated with books. However, it is not only about encoding and decoding printed texts, but rather is an ideological practice in reading and writing which reflects an individual's values, beliefs, and culture (Kenner 2004). It is found that children from Chinese, Arabic, and Spanish immigrant families in the UK expressed "their sense of living in multiple social and cultural worlds" and studied different reading resources and writing systems at home (Kenner 2004: 118).

Rather than copying one Chinese character multiple times, Y copied examples of Chinese essays and poems. She also created words and phrases. She particularly liked writing the words 中国 [China] and 中国人 [Chinese people] in Chinese characters, even in her writing and drawing work in an English context. The activity of writing Chinese characters helped Y generate a sense of her being Chinese. Through literacy practice, her hidden Chinese identity in the Japanese society could be expressed.

8.2.2 Making cross-linguistic associations among written forms

Children at five or a later age can make judgments about language out of context, predicting the consequences of using particular forms and reflecting on the product of an utterance (Clark 1978). One's multilingual repertoire is a rich resource for one to compare different linguistic elements at different levels, such as phonetic, lexical, morphosyntactic, pragmatic, and discursive levels, and to use these resources cross-linguistically (Cenoz and Gorter 2011). As her metacognitive skills developed, Y started to think about the connections between the linguistic aspects of her three languages. Taking English loanwords in Japanese as an example, she would guess the original English word by referring to its Japanese pronunciation (e.g. "What's 'pants' in Japanese? パンツ [pants]?") (3;7). She also understood that English loanwords in Japanese were written in *katakana* symbols, as shown in Example 105.

Example 105 is from a diary entry (3;10).
Situation: Y saw guitars in a shop.
1 CHI: ギター?
[Guitar?]
2 MOT: Yes, guitar.
3 CHI: カタカナ?
[Katakana?]
4 MOT: Yes. It's written in カタカナ.
[Yes, it's written in *katakana*.]

This example shows Y was aware that an English loanword in Japanese was similar in pronunciation to its original English form (Turn 3). From the age of three, Y showed a growing recognition that Chinese characters in Mandarin and *kanji* in Japanese differed in terms of their sounds, forms, and meanings. Differentiating the forms of a Chinese character and a *kanji* in Japanese required practice on the part of both Y and her parents. For example, when Y wrote the Mandarin character, 马 [horse], on the whiteboard, her mother added its *kanji*, 馬 [horse], and explained to her, "马, 是simplified character, 现在的中国人用的。古代的中国人用的是traditional character, 馬, 也是现在的日本人用的。" [This simplified Chinese character, 马, is used in China nowadays. This traditional Chinese character, 馬, was used by ancient Chinese people and is used nowadays by Japanese people.] (3;10). Making such cross-linguistic connections helped Y deepen her understanding of Chinese characters and their Japanese equivalents. Her understanding of two linguistic forms of a Chinese character is also shown in Example 106.

Example 106 is from a diary note (5;5).
Situation: Y's mother was about to write a word on the whiteboard.
CHI: 你是写中国汉字还是日本汉字?
[Will you write Chinese characters in Mandarin or *Kanji* in Japanese?]

In the above example, Y asked her mother whether she was going to model the two Chinese characters, 関西 [the south-central region of Japan's main island], in either the Chinese or Japanese way of writing. This shows her growing awareness of the difference between the two forms. Before turning four, Y read Japanese books written only in *kana* script, but she started to read books that included both *kanji* and *kana* scripts after she remarked that she "can read Chinese books." (4;2). Meanwhile, Y's understanding of a language's written form developed further through reading and writing practices, which is shown in Example 107.

Example 107 is from an observation note (5;6).
CHI: Do people write in Mandarin the same thing when people speak your dialect?
MOT: Are the written form of Mandarin and that of a Chinese dialect the same? Yes, people write in the exactly same way.

The above example shows that Y gradually came to understand that Chinese speakers whose regional dialect varieties were unintelligible to one another were connected by a shared written form. Y's understanding of written language was further enhanced by direct instruction by her mother. For instance, the mother explained a Chinese character, 休 [rest], that was written by Y on the whiteboard, as shown in Example 108.

Example 108 is from a diary entry (4;4).
左边一个单人旁, 右边一个 "树木" 的 "木", 一个人靠在一棵树上, 是 "休息" 的 "休"。日文里くんよみ是 "休み"(やすみ)。还有另一种读音, 用汉字写的词会用おんよみ的读音。比如 "休日"(きゅうじつ) 的 "休"(きゅう), やすみの日, holiday, 这个 きゅう 和拼音 xiū 读音很像。
[The left radical is 亻 [people] and the right is 木 [tree]. 休 (xiū) means a person leans on a tree taking a rest. This character is read as *yasumi* following the Japanese reading of a Chinese character. There is another way of reading a Chinese character in Japanese which follows a variety of Chinese pronunciation. For example, the sound of *kyu* in the word *kyu-jitsu* [holiday] is very similar to its Mandarin pronunciation, *xiū*.]

In this example, her mother taught her two different types of *kanji* pronunciation in Japanese, one of which is associated with the Mandarin *pīnyīn* pronunciation of that character. Y's growing awareness of cross-linguistic associations in connection with sounds was increasingly apparent after she started to read and write, as illustrated in Examples 109 and 110.

Example 109 is from a diary note (4;3).
CHI: "人" 有3种读音, ひと, にん, じん。那在日本, how do I know which one?
[There are three pronunciations of the Chinese character "people": *hito*, *nin*, and *jin*? How do I know which one I should use in Japanese?]

Example 110 is from the mother's diary note (4;5).
1 CHI: 本子 (běn zi) 的 本 (běn) 怎么写?
[How should I write the Chinese character, book, in the word, notebook?]
2 MOT: 问爸爸。
[Ask daddy.]

3 CHI: Daddy, how to write 絵本 (ehon) の 本 (hon). Only 本 (hon).
         [Daddy, how do you write the Chinese character, book, in the word, picture book? Only the Chinese character, book.]

The Chinese character, 本 (*běn*) [book], in the Mandarin word, 本子 (*běn zi*) [notebook] (Example 110, Turn 1), and the *kanji*, 本 (*hon*) [book], in the Japanese word, 絵本 (*ehon*) [picture book] (Example 110, Turn 3), are the same Chinese character. The above examples clearly show that Y knew the connections between Mandarin and Japanese in terms of Chinese characters. She was able to distinguish different sounds and meanings of a character used in Mandarin and Japanese. Collier (1992) considers that the stronger a child's academic ability in his/her heritage language, the faster the child will learn the society's majority language, which appears to be true of Y. Moreover, in the case where children have become bilingual consecutively, the reading proficiency in their first language is expected to transfer to some degree to the second (Cummins 1991). Y's reading abilities will be discussed in the next section.

8.3 Reading as a means of language socialization

There are many more factors supporting home language maintenance in addition to convergent choice conversations. Parents have different supplemental educational options to support their children's heritage language learning such as registering them in a supplementary language school or program. Parents can also choose home activities that would interest their children, such as joint book reading, listening to story and rhyme recordings, etc. Such frequent and qualitatively high home language and literacy input is crucial. Applying the OPOL policy, each parent can help their child read and write in his/her native language.

It is clear that Y had already achieved a high level of communication and academic skills in English before she went to Scotland (at 4;10). It is also true that her English reading and writing abilities continued to improve rapidly after she returned from Scotland (at 5;10). Because Y was getting almost no English practice outside the home in Japan, the most reasonable explanation for her further literacy development is the two hours' daily reading and writing practices done at home.

8.3.1 Becoming an independent reader

Books and other written materials were important tools in Y's language learning. She enjoyed reading books, either together with her parents before three years old or primarily on her own after that age. Her parents encouraged her to read on a diverse set of topics and supported her writing in different styles. It was a gradual but natural process for Y to become an efficient and excellent reader in her childhood.

Y's parents found that reading books to Y was the best means of teaching her to read at the beginning. Even before she could produce understandable words, her parents developed some effective strategies to involve her in interactive reading activities; for example, her father read a storybook called *David goes to school* and checked her understanding by eliciting non-verbal responses from her. Eliciting words from her and reading together with her were other ways in which Y's parents helped her develop reading skills. Her parents normally read slowly and let her repeat their words, or they skipped key words and prompted her to say them. Moreover, her parents adapted stories for Y. For example, they changed the story of *David goes to school* to a revised one, "Y goes to school", as follows, "Please stand up, Y. Please put down your hand, Y. Please be quiet, Y. Well done, Y." (0;11). Y was very motivated by such reading activities. Besides, the whole family often sat together, her parents reading to her, listening to her reading, and discussing stories with her. Listening to a book's attached CD while looking at the book was another way of reading that could be done unassisted. Last but not least, the local library provided a location for extensive reading. Y's mother began to take her to the library to read or "play" nearly every day before she turned one. After she entered a full-time nursery at two, they visited the library about three times a week. Frequently visiting libraries and witnessing other family members reading emphasized reading as a family value and convention.

From one and a half years old, Y spent about an hour every day looking at books. From three years old, she became an independent and effective reader in English (reading fiction and non-fiction books) and Japanese (reading books written in *kana* script with some Chinese characters). She could also read Mandarin books which had *pīnyīn* written above the Chinese characters, but found the books which were printed only in Chinese characters difficult. Although Y often said, "I want to write *pīnyīn* (above the Chinese characters) then I can read (more books)" (4;2), books designed for school children (third graders and above) in China rarely used *pīnyīn* in the text.

From four years old, Y started to read English chapter books covering a variety of topics. She demonstrated good reading comprehension skills in discussions with her parents. Since the input and use of Japanese dramatically decreased while the family temporarily resided in Scotland, reading and discussion became the main practices for maintaining the Japanese language. Y's father invited her to read stories with him in turns and discussing and retelling the stories. She was at first reluctant to allow interruptions for discussion in the middle of a story and protested, "やめて、はやくよんで。" [Stop it, quickly read the story.] (4;10). After a couple of such sessions, she got used to this practice and allowed herself to become involved in the Japanese discussions.

Y's parents initially did not expect her to read English literature or history as a preschooler. Neither did they have much expectation for her writing skills in Mandarin. However, seeing Y's rapidly developing trilingual competences, her parents reconsidered and amended their language policies. New literacy policies were then planned to help Y with her discussion and presentation skills, as well as with her higher reading and writing abilities. A discussion of Y's writing skills will be introduced in Section 8.4.

8.3.2 Imagination and using language from books in daily speech

Vygotsky (2004) points out that there is an enormous significance for imagination in general and for children's imagination in particular. The experience of reading and adopting what was read in everyday life were important for Y to make a connection between a fantasy world from literature and a realistic sociolinguistic world through the means of imagination. Even at one year old, she could remember some book lines and song lyrics, and adapt them to her daily speech, as illustrated in Example 111.

Example 111 is from a video clip (1;4).
CHI: Moon.
        (Y was looking at the moon.)
MOT: Yes, moon.
CHI: Papa, moon.
MOT: Yes. *Papa, please get the moon for me.*

Here, Y remembered the content of the story, *Papa, please get the moon for me*, and some of the language on each page through reading. She also sometimes rephrased lines from books and used them in suitable interactions. For example, when she asked her parents what they could see, she would say, "Mummy, mummy, daddy, daddy, what do you see?" (1;6). Y retold the stories from an English storybook called *Brown bear, brown bear, what do you see?* using her own language. In a different example, when her parents saw ants and asked her,

"What are they?", she answered, "ありさん, こつつんこ" [Ants bumped each other]. Y rephrased the language in a Japanese song called おつかいありさん [The ants have to run some errands].

Reading influenced Y's way of thinking, as reflected in the language she adopted to describe the surroundings. Her passion for imagination is well reflected in fairy tale images. This is seen in Examples 112 and 113.

Example 112 is from an observation note (3;8).
MOT: 为什么只穿一只鞋?
 [Why are you wearing only one slipper?]
CHI: 因为我是灰姑娘。
 [Because I'm Cinderella.]

Example 113 is from an observation note (4;0).
Situation: Y saw an orange cat outside.
MOT: What's that?
CHI: Ginger.
 ("Ginger" was the name of an orange cat in Spot books. Spot is a book character.)

In the above examples, Y adapted the story scenarios to real life situations using her child-like imagination. Children imagine because they want to see things in a fantastic form in that the imagination corresponds to their internal needs (Vygotsky 2004). The choice of appropriate language from books, in turn, reflected Y's acquired knowledge through reading. Many difficult words which are generally used in a more formal situation were learned by her through extensive reading. For example, she learned and used such Mandarin words as 优雅美丽 [pleasing and graceful] (4;5) and such English expressions as "Indeed, it is." (4;8). Although her parents tended to use more formal English language, which was affected by their own English learning and working experiences, Y's mother did not often use the above-mentioned Mandarin word in daily conversations with her. This suggests that reading was an important source of language input in Y's language development, which can also be seen in Examples 114 and 115.

Example 114 is from an observation note (3;5).
MOT: Look at your big tummy.
CHI: These are pure muscles.
 ("Pure muscles" are words from Peppa Pig books. Peppa Pig is a book character.)
MOT: Make it smaller.

CHI:	Getting smaller means "shrink".
MOT:	How do you know that?
CHI:	Peppa said it.

Example 115 is from an observation note (7;10).
CHI: 我知道"既生瑜,何生亮"是什么意思。我读了《三国演义》。
[I know the meaning of "After making me, *Zhou Yu*, did you have to make *Zhuge Liang*?" I learned it from *Three Kingdoms*.]

As shown in the above, Y acknowledged the role of reading in her language acquisition. Moreover, an English native-speaking parent whose child and Y were in the same class in Scotland said to Y's mother, "I was surprised at Y's way of speaking, very formal and British." However, after the parent learned how much Y had loved the *Oxford Reading Tree* series from two years old, she felt this made sense. Y's parents stopped reading bedtime stories to her after she grew into an independent reader at four. Instead, they would pick up some parts from books and clarify the meaning where necessary, introduce the background of the story, and extend the topic. Her parents would discuss the content between themselves as well as involving Y in the discussion. The more Y read, the more words she came to use, most of which would not be used in daily communication or ordinary child language.

8.3.3 Narrating

Narrating includes both the daily routine of bedtime storytelling and impromptu storytelling. Vygotsky (2016) considers that when making up stories, children create a situation and combine the old elements in new ways. Y loved telling stories more than her parents and started to make up stories from as early as one year old. She was good at describing an object or an event. For example, seeing a picture of an indoor swimming pool, she said, "I like swimming pool. I like swimming. So many fish. Small fish. Middle fish. Big fish." (1;8). This elaboration was a retelling of a storybook about fish. Y also liked revising stories. She retold a Japanese story こぶた [Baby pig] as follows, "お父さんはぶた、お母さんもぶた、こどもぶた。Daddyはぶた, mummy はぶた, Yはぶた." [Daddy is a pig. Mummy is also a pig. Children are also pigs. Daddy is a pig. Mummy is a pig. Y is a pig.] (1;8).

From three years old, Y started to tell more complicated stories using her own language in addition to borrowing key words from books. This practice is as shown in Example 116.

Example 116 is from a video clip (3;1).
灰姑娘。 很久很久以前，有一个爸爸，他的妻子很早就死了。他有一个女儿叫灰姑娘。后来爸爸又和一个女人结婚了，这个女人是灰姑娘的后妈......
[Cinderella. A long time ago, there was a father. His wife died young. He had a daughter called Cinderella. The father married another woman. This woman was Cinderella's stepmother . . .]

Thanks to her parents' deep affection for English culture and their own overseas educational and working experiences, Y had an opportunity to learn about Western culture. In her family, history and culture stories were purposefully chosen and told, which enabled her to access the English and Chinese cultures while learning both languages and literacies. While her parents introduced historic figures and events through reading, Y displayed a strong interest in learning about them and enjoyed reading and telling stories based on the books she read.

At four years old, Y's favorite Chinese history stories were *Mulan* and *China's First Emperor*. Her favorite English history stories were *Queen Elizabeth I* and *Mary Queen of Scots*. Her knowledge of British history, literature, and society steadily grew in line with the development of her English reading skills in the first five years of her life in Japan, and were reinforced during the one year stay in Scotland. For example, she had read and told one of her favorite Scottish culture stories, *Mary Queen of Scots*.

Example 117 is from a diary note (4;11).
CHI: I read *Mary Queen of Scots* today. Her son is called James the first of England and James the sixth of Scotland (. . .).

Y told stories in her three languages every day on the way to and back from the Japanese nursery or the Scottish school. Her parents normally acted as a patient audience and only provided help when they were required to do so.

Starting around two and a half years old, Y began to prepare props and give shows at home. In her shows, she mainly spoke in English or Mandarin and occasionally in Japanese. Her choice of a language did not appear to be related to the themes of the games. For example, Y built the *Frozen* LEGO models and mimicked the characters' talking in Mandarin. However, she had actually read the *Frozen* books and watched the *Frozen* films mainly in English and Japanese. This positive self-talk greatly improved her language fluency in English and Mandarin.

8.3.4 Translating books

As discussed in Section 5.3.4, translating was a common input strategy that Y's parents used to help her acquire different forms of a word, a discourse strategy used by Y to socialize her parents into her planned interactions, and an effective way to involve every family member in clarifying meaning, transferring knowledge, and learning new languages. Examples in this section show that Y also enriched her oral language by translating and adapting book language to daily conversations. From as young as one year old, Y showed an awareness of the linguistic abilities of the characters in the books she read. She would translate what a character said from one language into another, as shown in example 118.

Example 118 is from a diary entry (1;10).
MOT: ノンタン是不是说 "一起玩啊?"
 [Did *Nontan*, a book character, say "Let's play" (in Mandarin)?]
CHI: 不是, ノンタン说: "あそびましょう。"
 [No. *Nontan* said, "Let's play" (in Japanese).]

In a Japanese storybook, *Nontan* spoke in Japanese. When Y described what *Nontan* said in a Mandarin conversation, she felt Mandarin was not the right code to use and thus she translated the words from Mandarin into Japanese. During the parent-child reading session, Y's parents sometimes asked her to translate what they had read or experienced in one language into the other. This can be seen in Example 119.

Example 119 is from a diary entry (1;10).
MOT: What do you want to read?
CHI: Spot.
MOT: If daddy buys you an ice cream, what should you say?
CHI: Thank you, daddy.
MOT: If you were 小波 [Spot], what would you say?
 (小波 is the Mandarin translation of the name Spot.)
CHI: 谢谢爸爸。
 [Thank you, daddy.]

As shown in the above, translating was frequently employed in Y's family for fulfilling daily communication functions or for the purpose of language practice. Many books in Y's home were bilingual books (English-Mandarin or English-Japanese) and some were published in all of her three languages (in three separate versions), such as the Disney stories series and classic novels. Y was able to distinguish the three writing systems when she was two. For example, her mother showed her a bilingual book with the text printed in both English and Chinese on the same page and asked her, "Which line is English? Which one is Chinese?" (1;6). Y answered correctly every time.

The one-person-one-language and one-person-two-languages strategies were extensively employed in Y's early reading. Using the one-person-one-language strategy, one of her parents would have a book in one language and the other have a translated version in a different language, and they would read simultaneously or read page by page consecutively. As a two-year-old, Y could read most of her picture books that had been translated from English to Japanese, or from Japanese to English, on her own. However, she was not able to read all of the books that had been translated into Mandarin. For this reason, Y always chose the English or Japanese version and gave the Mandarin equivalent to her mother. For example, she gave the Mandarin story – 蚂蚁和西瓜 [The ant and the watermelon], which she called 妈妈的书 [mum's book], to her mother, while she held the same story's Japanese version – ありとすいか [The ant and the watermelon]. Y would turn the Japanese version page by page following her mother's reading in Mandarin line by line (2;1). It was also common for each family member to choose a version published in their preferred language and read in turns. After a while, Y told her father, "Let's swap. I read in Japanese and you read in English." (5;0). Moreover, using the strategy of one-person-two-languages, one of her parents would read two versions of the same story on his/her own, or the parent would translate some parts of the story during reading. This is shown in Example 120.

Example 120 is from a diary entry (1;6).
Situation: Y found a bilingual English-Mandarin book called *Spot goes on a holiday*.
1 MOT: Do you want me to read in English or Chinese?
2 CHI: English.
3 MOT: Ok.
4 CHI: 小玻.
[Spot.]
(After her mother read a few pages in English, Y wanted the mother to read the story in Mandarin.)

Y's awareness of her parents' language abilities is shown in the above example, in which she requested her mother to switch to the translated equivalent during reading (Turn 4). Y would also look at an English book and its translated version at the same time on her own, looking at the two books page by page and comparing their languages and stories (1;6). At other times, she would listen to a book's attached CD in one language and read a translated version of the book in a different language. Moreover, Y sometimes read a book in one language even though the book itself was written in a different language. For example, when she was looking at a Japanese storybook called くまさん くまさん なに みてるの? [*Brown bear, brown bear, what do you see*?], she "read" it in English. Moreover, even for books which were originally published in only one language, Y would translate them into other languages as she "read" them. This is shown in Example 121.

Example 121 is from a video recording (3;0).
Situation: Y was about to read an English book called *No Roses for Harry*. She didn't have the Mandarin or Japanese version of the book.
1 CHI: 我用中文读。
 [I am going to read it in Mandarin.]
2 MOT: Isn't it an English book?
3 CHI: 外婆买了一件新衣服 . . .
 [Grandma bought a new dress . . .]

In the above example, Y "read" an English book, *No Roses for Harry*, which did not have a Mandarin version, using her own translated Mandarin language (Turn 3). As a multilingual speaker, Y perceived the world around her to be multilingual and multiliterate, and she regarded translating as a reflection of this function.

Data provided so far demonstrate that having a high level of triliteracy greatly reinforced Y's trilingual competence. Using collaborative practices like translating and translanguaging provided her with more opportunities to use a language in different contexts for different purposes. This is particular true for the development of her two non-societal languages – English and Mandarin when living in Japan or Japanese and Mandarin when living in Scotland.

8.4 Writing as a means of language socialization

A child's connections with the immediate environment and with those around them become more complex as they grow older, as compared to those in the earlier years of childhood (Vygotsky 2004). One obvious change is reflected in creative writing – that is, emotionality is a trait commonly shown in adolescence, but was observed in Y as a preschooler. As her external experience increased, Y replaced the simple, superficial drawing – once the only form of creative activity – with creative writing alongside contextual-related drawing. Using written language helped her express complex inner relationship with and complicated attitude toward the external world.

Mason (1984) notes that children begin to write at the same time that they begin to recognize words. Writing can potentially promote learning in terms of constructing meanings and thinking about linguistic structures (Gort 2012). Writing is surrounded by talk; writing practices thus provide communication ideas, a source of language, and an enactment of cognitive activation in spoken language practice (Gort 2012). In the present study, doing literacy activities created a new and a more formal domain for Y's language acquisition. Collaboration among family members acknowledged Y as knowledgeable about the use of her entire languages, as well as advocating the family's efforts to support the development of the two non-school languages, English and Mandarin. Writing built a new space for family socialization involving both oral and written texts in Y's home, and, moreover, bolstered her family ties.

8.4.1 Guided writing

Children's creative writing may be stimulated and guided by adults. Y started to write stories and make picture books around three years old. Before she became an independent writer, a piece of writing was usually completed in the expected language but discussions on writing would involve different languages. This cognitive processing is seen as useful for emergent trilingualism. Baker (2011: 289) points out that "to read and discuss a topic in one language, and then to write about it in another language, means that the subject matter has to be processed and 'digested'".

Dynamic language practice in speech as a pedagogical practice does not only promote a deeper understanding of the written content, but also develops skills in a different language relating to the one that is required for writing. The following example (Figure 11) illustrates the process through which a story called うさぎの

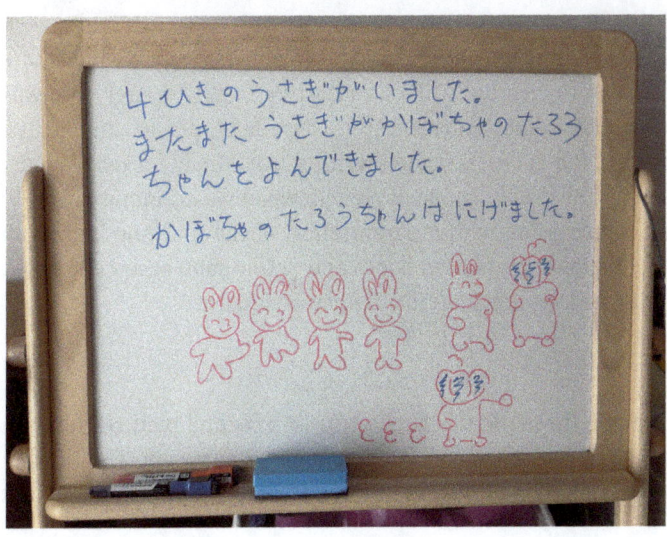

Figure 11: Plotting a story with her father (3;10).

おやま [Rabbit mountain] was developed. Y and her father first discussed the plot of the story in English after Y came up with the idea of "I want to write a story. Think some words." (3;10). Y told the whole story in Japanese and her father wrote down what she said on the whiteboard.

Y and her father collaborated on the above writing task, discussing the stories and negotiating the meaning of words using English and Japanese. They went back and forth to revise the grammar and the meaning of each sentence; for example, her father asked her, "How many rabbits are there?" following Y's statement of "うさぎがいました" [There were rabbits.] After she replied, "four", the father retold her answer but in Japanese and then wrote it down on the whiteboard ("4ひきのうさぎがいました。" [There were four rabbits.]) Questions and comments were frequently made by her father in English regarding Y's contributions in Japanese, some of them requesting a logical flow of the story while others an accuracy in language usage. Seeing languages as referential resources and using them as tools, translanguaging enabled Y and her father to clarify the meanings of the story. In this way, her trilingual competence was empowered through the contextual discursive and writing practices, as well as the pedagogical practices with oral and written texts. Moreover, translanguaging in guided writing required good cooperation and commitments from Y and her parents, and it in turn improved the parent-child relationship.

8.4.2 Creative writing

Y showed more and more interest in writing and made writing a daily activity from four years old. She turned out to be an effective English writer who was keen on writing storybooks, diary entries, letters, fairy tales, poems, and essays. Even before Y attended the Scottish school, writing was already a job that she completed on her own. It was only occasionally followed by a grammar check by a parent or a content discussion with a parent; most of the time she looked up unknown words in a dictionary and used books and online sources as references. Y wrote in all of her three languages but did the best in English.

Storybooks
In the following, Y made three picture books with stories and pictures on each page. Figures 12 to 14 show a few pages of each book respectively. The titles of the three books were Peppa Pig, 灰姑娘 [Cinderella], and うさぎのやま [Rabbit mountain].

8.4 Writing as a means of language socialization — 157

Figure 12: The story of Peppa Pig (4;6).

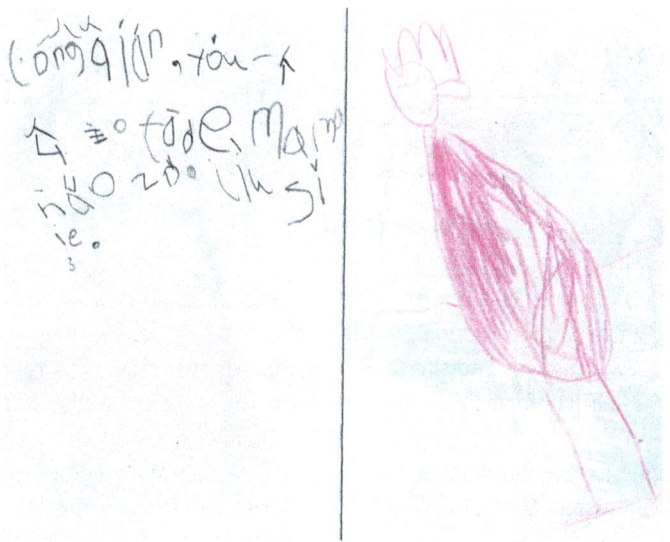

Figure 13: The story of *Huī gū niang* [Cinderella] (4;6).

Y completed the following story, うさぎのやま [Rabbit mountain], eight months later (4;6) after writing the story with the same title guided by her father at 3;10 (as shown in Figure 11). This time she was able to complete the whole story independently. The content of the new story (Figure 14) was entirely different from the previous one (Figure 11).

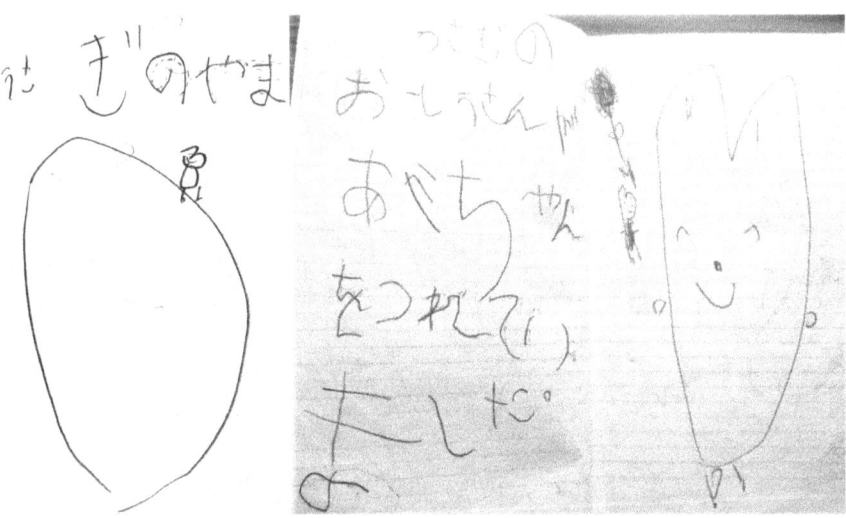

Figure 14: The story of うさぎのやま [Rabbit mountain] (4;6).

The three storybooks (Figures 12–14) written by Y were stored along with other books on a bookshelf as a good motivation for her to keep writing. As Y grew older, her stories grew in length and the content became more complex. A relative richness of grammatical forms also developed. One example is as shown in Figure 15.

It was interesting to see that Y often started to write a new story before the previous one was completed. She once started three stories within the same week ("Snow White", "Frozen I", and "Frozen II"). The same habit was also noticed when she wrote "adventure series" (similar to a series called *Magic Tree House*) or "chapter books". As for chapter books, such as a one called *The big book about animals* (7;1), she wrote one chapter at a time for a different animal. Figures 16 and 17 are two examples of this kind.

It took her some effort to refer to different reference books in four languages (English, Japanese, Mandarin, and Spanish) in order to "publish" multilingual books. Y said, "It's for learning." (7;2). She meant that multilingual books were good for children to learn different languages. As shown in Figures 16 and 17, at

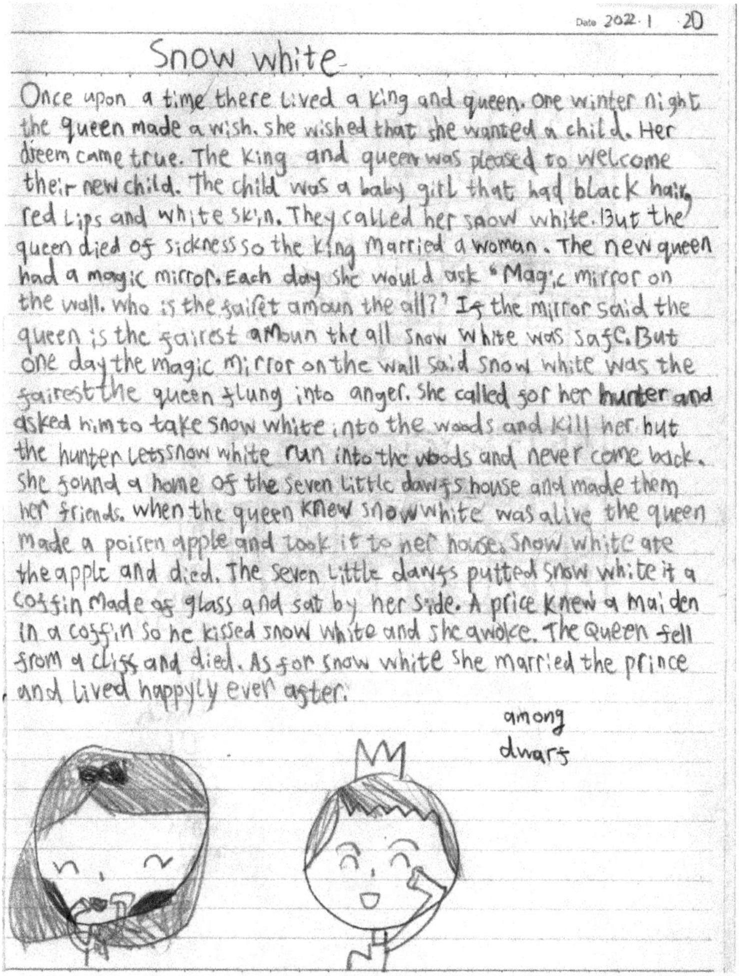

> Date 2022·1·20
>
> ## Snow white
>
> Once upon a time there lived a king and queen. One winter night the queen made a wish. she wished that she wanted a child. Her dreem came true. The king and queen was pleased to welcome their new child. The child was a baby girl that had black hair, red lips and white skin. They called her snow white. But the queen died of sickness so the king married a woman. The new queen had a magic mirror. Each day she would ask "Magic mirror on the wall. who is the fairet amoun the all?" If the mirror said the queen is the fairest amoun the all snow White was safe. But one day the magic mirror on the wall said snow white was the fairest the queen flung into anger. She called for her hunter and asked him to take snow white into the woods and kill her. but the hunter lets snow white run into the woods and never come back. She found a home of the seven little dawfs house and made them her friends. When the queen knew snow white was alive the queen made a poisen apple and took it to her house. Snow white ate the apple and died. The seven little dawfs putted snow white it a coffin made of glass and sat by her side. A price knew a maiden in a coffin so he kissed snow white and she awoke. The Queen fell from a cliss and died. As for snow white she married the prince, and lived happyly ever after.
>
> among dwarfs

Figure 15: The story of Snow White (7;8).

the end of each chapter, she specified the Japanese equivalent words for the English terms, dinosaur [きょうりゅ] and panda [パンダ]. Moreover, a special location noun, Wolong, was enunciated following the way of teaching sounds to native English speakers ("say wo-lo-ng") (Figure 17). In her other "chapter books", she also inserted footnotes, created a glossary, or listed reading comprehension questions to make readers think.

The three examples (Figures 15–17) also show how Y's skills of using description, elaboration, and specification had been steadily improving with an increase in life experience and language ability. Such skills were not only shown in her

Figure 16: A page from a chapter book (7;1).

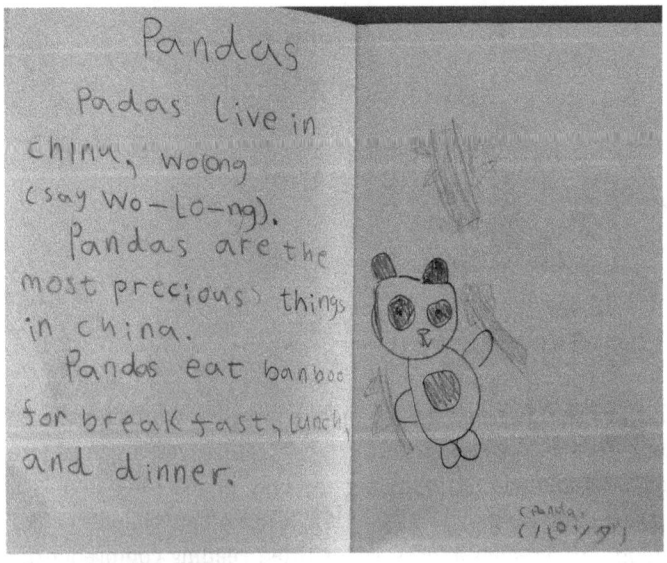

Figure 17: A page from a chapter book (7;1).

English and Japanese texts, but also in her Mandarin text. The Mandarin version of the story, Peppa Pig, was written at the age of 7;3 (Figure 18). Direct speech, which was not used in the English version of the story (Figure 12), now appeared.

Figure 18: One day of Peppa Pig (7;3).

As for writing skills, in addition to using direct speech, a sense of employing the past tense and the future tense in English and Japanese emerged as more writing was done in these two languages. As regards writing topics, Y revealed more and more about what she had experienced and encountered.

Diary entries
In multilingual practices, children play with linguistic resources and new technologies to make sense of their multilingual world (Danjo 2021). Deeply influenced by her mother, Y started to write diary entries when she was a preschooler. A diary record from her immediate environment reflected what she saw, heard, read, and thought about. She was able to describe her inner world using this type of writing. She either wrote an event in a notebook or typed about it in a Word document. Figure 19 is one page from her diary entries.

Y enjoyed keeping a diary every day, mainly in English and Japanese. The more she wrote, the better she learned how to express her feelings through written language. Keeping a diary became one of her habits. Although she wrote primarily in English and Japanese on paper, she could type in Mandarin speedily

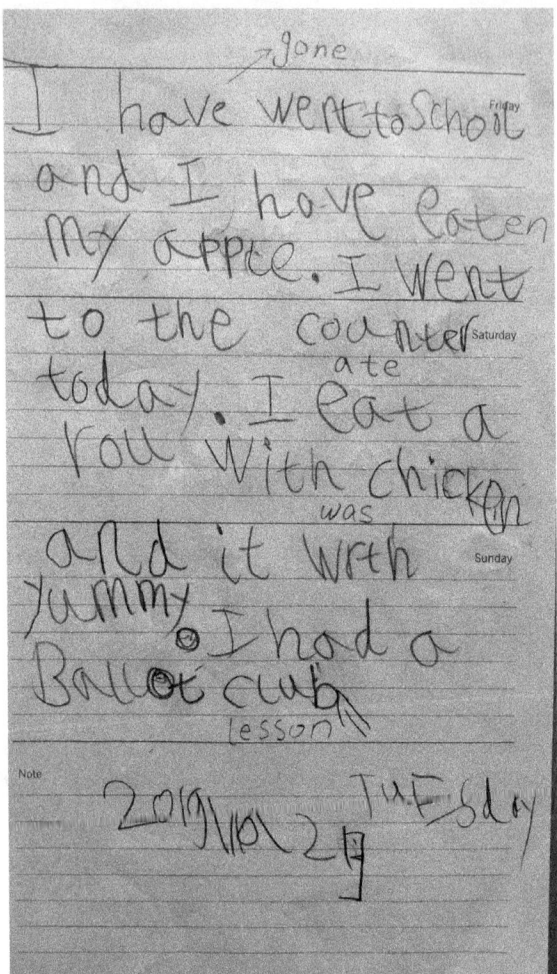

Figure 19: Y's diary (5;5).

and accurately on her laptop. The flexible use of her entire linguistic knowledge in writing is shown in Figure 20.

In her diary entry, Y considered her three languages as resources. The flexible language use enabled her to clarify the meaning of unfamiliar expressions in the familiar language. Canagarajah (2011) used the term *translingual* practice to refer to the coexistence of different linguistic repertoires in writing. This type of pedagogic strategy demonstrates how learners alternate languages in writing to fit their cognitive processing as well as linguistic preferences and constraints. Figure 21 is another page from Y's diary entries which shows a different function of translingual practice

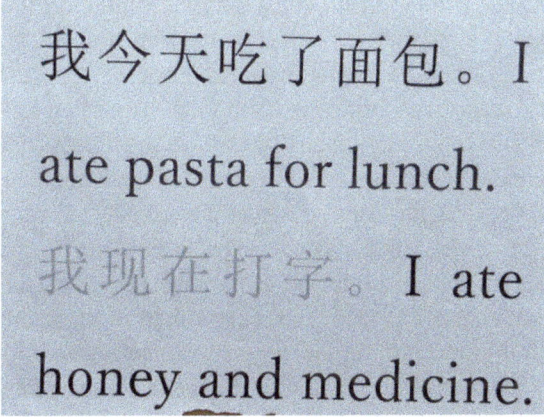

Figure 20: Y's diary (4;6).

in the written text. Translating used in the following piece of writing shows Y's metalinguistic awareness as well as her metacognitive ability in using appropriate features of her whole repertoire in different communicative circumstances.

Figure 21: A piece of writing (6;2).

The example in Figure 21 clearly shows that Y had a sense of translation. She even wrote "translaito (translate) Japanese". When being questioned about the motivation for doing translation in her diary, she explained, "かいとうU (*Kaito U*) is Japanese. I want to put *romaji* above Japanese. Then English speakers can read Japanese." (6;2). The Japanese translation immediately following the English words, "he's a baddy", also revealed Y's awareness of her readers' language abilities. Song (2016) suggests that providing translations from the stronger or more familiar language to the weaker or less familiar language helps children expand their linguistic repertoires. This is also true in the case of Y's learning.

From six years old, as Y came to read much more and to read much higher levels of books in Mandarin and particularly in Japanese, her knowledge of Chinese characters dramatically increased. A strong desire to write in Mandarin developed accordingly. In order to make sure every Chinese character was correctly formed, Y habitually referred to an electronic dictionary. A page from her Mandarin diary is shown in Figure 22.

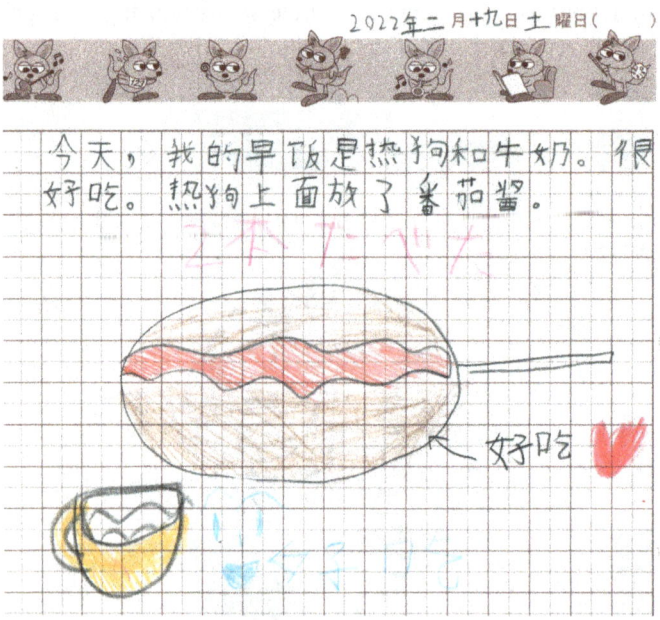

Figure 22: Y's diary (7;9).

In this piece of Y's diary work, a picture of a hotdog was drawn to support the meaning of the Mandarin text. The Japanese text ("2本たべた" [I ate two (hotdogs)]) appeared above the picture and could be seen as a part of the illustration. Rather than separately investigating the meaning of each language itself, using translanguaging in this writing softened the rigid boundaries between named languages. The text and images in Figure 22 could be easily understood based on their semiotic meaning beyond the surface text. By enacting her fluid trilingualism, Y set up a collaborative space using her entire linguistic resources for thinking, communicating, and constructing meaning. Encompassing different forms of language within one entity reflected an integrated use of her three languages, which challenged the traditional monolithic view of language policy and practice in multilingual education.

Children have a great ability to imitate. Adults' spoken and written form frequently influence children's written language. For those who are keen readers, the literary style of books also influences them greatly. Y was enthusiastic about world history and read a great deal of history-related literature since she was a preschooler. At seven years old, she started to write under a pseudonym, YY. Using a pseudonym in writing appeared to be related to her influence from a book called *The diary of Anne Frank*. It was found that there was an upward trend in using the third person pronouns and passive voice in her diary entries. The number of reflective questions also increased as a result of her imitating the language of books and the speech of her parents.

Although Y still wrote, but selectively, about some daily events, more and more she showed an interest in recording her ideas about social and cultural issues in her diary. For example, she considered the topic of war and peace, and showed concern with the coronavirus situation, as well as thinking about how to live a happy life. Writing about these subjects was a reflection of her internal world on the external world.

Letters and messages
Being trilingual and tricultural means that there are a lot of events to celebrate within a year. Y made cards for each festival in each culture. She would also find time to celebrate with her parents. Figure 23 is a Mother's Day card (5;11) and Figure 24 is an invitation card (6;7).

Y's parents read through what she wrote and occasionally corrected some spelling mistakes. They appreciated her motivation and were supportive of her taking initiative in writing practices. Translanguaging was again used as a learning approach in Y's writing. In her greeting card (Figure 25), she translated the Japanese

Figure 23: A Mother's Day card (5;11).

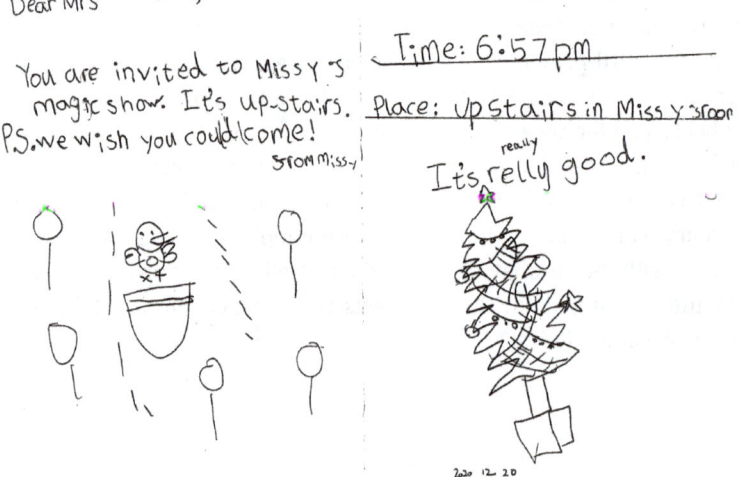

Figure 24: An invitation card (6;7).

text into English. It might be seen as a way to emphasize her emotions by repeating the same message in more than one language.

Emotions are a part of multilingual trajectories (Gort and Sembiante 2015). Multilingual speakers may have more feelings relating to the use of some languages than the use of others (Gort and Sembiante 2015). In the example shown in Figure 25,

8.4 Writing as a means of language socialization

Figure 25: A card to her mother (6;7).

Y might have felt that her fondness for her mother was more salient when she expressed it in English and that the translation behavior most accurately reflected her emotion. Translanguaging thus demonstrated her rich linguistic experience, cognitive thinking, multilingual identities, individual emotions, and strong family ties.

Thanks to the family intimacy, Y and her parents were able to spend a lot of valuable time together, such as by working separately in the same room and going outside together frequently. Shopping was a family activity. Although it might just take about 20 minutes to complete the whole shopping, it nevertheless was a good opportunity to involve every member in this family activity. For example, they would negotiate when and where to go and what to buy, and Y would then make a shopping list such as the English one shown in Figure 26.

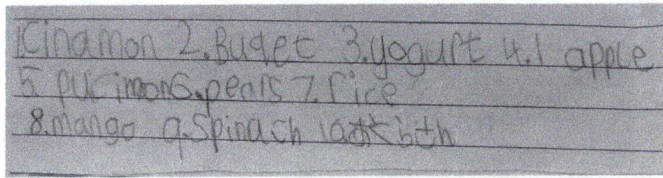

Figure 26: A shopping list (5;5).

When making a shopping list in English, Japanese vocabulary would sometimes be chosen intentionally or inadvertently. For example, the last item in the above list, おくらさん [okra], was written in Japanese. Y's mother reminded her that お

くら [okra] was the Japanese phonological translation of the English word, okra. In other words, the mother provided a hint for the English spelling of the word. However, Y still chose to write it in Japanese. さん (san), a Japanese language suffix, was added to indicate the word's Japanese nature. Okra is commonly sold in Japanese supermarkets and the pronunciation of the vegetable sounds like a Japanese name. Offering a Japanese translation reflected Y's belief about the link between the language and its culture. Translanguaging thus contributed to the formation of Y's metalinguistic knowledge and metacognitive ability. Similarly, Gort (2006), for example, noticed that Spanish-English first graders used strategic code-switching in their talking and writing during the classroom writing practices, which was evidence of their phonological and alphabetical knowledge of textual resources in the Spanish and English texts.

Modern technology and digital communication are employed to advocate parents' language beliefs, as these media bring new access to the use of the heritage language (Lanza and Gomes 2020). Importantly, literacy practice can also encompass digital practice as a significant mediational tool (Palviainen 2020). Tablet and PC, for example, remarkably support people's daily communication. Y learned to use these tools and could freely access them every day as long as her parents were able to guide her activity. Parents' behavior was again imitated by Y and reflected in her daily reading and writing routines. For example, when her mother kept a diary in a notebook, Y copied what the mother wrote and wrote her own diary entries; when her mother typed her work on the computer, Y also typed everything in Word files on her own laptop (from three years old).

Moreover, internet provides the best opportunity for culturally diverse families to make a regular contact with their extended family members, who live in their own home country and whose emotional support is critical in child development. Y frequently sent text messages to her Chinese grandparents, as shown in Figures 27. She also sent text messages and emails to her parents when they were away from home. This is shown in Figures 28 and 29.

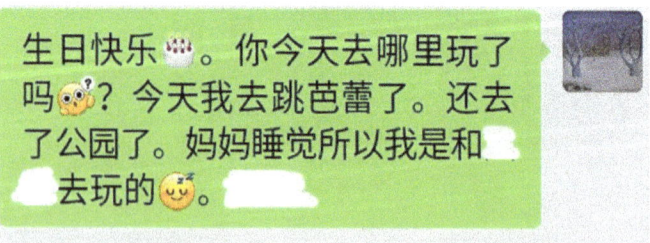

Figure 27: A text message to her grandfather (7;9).

Daddy, when do you come back? What are you doing   ?we are waiting for you.
What are you buying dada?
If you want just tell us when you come back.
I love you daddy

Figure 28: An email to her father (4;11).

Saturday • 13:26

はいまアルディーにいきます。　は中国のたべもののおみせにいきます。　はおうちにかえります。　　ママさん。

Sat 13:27 • SMS

Figure 29: A text message to her mother (4;11).

In this way technologies played a supplementary and incentive role in Y's writing practices. Typing requires both linguistic knowledge and ICT skills. Through typing, she learned more about the connections between Chinese characters in Mandarin or *kana* script in Japanese and their corresponding sound systems. Typing also helped Y improve her English spelling and sentence writing skills, as shown in Example 122.

Example 122: A text message to a classmate (5;1)
Hello, we in vite you to our flat anee time you want. We can cook cure rise and spgeti. And we can play at the park.

Y was aware that the underlines indicated spelling mistakes in her message and looked for the correct forms in a dictionary after typing the above message. Thus, using modern technology was an effective means of practice. Nevertheless, there are many non-linguistic issues to be considered when children use the new technologies. For example, how to deal with child-inappropriate online information and how to keep the child's eyesight healthy. These issues affected her parents' practices such as their limiting the amount of time Y could use a computer.

It was a great comfort to her parents that their very young child had a sense of time management. Y was keen on making a daily or weekly schedule, which she began to do from five years old. Figure 30 is an example showing a self-check on completion of activities at the end of a day. She also scheduled some events for her parents (the last line in Figure 31) and evaluated them based on their fulfillment of tasks, as shown in Figure 32.

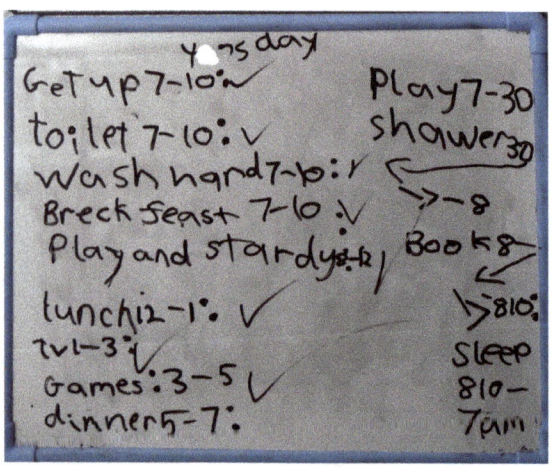

Figure 30: A time schedule (5;9).

It might be true that work that children do voluntarily and with interest yields greater results than work that they are required to do. Y's parents felt that the sense of self-management was more important than the actual completion and therefore rarely criticized her plans.

The greatest value of diary entries, letters, cards, and messages is that they bring children's creative writing into a child's life. Y began to understand why she wanted to write an email, send a text message, or make a time schedule. Writing therefore became a meaningful and necessary tool for her to communicate and to do tasks in real life. In addition to these more practical writing practices, she was also keen on writing in other different ways such as essays and poems.

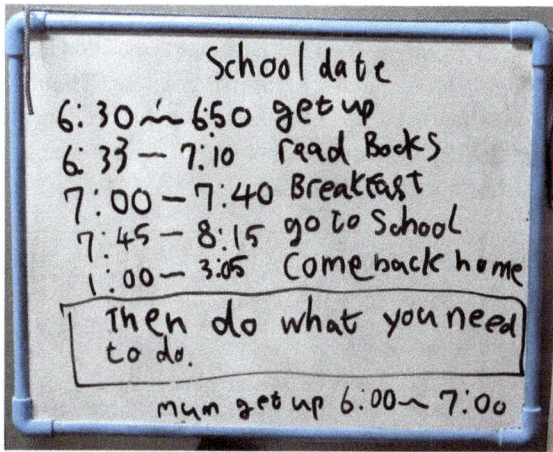

Figure 31: A time schedule (7;1).

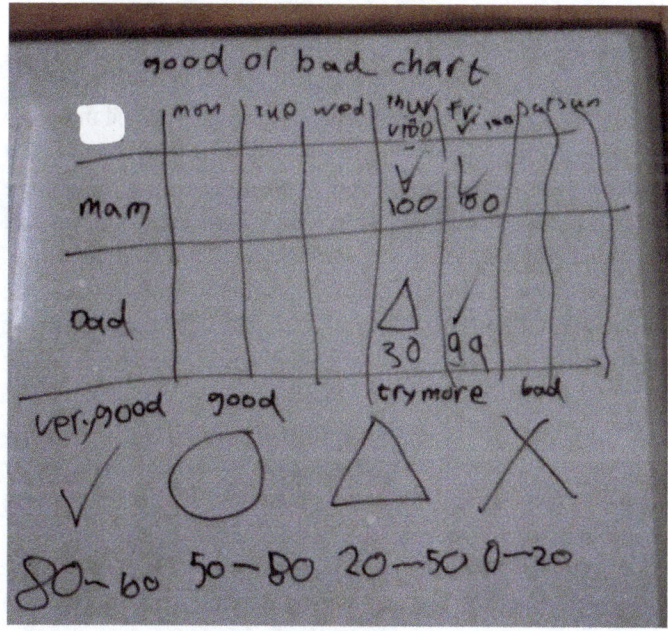

Figure 32: Good or bad chart (7;2).

General and argumentative essays

Having a strong interest in her mother's research on her language acquisition experience, Y paid a great deal of attention to the mother's research progress ("Mummy, have you finished Y's story?") (5;6). She tried to read the mother's published journal articles ("Where is Y? I want to read.") (5;6). Meanwhile, her mother encouraged her to write different types of essays, as shown in Example 123.

Example 123 is from a mother-child conversation (5;4).
CHI: Have you finished Y's story?
MOT: I finished two year old Y's story.
CHI: How about 10 year old Y?
MOT: I will write 6–12 year old Y when you are in primary school.
CHI: Then?
MOT: Then 12–18 year old Y.
CHI: Then?
MOT: Then you are going to write about yourself by yourself.

Inspired by her mother's research, Y started to write and type essays about her life from five years old. Most of the time, it was more convenient to write on paper. A short essay recording her early life is shown in Figure 33.

Similar essays titled "Y's Story" were repeatedly written as Y gained more life experience and had more to reflect on from the past and in the present. In a typed version of Y's story (876 English words and 32 Japanese symbols) (6;8), she described her friendship and neighborhood in Scotland. Examples of direct and indirect speech and conversational exchanges were enclosed in quotation marks. She also explained the background of her family's relocation to Scotland like this, "... Me and my family went to the UK for daddy's job ... So we stayed there for one year." (6;8). In addition, she described her time in the Japanese primary school and compared it with the Scottish school life.

Eventually, after Y had turned six, she came to write argumentative essays. This was also initially a guided activity supported by her parents. After a few times, her mother came to feel that this writing seemed not suitable for a young child. Even though the language Y wrote and the content of her essays were satisfactory, she showed no interest in this age-inappropriate style. However, after her seventh birthday she appeared to be willing to take on more challenges. She "sat" an English language test, *EIKEI*,[22] at home (7;9). The level of the test that she took was for advanced level English speakers in Japan. She completed it with

---

[22] *EIKEN* is an abbreviation of *Jitsuyo Eigo Gino Kentei* (Test in Practical English Proficiency). It is the most widely used English-language testing program in Japan.

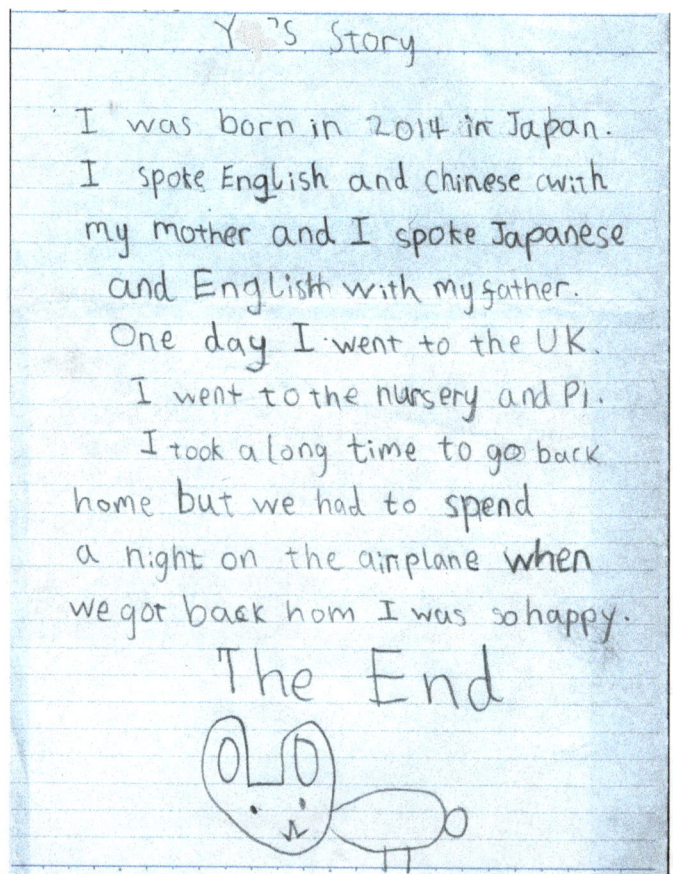

Figure 33: Y's story (5;10).

almost all of the items correct in the grammar, vocabulary, and reading comprehension parts. She also completed a 120–150 word English essay, stating a point and giving two supporting reasons. Her writing is shown in Figure 34.

People may consider Y's positive attitude toward writing argumentative essays as having emerged a result of her desire to pass the English levelling test. Nevertheless, it is also evidence of her growing academic skills and cognitive abilities. A piece of writing titled "How to pass" (Figure 35) further explains how she self-learned to write argumentative essays.

In Figure 35, Y highlighted the number of words required ("words 80~100"; "No more") and explained the structure of an argumentative essay ("1. Topic sentence"; "2. Supporting sentence"; and "3. Concluding sentence"). These highlighted parts, either underlined or circled in Figure 35, clearly demonstrated her understanding of a

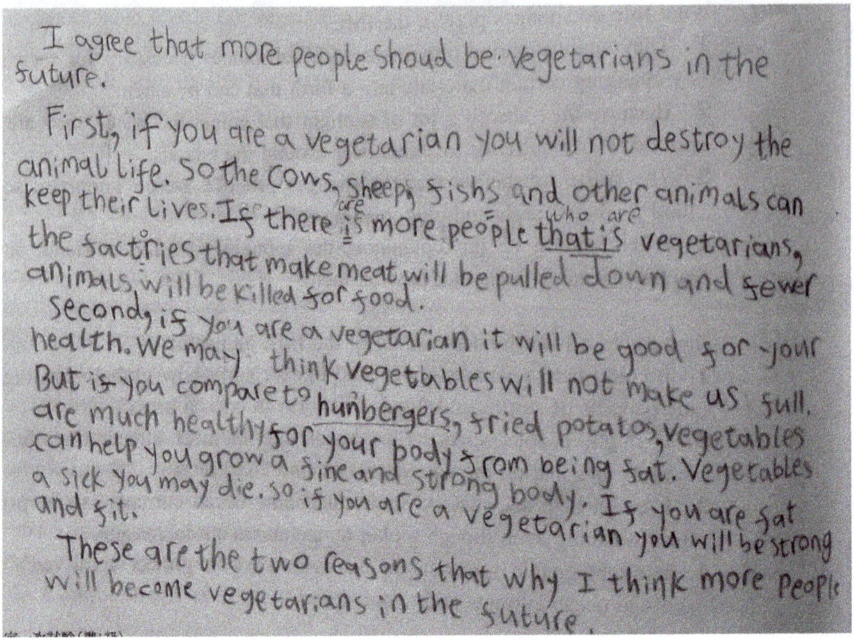

I agree that more people shoud be vegetarians in the future.
First, if you are a vegetarian you will not destroy the animal life. So the cows, sheeps, fishs and other animals can keep their lives. If there is more people that is vegetarians, the factries that make meat will be pulled down and fewer animals will be killed for food.
are
who are
Second, if you are a vegetarian it will be good for your health. We may think vegetables will not make us full. But if you compare to hunbergers, fried potatos, vegetables are much healthy for your body from being fat. Vegetables can help you grow a fine and strong body. If you are fat a sick you may die. so if you are a vegetarian you will be strong and fit.
These are the two reasons that why I think more people will become vegetarians in the future.

Figure 34: An argumentative essay (7;9).

How to pass
(2022) 2 月 7 日月 曜日
writing
2 resons Points 1. Education 2. Convenience 3. Safety. words 80~100
No more!
1. Topic sentence 2. Supporting sentence 3. Concluding sentence.
まとめの文
支持文
支持文
First

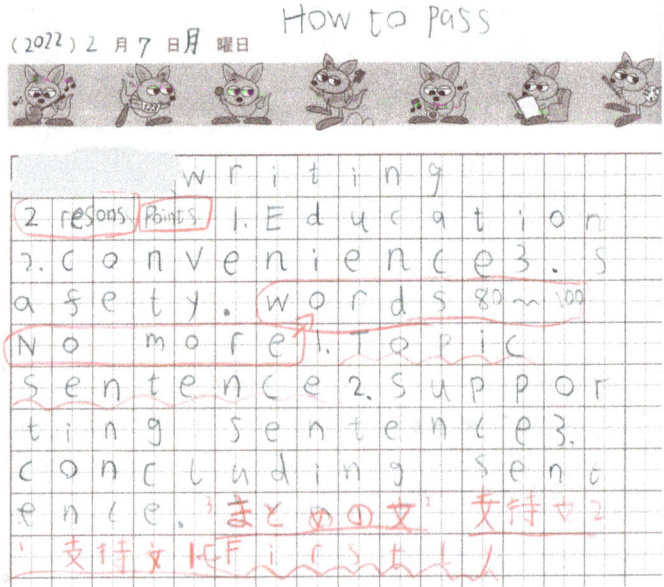

Figure 35: A piece of writing: how to pass (7;8).

more complex writing style. This piece of writing shows how Y's young mind organized and analyzed information using her reasoning and critical thinking skills.

Poems

The number of poems that Y wrote gradually increased after she turned seven years old. Although drama and poetry are not very common forms for children, Y seemed to be influenced by the books that she read such as *Romeo and Juliet*. Most of her poems in Mandarin and English would be more accurately described as rhymes. One of such rhymes, shown in Figure 36, was created at 7;4.

Figure 36: An English poem (7;4).

If writing poems in English and Chinese was a hobby, writing poems in Japanese was a more serious "job". Figure 37 is from *Mainichi Shougakusei Shinbun* [Daily Primary School Newspaper] which shows a *Haiku* [a genre of Japanese poetry] that Y had published.

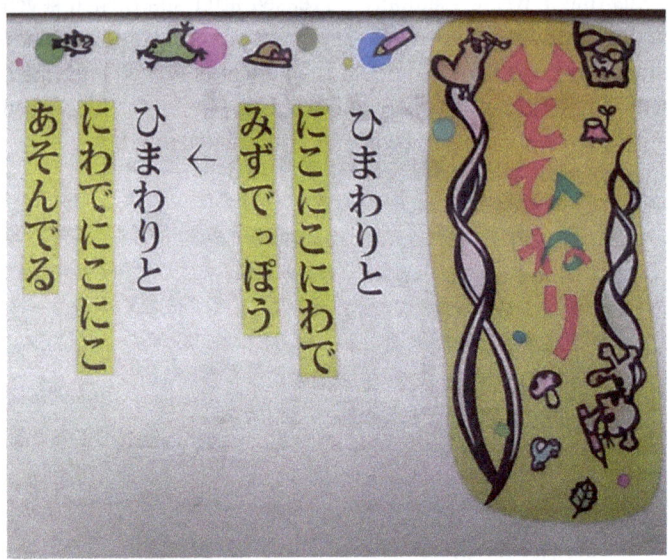

Figure 37: A published Japanese poem (7;3).

The three lines on the right side of the arrow are Y's original text and the three lines on the left show the revised version provided by the editor. From then on, Y continued submitting manuscripts to the same newspaper and published two more poems (accepted without corrections), as shown in Figures 38 and 39, at the age of 7;11 and 8;4 respectively.[23]

All of the above self-administered writing practices show that creative writing was more important for Y than literature itself. Children's writing has the same relationship to the writing of adults as a child's play has to life; in other words, writing is as necessary to the child as play is, for building a strong foundation in the young author (Vygotsky 2004). It would thus be unfair to judge the child's work from the viewpoint of adult writing criteria (Vygotsky 2004). By exercising her creative tendencies, Y formed and expressed her thoughts, emotions, and inner world. The significance of these creative endeavors lies in the

---

[23] Both poems were submitted and accepted before 8;0.

8.4 Writing as a means of language socialization

Figure 38: A published Japanese poem (7;11).

Figure 39: A published Japanese poem (8;4).

fact that they allow for the development and education of the child through the rest of her life (Vygotsky 2004).

8.5 Adding Spanish and Japanese sign language to trilingualism

After Y entered a local Japanese primary school at 6;10, her multilingual and multiliterate competences continued to develop. In addition to her existing three languages, she studied a fourth one, Spanish, on her own. Y learned Spanish from self-study using written materials and recordings rather than from talking to her peers or playing in the neighborhood. In addition, she came to teach Spanish to her parents, which was also a literacy activity, and the teaching practice contributed to her own learning.

While English had been naturally acquired as one of her first languages, Y's learning of Spanish took place in a second language learning context. As a part of the learning process, she made use of translanguaging, deploying her entire trilingual repertoire to make meaning of the new language and to further develop her multilingual competence and identities. Having a good knowledge of English and Japanese, and self-learning skills, Y practiced listening, speaking, and reading every day for about 10 minutes using bilingual English-Spanish or Japanese-Spanish resources. Inspired by cross-linguistic connections between Spanish and other romance languages, she was also motivated to become a polyglot ("If I can speak Spanish, I can also speak Italian.") (6;10).

The second language learning context was also implicit in the situation where Y acted as a Spanish teacher to her parents. Translanguaging was then used as a communicative strategy to promote learning and participation (García 2011). The following picture (Figure 40) catches a moment of a Spanish lesson given by Y using both English and Spanish. English translations of the Spanish terms were provided on the whiteboard as well as being explained verbally.

Through Spanish lessons given by Y on a regular basis, she and her parents studied this language together. In this way, a new multilingual space was established in family socialization involving members of varying multilingual competencies and experiences. Figure 41 is an example showing Y's mother's effort to learn Spanish.

The example in Figure 41 shows that at the end of a Spanish lesson, her mother was given a dictation of numbers, on which she tried her best to score "80%". Y enjoyed being an examiner and marking her mother's answers. In this way, most of Y's interests and talents were developed in the family context with limited or no outside influences, though the types of her home stimulation varied.

The most striking impression of Y's home stimulation was perhaps the high degree of parental involvement with the child. There are many good and successful

Figure 40: Teaching Spanish to her parents (6;10).

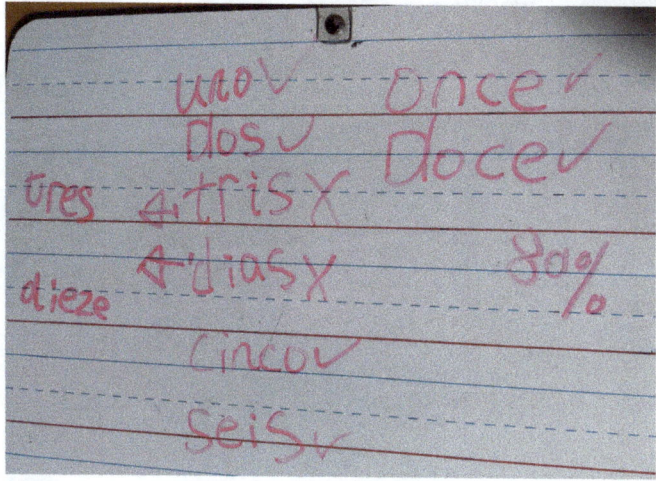

Figure 41: Giving her mother a Spanish test (7;6).

ways to work with creative children. For example, in the Spanish learning context, when reading together or having discussions in Spanish turned out not to be plausible for Y's parents, consistent encouragement, participation in the activities, listening to the child's talk, and asking and answering questions (even in a different language) were alternative ways to be stimulating and supportive.

When foreign language education is deployed as a strategy for language learning, it is usually in the hope that children will use the minority language not only in language classrooms, but also in critical informal domains, such as the family and neighborhood (Armstrong, 2014). The Spanish homeschooling led by Y and participated in by her parents created a new type of family socialization and bolstered the language development of both the child and her parents. Based on the activities of her self-learning Spanish and teaching Spanish to her parents (as shown in Figures 40 and 41), as well as cooking Spanish food (such as tortilla) with her father, Y wrote and published an article talking about her Spanish learning experience gained in the home context, as shown in Figure 42.

Figure 42: A published Japanese article (8;1).

The article, published by *Mainichi Shougakusei Shinbun* [Daily Primary School Newspaper], was titled 難しいから楽しい [Difficult but joyful] (The black vertical bold text in Figure 42). The three pictures and the article described three different Spanish practices involving different participants in different situations of family socialization, that is, teaching parents Spanish (top-left picture), reading Spanish books on her own (bottom-left picture), and making Spanish omelet (bottom-right picture). One of the motivations behind Y's desire to learn Spanish was her experience in Scotland, where she learned some Spanish songs in the first grade. After returning to Japan from Scotland, she decided to study Spanish on her own. She studied its phonics sounds, vocabulary, and grammar. She also read children's Spanish books, sang Spanish songs, and followed cooking books to cook Spanish food. This piece of writing indicates that Y's multilingual competency was never developed alone but part of her whole child well-being development. Learning a language through literacy-driven and other creative activities is thus an important aspect of language policy; these practices are part of the agency that Y called upon in her family socialization.

Similar child-led literacy-driven practices were also adopted when Y learned about Japanese sign language. She aimed to join the sign language club in her Japanese school (club members were usually 4th graders and above) and started to prepare when she was a first grader. She read books and newspaper articles and watched TV programs introducing this language. She also wrote sign language "books" and taught her parents to use this language at home. Moreover, she expanded these literacy-driven practices to broader language practices, for example, by convincing her classroom teacher that the class should perform collective greetings bilingually using Japanese sign language together with the regular Japanese spoken language. She also founded a sign language club and created a sign language corner in her classroom. Y's agency thus created a new multilingual space at home and a bilingual moment in the monolingual Japanese classroom, socializing her parents, peers, and teachers into the process of language learning through daily routines.

8.6 Reading newspapers and publishing articles

Reading newspapers and discussing news are other practices that helped establish a multilingual space in Y's home. Watching and listening to news at breakfast and dinner was originally a habit of her parents but now it had become a family activity. In addition to watching live news broadcasts in English or Japanese, Y also liked a recorded program which combined headlines reported by the main media of different countries, where each piece of news was reported in a different language that included Mandarin and Spanish. However, news in brief could not continually satisfy her curiosity, as Y came to desire more information and raise more questions on the current affairs. Seeing this, her parents subscribed to a Japanese newspaper for primary school year students when Y was 6;10, one that she had occasionally read in a local library when she was still a preschooler.

It has been found that in a multilingual space, more than one language will be intentionally used to support the development of different language and literacy skills. This "purposeful pedagogical alternation of languages in spoken and written, receptive and productive modes" is more often used to describe the majority language speakers learning a foreign language in classrooms, or to describe immigrant children learning a minority language at home (Hornberger and Link 2012: 262). However, a different purpose was displayed in Y's case, that is, learning the school language at home.

Formal news language in Japanese is different from that used for daily communication. Newspaper terms are frequently written in Chinese characters (*kanji*). Some of these *kanji* expressions share linguistic forms with their Mandarin equivalents, regardless of their deviant pronunciations or lexical meanings. Many of such newspaper words are typically not acquired by Japanese lower graders (P1 and P2 pupils); they do, however, more or less appear in the lower primary years' Mandarin textbooks and are used more commonly in less formal situations by fluent Mandarin speakers than by Japanese speakers. Y was able to read and understand lower grade Mandarin textbooks from five. That being the case, complex vocabulary in Japanese newspapers was *trans-enunciated* (the written form of one language being pronounced using the sound system of another language) (Song 2016) by her mother upon Y's request. In other words, her mother would read a Japanese word in its Mandarin's pronunciation.

Because Y had a broad vocabulary and read extensively in English and had the highest level of reading comprehension skills in this language, English was employed as the base language in discussions about the background of a piece of news. However, considering that *kanji* vocabulary was expected to be acquired as a part of higher-level academic Japanese language skills, *kanji* words and expressions were not translated into their English equivalents even in an English discussion. Translanguaging was thus drawn on in Y's family to support the understanding of news by integrating three sets of linguistic resources.

Reading newspapers also helped Y learn about many things that could not be directly witnessed, such as socio-political affairs, geographical features of an area, the history of a country, etc. In all of these cases, the function of imagination in one's mental activity, behavior, and development should not be overlooked (Vygotsky 2004). By imagining what one has not directly experienced or conceptualizing something from someone else's narration and description, a person's historical and social experience is deepened and broadened (Vygotsky 2004).

In addition to reading newspaper articles, Y had written and published two articles at eight years old (one of them is shown in Figure 42). Writing and revising drafts was a child-led family activity in which Y first wrote an article independently and her parents refrained from comment. There would then be discussions and corrections on ambiguous points and inappropriate language use. It was in the process of revising that Y learned to plan, structure, and organize her language and cognitive knowledge.

8.7 Doing research

Carrying out academic research provided a multilingual space for family communication. From the age of five Y demonstrated a strong interest in her mother's research about her journey to trilingualism. When her mother was writing her notes and diary entries or typing her research papers, Y always brought her own notebook and did her own "research", as she called it, next to the mother. Figure 43 shows a spelling test Y did on her own when she was 5;9.

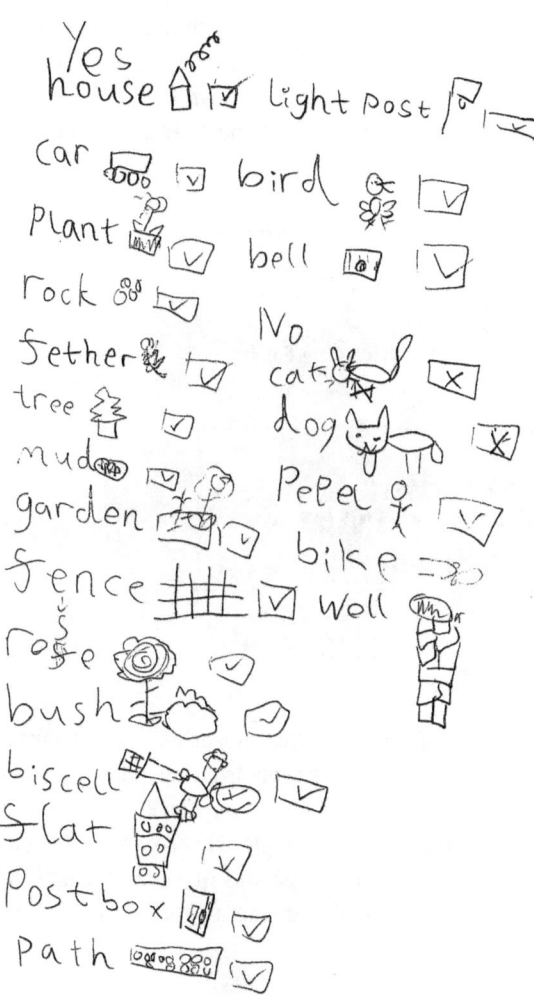

Figure 43: A self-administered spelling test (5;9).

When doing the above "research", instead of asking for help from her parents, Y referred to a paper dictionary to correct answers. She was taught and understood that an important part of doing research was being an independent thinker and problem solver. Taking an inquiry stance towards learning was significant to the overall development of her literacy and academic abilities. This interest eventually turned into a more serious research activity. With her growing writing skills and cognitive thinking abilities, at age eight Y decided to do some real research and started to collect data regularly in her classroom. For example, she raised two research questions – "Why do teachers don't want children to speak English?"[24] and "Even children go to *Kumon*,[25] why they can't speak English?" (8;1). She used the methods learned from her parents, such as observing, interviewing, and making conversations. She then wrote down field notes in a research diary kept at home. Data recorded in Figures 44 and 45 were from participant observation and conversations.

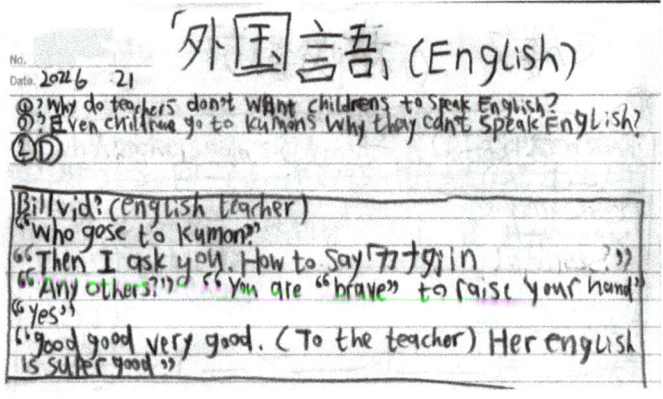

Figure 44: Research data (8;1).

In Figure 44 Y had jotted down direct speech of her English teacher,[26] Mr. B, putting it within double quotations marks. In Figure 45 the reply from a Japanese student, M, to Y's question was put within the Japanese quotation marks 「 」. When Y showed her data to her parents, they would ask some questions regarding the data and data collection methods, such as "Why do you ask this question?" and "What can you find from the data?" However, they did not attempt to guide or interfere in

---

24 "Why don't Japanese teachers want children to speak English in the classroom?"
25 *Kumon* is an educational institution based in Japan.
26 An English activity lesson (45 minutes) was taught to second-year students once a month.

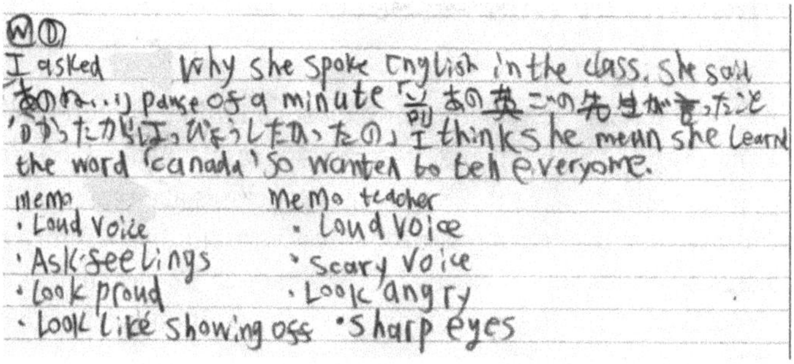

> ①②
> I asked why she spoke English in the class. She said
> 「ん…」pause of a minute 「あの表この字が下だった
> のだから、だからこっちした、た。」I think she meant she learn
> the word 'canada' so wanted to teh everyone.
>
> memo   memo teacher
> • Loud voice   • Loud voice
> • Ask feelings   • Scary voice
> • Look proud   • Look angry
> • Look like showing off • Sharp eyes

Figure 45: Research data (8;1).

her work, but mostly encouraged her to gather and record more and more varieties of accurate data. This is evidenced in Figure 45 in which Y added her own opinions ("I think . . .") to M's words as a supplemental explanation. She also observed the non-verbal communication of M and her Japanese teacher. Observing the teacher's "loud voice" could be seen as supportive evidence for Y's recorded data such as a comment given by the teacher – "ほかのみんなはいやなきもちになる" [Other students may feel offended.] Doing research in this way became a shared experience between Y and her parents which created a new type of family socialization.

This chapter has illustrated how Y's cognitive and literary creativity facilitated her language development. More importantly, it has provided new directions for the research on FLP and child agency. Y's specific interests and skills shaped the interaction between her and her family members. The examples provided have demonstrated how acquiring a language through reading and writing and other literacy-driven activities, in addition to daily conversations, contributed to the high level of Y's multilingual competence. These written language related socialization patterns show how literacy can ensure continuous and sustainable development of non-societal languages in Japan – including English, Mandarin, Spanish, and Japanese sign language. Generational order in Y's family was also reversed in literacy-related activities. Y first learned three writing systems in the parent-directed practices, then became an independent reader and writer, and finally socialized her parents into child-centered activities involving the reading and writing processes. Moreover, Y published articles and carried out academic research, both of which were highly independent work but she made them joint family activities. Y's parents recognized her abilities and appreciated her efforts, and eventually followed her lead and accommodated her rules. In this way, the child became the policy maker and language manager.

9 The contribution of this research

People who read this book may say they don't think most children could do what Y has done, or they may say that the outcome is strictly a result of her family's practices. There can be no claim that Y's developmental processes are representative of other children her age; in fact, she is probably representative of only a very small percentage of that population. Nevertheless, although Y's case may not directly inform other families regarding their language policies, it does offer new understandings of how parents and children negotiate language together in multilingual families.

Unlike many studies of family language socialization, which primarily focus on children's verbal communication abilities and are conducted from the parents' perspective, the present study has focused on self-directed aspects of a child's near simultaneous language and literacy development in the early years. In particular it has revealed a set of agentive strategies and skills that were used by the child to shape her own learning processes, as well as the family's language policies through which the child's perspective was accommodated. The rational, negotiable nature of child agency thus becomes a key concept in discussing language choices. As child agency is a relatively underdiscussed topic within FLP literature, and especially for trilingual children, the present study should make a valuable contribution to the literature in this area as well as to the study of individual differences in language learning.

It is in reality difficult for language acquisition to continue when literacy acquisition is not simultaneously promoted. The present study demonstrates how the opportunity for using a language is not limited to the spoken mode of that language; joint literacy-driven socialization creates equally important multilingual spaces. It is clear that Y has been very focused on written language in a primarily self-reliant way, which has been a key to her development. Her literacy-driven language learning experience appears different than what is seen in most studies of multilingual children. Literacy provides a rich context for the sustainable development of all of a child's languages, particularly the non-societal languages. Family members with unique language and cultural strengths gathering to talk about written texts and participate in events related to them create a productive daily routine; this also creates happy moments in which to share experiences and emotions from the day. It would thus be worthwhile for further research to focus more on children's literacy and the ways it influences their language development and sense of agency.

Not only are children socialized by listening to their parents and participating in the learning that the parents organize, but children also socialize their parents through their own guided activities. Children who have specific interests and skills are good at shaping the interactional contexts. While being very focused on their own concerns, they can shape the interaction that they have with other family members (Vygotsky, 2016). The present study shows how Y's productive use of her free time to do her favorite things, including reading, writing, playing, being a child teacher, and working on other things of interest, provided her with abundant opportunities to engage in creative and dynamic family interaction. Through this kind of activity, the conventional generational order can be challenged and even reversed when children assert their various types of agency and take a leadership role in socialization. It would thus be desirable for adults to accommodate their children's needs and share their interests, making the establishment of family language policies a collaborative achievement of both children and adults. There is very little, if any, research on children with special interests and skill sets, or on their parents' (or other family members') efforts to accommodate and support them through literacy development or other aspects of multilingual parenting.

It is generally recognized that children's specific cognitive skills may not be attributed to environment alone. The present child, in fact, showed a predisposition to learning alphabet letters and other aspects of literacy that is not present in all children and cannot be accomplished equally by all children even within a similar environment. With very little external support from the Japanese society where she was mainly raised, Y reached a high level of competency not only in Japanese but in her other two languages as well. She acquired native-like skills in the English language despite the fact that neither parent was a native speaker of it; this included native-like linguistic aspects that were lacking in her parents, including aspects of pronunciation, grammar, and language awareness.

From the present study, one can see how parents' support for their children and the creation of a harmonious, suitable learning setting are significant for children's language and cognitive development. It is found that establishing and socializing children in such a setting will greatly depend on children's agentive abilities and intergenerational relationship. As pointed out by Olszewski-Kubilius (2008), an unusual degree of closeness and a cohesive relationship among family members is a significant characteristic of families that nurture creative and talented individuals. A close family bond enables family members to make shared hobbies a multilingual space for language socialization. Y had good rapport with her parents and the entire family spent great quality time together, talking, playing, and learning. She self-learned Spanish and Japanese sign language and persuaded her parents to learn them as a family activity. Both parents were supportive of her, attending the language lessons that she taught, which included playing musical instruments, singing, and participating in activities following her instructions.

But rather than viewing these simply as a part of the child's language learning, her parents enjoyed the intimate family moments.

Most of the existing studies on child language learning have examined primarily the mother-child relationship; the compelling role of the father has not been much discussed in the literature on child language development. A major reason for the focus on mothers is that most of the research has been done from a Western point of view (in middle-class families) where the mother has traditionally been the main caregiver. However, paternal power and its impact on children cannot be replaced. In the present study, Y's father modelled a masculine way of thinking and acting and that broadened the child's scope of experience. The participation of fathers in their children's language and literacy development also supports children's learning in school (Gallo, 2014). Investigations balancing maternal and paternal bonds may help people understand more about children's unique behavioral, emotional, and psychological development.

An intimate family bond is sometimes associated with an unconventional parenting style, such as one through which children are given more freedom in order to boost their independent thoughts and independent actions (Olszewski-Kubilius 2008). In Y's family, adherence to the parents' values was not the major demand. Her parents supported her in various domains while still encouraging her to explore other appropriate fields that matched her special abilities and interests. Maintaining strong emotional ties while reducing parent-child identification fosters creativity, talent development, and psychological health in children (Olszewski-Kubilius 2008). Y and her parents together negotiated their family's beliefs and values, while creating unique individual identities and shared family identities. In addition, her parents adjusted their expectations for her when she showed high potential and talent in language learning; however, they did not expect to achieve their own unachieved goals through their child. They also helped her develop flexible attitudes toward different living environments. The present study thus evidences how children's interests and emotional needs can be supported in a stimulating family environment filled with happiness and respect. Children in such a situation can also be inspired to accept challenges and learn to deal with the stresses that arise from high expectations in and outside the home (Olszewski-Kubilius 2008).

Intergenerational intimacy underlies the success of Y's family's language policies. Children brought up in a child-centered and an intimate family environment can become independent thinkers and action takers. As these young minds develop, they may gain extensive knowledge through reading and life experience. They can and may also want to share some responsibilities for making decisions about family issues including language policies. Their ability to mediate and exert authority may be truly appreciated and highly respected by their parents, who may end up following the child's lead. These children are de facto policy co-makers and co-managers. Researchers engaging in outreach with parents and families therefore need to rethink the critical position of children as well as their agency. Research findings that highlight the role of child agency may redefine and contribute to the expansion of the traditional theoretic framework of family language policy.

Appendix 1: Videos taken between 2;0 and 5;10

Video	Age	Language	Participant	Activity
1	2;0	English	Child; Mother	Drawing and writing
2	2;1	English	Child; Father	Reading an English book
3	2;2	Mandarin	Child; Mother	Playing cooking games
4	2;3	English	Child; Father; Mother	Building LEGO modules
5	2;4	Mandarin	Child; Mother	Playing cooking games
6	2;5	English	Child; Father; Mother	Playing puzzle games
7	2;6	Mandarin	Child; Grandparents; Mother	Building LEGO models
8	2;7	English	Child; Grandparents; Mother	Playing cooking games
9	2;8	English	Child; Father; Mother	Playing cooking games
10	2;9	English; Japanese	Child; Father; Mother	Learning Japanese *hiragana*
11	2;10	English	Child; Father; Mother	Doing a role play
12	2;11	Mandarin	Child; Mother	Having a dinner conversation
13	3;0	Mandarin	Child; Mother	Playing cooking games
14	3;1	Mandarin	Child; Father; Mother	Doing math activities
15	3;2	English; Mandarin	Child; Father; Mother	Reading a book called *The very hungry caterpillar*
16	3;3	English	Child; Mother	Doing English phonics homework
17	3;4	Mandarin	Child; Mother	Reading Mandarin books
18	3;5	English	Child; Father	Doing math problems
19	3;6	Japanese; English	Child; Father	Teaching father *hiragana*
20	3;7	English; Mandarin	Child, Mother	Teaching and learning *pīnyīn*
21	3;8	Mandarin	Child; Mother	Telling a Chinese story
22	3;9	English; Mandarin	Child; Father; Mother,	Reading
23	3;10	English, Mandarin	Child, Mother	Learning Chinese characters
24	3;10	English	Child; Mother; Father	Doing addition problems
25	3;11	English; Japanese	Child, Father	Teaching father *hiragana*

https://doi.org/10.1515/9783111003092-010

(continued)

Video	Age	Language	Participant	Activity
26	4;0	English; Mandarin	Child; Father; Mother	Teaching father Mandarin
27	4;1	English; Mandarin	Child; Father; Mother	Teaching father *pīnyīn*
28	4;2	English; Japanese	Child; Father	Making a Japanese storybook
29	4;3	English; Japanese; Mandarin	Child; Father; Mother	Teaching father Chinese characters
30	4;4	Japanese; English	Child; Father	Reading Japanese books to father
31	4;5	English	Child; Mother	Doing math problems
32	4;6	Mandarin	Child; Mother	Reading and having a discussion
33	4;7	English; Mandarin	Child; Mother	Making an English storybook
34	4;8	English	Child; Father; Mother	Teaching father to play the piano
35	4;9	English; Mandarin	Child; Mother	Reading and having a discussion
36	4;10	English	Child; Father; Mother	Talking about school life
37	4;11	Mandarin	Child; Mother	Reading a Mandarin book
38	5;0	English	Child; Mother	Telling a story
39	5;1	Mandarin	Child; Mother	Writing Chinese characters
40	5;2	Japanese; English	Child; Father; Mother	Reading and having a discussion
41	5;3	English; Mandarin	Child; Mother	Reading and having a discussion
42	5;4	Japanese; English	Child; Father; Mother	Reading and having a discussion
43	5;5	Japanese	Child; Father; Mother	Having a discussing about a Japanese book
44	5;6	Japanese	Child; Father	Doing a role-play
45	5;7	Mandarin	Child; Mother	Reading a Mandarin story
46	5;8	Mandarin; Japanese	Child; Mother	Learning Chinese characters
47	5;9	English	Child; Mother	Doing English phonics homework
48	5;10	English; Mandarin	Child; Father	Teaching father to read a Mandarin book

Appendix 2: Transcription conventions in the example of two coded transcripts

Situation	situational information
[ ]	English translations are shown in the square brackets
( )	General purpose comments are shown in the round brackets
0	no verbal response
E	English coded in roman letters
J	Japanese coded in ひらかな (*hiragana*) and カタカナ (*katakana*)
M	Mandarin coded in Chinese characters

Example 1

CHI:	What's the weather like today?
GrM:	用中文说一遍。
	[Say it in Mandarin.]
CHI:	(0).
	(No response from the child.)

Example 2

Situation:	Y and her Chinese grandmother were assembling puzzles.
CHI:	できない。
	[You can't do it.]
GrM:	我会的。
	[I can.]

References

Abebe, Tatek. 2019. Reconceptualising children's agency as continuum and interdependence. *Social Sciences* 8(3). 1–16.
Ahearn, Laura. 2001. Language and agency. *Annual review of anthropology* 30. 109–137.
Antonini, Rachele. 2016. Caught in the middle: child language brokering as a form of unrecognised language service. *Journal of Multilingual and Multicultural Development* 37(7). 710–725.
Armstrong, Timothy. 2014. Naturalism and ideological work: how is family language policy renegotiated as both parents and children learn a threatened minority language? *International Journal of Bilingual Education and Bilingualism* 17(5). 570–585.
Baker, Colin. 2000. *A parents' and teachers' guide to bilingualism*. Bristol: Multilingual Matters.
Baker, Colin. 2011. *Foundations of bilingual education and bilingualism*, 5th edn. Bristol: Multilingual Matters.
Baker, Colin & Wayne E. Wright. 2017. *Foundations of bilingual education and bilingualism*, 6th edn. Bristol: Multilingual Matters.
Barnes, Julia. 2006. *Early trilingualism: a focus on questions*. Bristol: Multilingual Matters.
Barnes, Julia. 2011. The influence of child-directed speech in early trilingualism. *International Journal of Multilingualism* 8(1). 42–62.
Barron-Hauwaert, Suzanne. 2004. *Language strategies for bilingual families: the one-parent-one-language approach*. Bristol: Multilingual Matters.
Baxter, Pamela & Susan Jack. 2008. Qualitative case study methodology: study design and implementation for novice researchers. *The Qualitative Report* 13. 544–559.
Berg, Lawrence. 2001. *Qualitative research methods for the social sciences*, 4th edn. Boston: Allyn and Bacon.
Bergroth, Mari & Åsa Palviainen. 2017. Bilingual children as policy agents: language policy and education policy in minority language medium early childhood education and care. *Multilingua: Journal of Cross-Cultural and Interlanguage Communication* 36(4). 375–400.
Bialystock, Ellen. 2001. *Bilingualism in development: language, literacy, and cognition*. Cambridge: Cambridge University Press.
Blackledge, Adrian & Angela Creese. 2010. *Multilingualism: a critical perspective*. London: Continuum International.
Blommaert, Jan. 2010. *The sociolinguistics of globalization*. Cambridge: Cambridge University Press.
Boutakidis, Ioakim, Ruth Chao & James Rodríguez. 2011. The role of adolescents' native language fluency on quality of communication and respect for parents in Chinese and Korean immigrant families. *Asian American Journal of Psychology* 2(2). 128–139.
Bourdieu, Pierre. 1990. *The logic of practice*. Cambridge: Polity.
Bourdieu, Pierre. 1997. The forms of capital. In Halsey Albert, Hugh Lauder, Phillip Brown, Amy Wells (eds.), *Education, culture, and society*, 46–58. Oxford: Oxford University Press.
Boyatzis, Richard. 1998. *Transforming qualitative information: thematic analysis and code development*. Thousand Oaks, London, New Delhi: Sage Publications, Inc.
Braun, Andreas & Tony Cline. 2010. Trilingual families in mainly monolingual societies: working towards a typology. *International Journal of Multilingualism* 7(2). 110–127.
Braun, Virginia & Victoria Clarke. 2006. Using thematic analysis in psychology. Qualitative Research in Psychology 3(2), 77–101.
Caldas, Stephen. 2006. *Raising bilingual-biliterate children in monolingual cultures*. Bristol: Multilingual Matters.

Caldas, Stephen. 2012. Language policy in the family. In Bernard Spolsky (ed.), *The Cambridge handbook of language policy*, 3rd edn, 351–373. Cambridge: Cambridge University.

Caldas, Stephen & Caron-Caldas Suzanne. 2002. A sociolinguistic analysis of the language preferences of adolescent bilinguals: shifting allegiances and developing identities. *Applied Linguistic* 23(4). 490–514.

Canagarajah, Suresh. 2008. Language shift and the family: questions from the Sri Lankan Tamil diaspora. *Journal of Sociolinguistics* 12(2). 143–176.

Canagarajah, Suresh. 2011. Translanguaging in the classroom: emerging issues for research and pedagogy. *Applied Linguistics Review* 2. 1–27.

Canagarajah, Suresh. 2013. *Translingual practice: global Englishes and cosmopolitan relations*. London/New York: Routledge.

Cenoz, Jasone & Durk Gorter (eds.). 2011. A holistic approach in multilingual education: introduction. *Special issue: toward a multilingual approach in the study of multilingualism in school contexts, The Modern Language Journal* 95(3). 339–343.

Cenoz, Jasone & Durk Gorter. 2017. Minority languages and sustainable translanguaging: threat or opportunity? *Journal of Multilingual and Multicultural Development* 38(10). 901–912.

Chevalier, Sarah. 2012. Active trilingualism in early childhood: the motivating role of caregivers in interaction. *International Journal of Multilingualism* 9(4). 437–454.

Chevalier, Sarah. 2015. *Trilingual language acquisition: contextual factors influencing active trilingualism in early childhood*. Amsterdam: John Benjamins.

Chinen, Kiyomi & G. Richard Tucker. 2006. *Heritage language development: understanding the roles of ethnic identity, schooling and community*. Amsterdam: John Benjamins Publishing Company.

Clark, Eve. 1978. Awareness of language: some evidence from what children say and do. In Anne Sinclair, Robert Jarvella & Willem Levelt (eds.), *The child's conception of language*, 17–43. New York: Springer.

Collier, Virginia. 1992. A synthesis of studies examining long-term language minority student data on academic achievement. *Bilingual Research Journal* 16(1–2). 187–212.

Creese, Angela & Adrian Blackledge. 2010. Translanguaging in the bilingual classroom: a pedagogy for learning and teaching. *The Modern Language Journal* 94. 103–115.

Creswell, John. 2009. *Research design: qualitative, quantitative, and mixed methods approaches*, 3rd edn. Thousand Oaks, CA: Sage Publications.

Creswell, John. 2013. *Qualitative inquiry & research design: choosing among five approaches*, 3rd edn. Thousand Oaks, CA: Sage Publications.

Creswell, John. & Cheryl Poth. 2018. *Qualitative inquiry & research design: choosing among five approaches*, 4th edn. Los Angeles, CA: Sage Publications.

Cross, Russell. 2009. A sociocultural framework for language policy and planning. *Language Problems & Language Planning* 33(1). 22–42.

Cruz-Ferreira, Madalena. 2006. *Three is a crowd? Acquiring Portuguese in a trilingual environment*. Cleveland: Multilingual Matters.

Cummins, Jim. 1991. Language development and academic learning. In Lilliam Malave & Georges Duquette (eds.), *Language, culture and cognition*. Clevedon: Multilingual Matters.

Curdt-Christiansen, Xiao Lan. 2009. Invisible and visible language planning: ideological factors in the family language policy of Chinese immigrant families in Quebec. *Language Policy* 8(4). 351–375.

Curdt-Christiansen, Xiao Lan. 2013a. Editorial: family language policy: sociopolitical reality versus linguistic continuity. *Language Policy* 12(1). 1–6.

Curdt-Christiansen, Xiao Lan. 2013b. Negotiating family language policy: doing homework. In Mila Schwartz & Anna Verschik (eds.), *Successful family language policy: parents, children and educators in interaction*, 277–295. Dordrecht: Springer.

Curdt-Christiansen, Xiao Lan. 2014a. Family language policy: is learning Chinese at odds with learning English. In Xiao Lan Curdt-Christiansen & Andy Hancock (eds.), *Learning Chinese in disporic communities: many pathways to being Chinese*. Amsterdam: John Benjamins.

Curdt-Christiansen, Xiao Lan. 2014b. Planning for development or decline? Education policy for Chinese language in Singapore. *Critical Inquiry in Language Studies* 11(1). 1–26.

Curdt-Christiansen, Xiao Lan. 2015. Family language policy in the Chinese community in Singapore: a question of balance? In Wei Li (ed.), *Multilingualism in the Chinese diaspora worldwide*, 255–275. London: Routledge.

Curdt-Christiansen, Xiao Lan. 2016. Conflicting language ideologies and contradictory language practices in Singaporean bilingual families. *Journal of Multilingual and Multicultural Development* 37(7). 694–709.

Curdt-Christiansen, Xiao Lan & Jing Huang. 2020. Factors influencing family language policy. In Andrea Schalley & Susana Eisenchlas (eds.), *Handbook of home language maintenance and development: social and affective factors*, 174–193. Berlin/Boston: De Gruyter Mouton.

Danjo, Chisato. 2021. Making sense of family language policy: Japanese-English bilingual children's creative and strategic translingual practices. *International Journal of Bilingual Education and Bilingualism* 24(2). 292–304.

De Houwer, Annick. 1990. *The acquisition of two languages from birth*. Cambridge: Cambridge University Press.

De Houwer, Annick. 1999. Environmental factors in early bilingual development: the role of parental beliefs and attitudes. In Guus Extra & Ludo Verhoeven (eds.), *Bilingualism and migration*, 75–96. New York: Mouton de Gruyter.

De Houwer, Annick. 2007. Parental language input patterns and children's bilingual use. *Applied Psycholinguistics* 28(3). 411–424.

De Houwer, Annick. 2009. *Bilingual first language acquisition*. Bristol: Multilingual Matters.

De Houwer, Annick. 2017. Bilingual language acquisition. In Paul Fletcher & Brian MacWhinney (eds.), *The handbook of child language*, 219–250. Oxford: Blackwell Publishing Ltd.

De Houwer, Annick. 2020. Harmonious bilingualism: well-being for families in bilingual settings. In Andrea Schalley & Susana Eisenchlas (eds.), *Handbook of home language maintenance and development: social and affective factors*, 63–83. Berlin/Boston: De Gruyter Mouton.

De Houwer, Annick & Marc H. Bornstein. 2003. Balancing on the tightrope: language use patterns in bilingual families with young children. Fourth International Symposium on Bilingualism, Tempe, Arizona, USA, April 30–May 3, 2013.

Delamont, Sara. 2012. 'Traditional' ethnography: peopled ethnography for luminous description. In Sara Delamont (ed.), *Handbook of qualitative research in education*, 342–353. Cheltenham, UK/Northampton, MA. USA: Edward Elgar.

Denzin, Norman. 2009. The elephant in the living room: or extending the conversation about the politics of evidence. *Qualitative Research* 9. 139.

Dodson, Charles Joseph. 1985. Second language acquisition and bilingual development: a theoretical framework. *Journal of Multilingual and Multicultural Development* 6(5). 325–346.

Donaldson, Julia & Axel Scheffler. 2012. The gruffalo in Scots. Edinburgh: Black & White Pub Ltd.

Döpke, Susanne. 1992. *One parent, one language: an interactional approach*. Amsterdam. Philadelphia: J. Benjamins.

Doyle, Colm. 2013. To make the root stronger: language policies and experiences of successful multilingual intermarried families with adolescent children in Tallinn. In Mila Schwartz & Anna Verschik (eds.), *Successful family language policy: parents, children and educators in interaction*, 145–175. Dordrecht: Springer.

Dyson, Anne Haas. 1997. Rewriting for, and by, the children: the social and ideological fate of a media miss in an urban classroom. *Written Communication* 14(3). 275–312.

Fantini, Alvino. 1985. *Language acquisition of a bilingual child: a sociolinguistic perspective*. Bristol: Multilingual Matters.

Fetterman, David. 2010. *Ethnography: step-by step guide*, 3rd edn. Los Angeles: Sage Publications.

Ferguson, Jenanne. 2015. "Is it bad that we try to speak two languages?": language ideologies and choices among urban Sakha bilingual families. *Sibirica* 14(1). 1–27.

Fillmore, Lily. 1991. When learning a second language means losing the first. *Early Childhood Research Quarterly* 6(3). 323–346.

Fillmore, Lily. 2000. Loss of family languages: should educators be concerned? *Theory into Practice* 39 (4). 203–210.

Finkbeiner, Matthew, Tamar Gollan & Alfonso Caramazza. 2006. Lexical access in bilingual speakers: what's the (hard) problem? *Bilingualism: Language and Cognition* 9(2). 153–165.

Fishman, Joshua. 1965. Bilingualism, intelligence and language learning. *The Modern Language Journal* 49(4). 227–237.

Fishman, Joshua. 1970. *Sociolinguistics: a brief introduction*. Rowley. MA: Newbury House.

Fishman, Joshua. 1991. *Reversing language shift: theoretical and empirical foundations of assistance to threatened languages* 76. Bristol: Multilingual Matters.

Fishman, Joshua. (ed.). 2001. *Can threatened languages be saved? Reversing language shift, revisited: a 21st century perspective*. Clevedon, UK: Multilingual Matters.

Fishman, Joshua. 2006. *Do not leave your language alone: the hidden status agendas within corpus planning in language policy*. New York: Routledge.

Fogle, Lyn Wright. 2012. *Second language socialization and learner agency: adoptive family talk*. Bristol: Multilingual Matters.

Fogle, Lyn Wright & Kendall King. 2013. Child agency and language policy in transnational families. *Issues in Applied Linguistics* 19. 1–25.

Fotos, Sandra. (1995). Japanese-English conversational codeswitching in balanced and limited-proficiency bilinguals. *Japan Journal of Multilingualism and Multiculturalism* 1. 2–16.

Gafaranga, Joseph. 2010. Medium request: talking language shift into being. *Language in Society* 39(2). 241–270.

Gallagher, Joseph. 2008. Psychology, psychologists, and gifted students. In Steven Pfeiffer (ed.), *Handbook of giftedness in children: psychoeducational theory, research, and best practices*, 1–12. New York: Springer.

Gallo, Sarah. 2014. The effects of gendered immigration enforcement on middle childhood and schooling. *American Educational Research Journal* 51(3). 473–504.

García, Ofelia. 2009. *Bilingual education in the 21st century: a global perspective*. Malden: Wiley Blackwell.

García, Ofelia. 2011. Educating New York's bilingual children: constructing a future from the past. *International Journal of Bilingual Education and Bilingualism* 14(2). 133–153.

García, Ofelia & Wei Li. 2014. *Translanguaging: language, bilingualism and education*. Basingstoke, UK: Palgrave Macmillan.

Geertz, Clifford. 1973. *The interpretation of cultures: selected essays*. New York: Basic Books.

Genesee, Fred, Elena Nicoladis & Johanne Paradis. 1995. Language differentiation in early bilingual development. *Journal of Child Language* 22(3). 611–631.

Gyogi, Eiko. 2014. Children's agency in language choice: a case study of two Japanese-English bilingual children in London. *International Journal of Bilingual Education and Bilingualism* 18(6). 749–764.

Goetz, Judith & Margaret LeCompte. 1984. *Ethnography and qualitative design in education research.* London: Academic Press.

Gomes, Rafael Lomeu. 2018. Family language policy ten years on: a critical approach to family multilingualism. *Multilingual Margins* 5(2). 50–71.

Goodson, Ivor. 2013. *Developing narrative theory: life histories and personal representation.* Abingdon: Routledge.

Goodwin, Glenn. 2006. The structure of social theory. *Contemporary Sociology* 35(3). 308–309.

Goodz, Naomi. 2006. Parental language mixing in bilingual families. *Infant Mental Health Journal* 10. 25–44.

Gort, Mileidis. 2006. Strategic codeswitching, interliteracy, and other phenomena of emergent bilingual writing: lessons from first grade dual language classrooms. *Journal of Early Childhood Literacy* 6(3). 323–354.

Gort, Mileidis. 2012. Code-switching patterns in the writing-related talk of young emergent bilinguals. *Journal of Literacy Research* 44(1). 45–75.

Gort, Mileidis & Sabrina Sembiante. 2015. Navigating hybridized language learning spaces through translanguaging pedagogy: dual language preschool teachers' languaging practices in support of emergent bilingual children's performance of academic discourse, *International Multilingual Research Journal* 9(1). 7–25.

Grosjean, François. 1982. *Life with two languages: an introduction to bilingualism.* Cambridge, MA, USA: Harvard University Press.

Grosjean, François. 1998. Transfer and language mode. *Bilingualism: Language and Cognition* 1(3). 175–176.

Grosjean, François. 2001. The bilingual's language modes. In Janet Nicol (ed.), *One mind, two languages: bilingual language processing*, 1–25. Oxford: Blackwell.

Grosjean, François. 2008. *Studying bilinguals.* Oxford: Oxford University Press.

Grosjean, François. 2010. *Bilingual: life and reality.* Cambridge, MA, USA: Harvard University Press.

Gumperz, John. 1982. *Discourse strategies.* Cambridge: Cambridge University Press.

Hammersley, Martyn & Paul Atkinson. 2007. *Ethnography: principles in practice.* London: Routledge.

Harris, Judith Rich. 1995. Where is the child's environment? A group socialization theory of development. *Psychological Review* 102(3). 458–489.

Heath, Shirley Brice. 1983. *Ways with words: language, life, and work in communities and classrooms.* Cambridge: Cambridge University Press.

Hoff, Erika & Rosario Rumiche. 2012. Studying children in bilingual environments. In Erika Hoff (ed.), *Research methods in child language: a practical guide*, 300–316. Chichester, UK: Blackwell Publishing Ltd.

Hoffmann, Charlotte. 2001. Towards a description of trilingual competence. *International Journal of Bilingualism* 5(1). 1–17.

Hoffmann, Charlotte. 2010. Language acquisition in two trilingual children. *Journal of Multilingual and Multicultural Development* 6(6). 479–495.

Hoffmann, Charlotte & Stavans, Anat. 2007. The evolution of trilingual codeswitching from infancy to school age: the shaping of trilingual competence through dynamic language dominance. *International Journal of Bilingualism* 11(1). 55–72.

Hornberger, Nancy & Holly Link. 2012. Translanguaging and transnational literacies in multilingual classrooms: a biliteracy lens. *International Journal of Bilingual Education and Bilingualism* 15. 261–278.
Hulk, Aafke & Natascha Müller. 2000. Bilingual first language acquisition at the interface between syntax and pragmatics. *Bilingualism: Language and Cognition* 3(3). 227–244.
Iannacci, Luigi. 2008. Beyond the pragmatic and the liminal: culturally and linguistically diverse students code-switching in early-years classrooms. *TESL Canada Journal* 25(2). 103–123.
Johnson, David. 2011. Critical discourse analysis and the ethnography of language policy. *Critical Discourse Studies* 8(4). 267–279.
Kasuya, Hiroko. 1998. Determinants of language choice in bilingual children: the role of input. *International Journal of Bilingualism* 2(3). 327–346.
Kendall, Tyler. 2008. On the history and future of sociolinguistic data. *Language and Linguistics Compass* 2. 332–351.
Kenner, Charmian. 2004. *Becoming biliterate: young children learning different writing systems*. Stoke-on-Trent, UK: Trentham Books.
King, Kendall. 2013. A tale of three sisters: language ideologies, identities, and negotiations in a bilingual, transnational family. *International Multilingual Research Journal* 7(1). 49–65.
King, Kendall. 2016. Language policy, multilingual encounters, and transnational families. In Elizabeth Lanza & Wei Li (eds.), Multilingual encounters in transcultural families. *Journal of Multilingual and Multicultural Development* 37(7). 726–733.
King, Kendall & Lyn Wright Fogle. 2006. Bilingual parenting as good parenting: parents' perspectives on family language policy for additive bilingualism. *International Journal of Bilingual Education and Bilingualism* 9(6). 695–712.
King, Kendall & Lyn Wright Fogle. 2013. Family language policy and bilingual parenting. *Language Teaching* 46(2). 172–194.
King, Kendall & Lyn Wright Fogle. 2018. Family language policy. In Teresa MaCarty & Stephen May (eds.), *Language policy and political issues in education*. New York: Springer.
King, Kendall, Lyn Wright Fogle & Aubrey Logan-Terry. 2008. Family language policy. *Language and Linguistics Compass* 2(5). 907–922.
King, Kendall & Elizabeth Lanza. 2019. Ideology, agency, and imagination in multilingual families: an introduction. *International Journal of Bilingualism* 23(3). 717–723.
Kirsch, Claudine. 2012. Ideologies, struggles and contradictions: an account of mothers raising their children bilingually in Luxembourgish and English in Great Britain. *International Journal of Bilingual Education and Bilingualism* 15. 95–112.
Kopeliovich, Shulamit. 2010. Family language policy: a case study of a Russian-Hebrew bilingual family: toward a theoretical framework. *Diaspora, Indigenous, and Minority Education* 4(3). 162–178.
Kuczynski, Leon. 2003. Beyond bidirectionality: bilateral conceptual frameworks for understanding dynamics in parent-child relations. In Leon Kuczynski (ed.), *Handbook of dynamics in parent-child relations*, 3–24. Thousand Oaks, CA: SAGE Publishing.
Kuczynski, Leon & Jan De Mol. (2015). Dialectical models of socialization. In Willis Overton & Prter Molenaar (eds.), *Theory and method. Volume 1 of the handbook of child psychology and developmental science*, 7th edn. Hoboken, NJ: Wiley.
Kuczynski, Leon, Robyn Pitman, Loan Ta-Young & Lori Harach. 2016. Children's influence on their parent's adult development: mothers' and fathers' receptivity to children's requests for change. *Journal of Adult Development* 23(4). 193–203.
Lanza, Elizabeth. 1992. Can bilingual two-year-olds code-switch? *J Child Lang* 19(3). 633–658.

Lanza, Elizabeth. 1997. *Language mixing in infant bilingualism: a sociolinguistic perspective.* Oxford: Oxford University Press.

Lanza, Elizabeth. 2004. Language socialisation of infant bilingual children in the family: quo vadis? In Xoán Paulo Rodríguez-Yáñez, Anxo M. Lorenzo Suárez & Fernando Ramallo (eds.), *Bilingualism and education: from the family to the school*, 21–39. Munich: Lincom Europa.

Lanza, Elizabeth. 2007. Multilingualism and the family. In Peter Auer & Wei Li (eds.), *Handbook of applied linguistics 5: multilingualism*, 45–67. Berlin: Mouton de Gruyter.

Lanza, Elizabeth & Curdt-Christiansen, Xiao Lan. 2018. Multilingual families: aspirations and challenges. *International Journal of Multilingualism* 15(3). 231–232.

Lanza, Elizabeth & Rafael Lomeu Gomes. 2020. Family language policy: foundations, theoretical perspectives and critical approaches. In Andrea Schalley & Susana Eisenchlas (eds.), *Handbook of home language maintenance and development*, 153–173. Berlin: Mouton De Gruyter.

Lewis, Gwyn, Bryn Jones & Colin Baker. 2012. Translanguaging: developing its conceptualisation and contextualisation. *Educational Research and Evaluation* 18(7). 655–670.

Li, Wei. 1994. *Three generations, two languages, one family: language choice and language shift in a Chinese community in Britain.* Clevedon: Multilingual Matters.

Li, Wei. 2018. Translanguaging as a practical theory of language. *Applied Linguistics* 39(1). 9–30.

Lightbown, Patsy & Nina Spada. 2013. *How languages are learned.* Oxford: Oxford University Press.

Liu, Lu. 2018. "It's just natural": a critical case study of family language policy in a 1.5 generation Chinese immigrant family on the east coast of the United States. Maarja Siiner, Francis M. Hult, & Tanja Kupisch (eds.), *Language policy and language acquisition planning*, 13–31. Cham: Springer.

Luykx, Aurolyn. 2003. Weaving languages together: family language policy and gender socialization in bilingual aymara households. In Robert Bayley & Sandra Schecter, *Language socialization in bilingual and multilingual societies*, 25–43. Bristol: Multilingual Matters.

Luykx, Aurolyn. 2005. Children as socializing agents: family language policy in situations of language shift. In James Cohen, Kara McAlister, Kellie Rolstad & Jeff MacSwan (eds.), *ISB4: Proceedings of the 4th International Symposium on Bilingualism, Arizona, USA, 2005*, 1407–1414. Somerville, MA: Cascadilla Press.

Mackey, Alison & Susan Gass. 2015. *Second language research: methodology and design*, 2nd edn. London: Routledge.

MacWhinney, Brian. 2017."The CHILDES project: tools for analyzing talk – electronic edition part 1:the CHAT transcription format." http://talkbank.org/manuals/CHAT.pdf. (accessed 15 July 2017)

Mason, Jana. 1984. Early reading from a developmental perspective. In Rebecca Barr, Michael Kamil, Peter Mosenthal & P. David Pearson (eds.), *Handbook of reading research*, 505–544. White Plains, NY: Longman.

Maxwell, Joseph. 2012. The importance of qualitative research for causal explanation in education. *Qualitative Inquiry* 18(8). 655–661.

McCarty, Teresa (ed.). 2011. *Ethnography and language policy.* New York: Routledge.

McClure, Erica. 1977. Aspects of code-switching in the discourse of bilingual Mexican American children. In Muriel Saville-Troike (ed.), *Georgetown University round table* on *languages* and *linguistics*.Washington, D.C.: Georgetown University Press.

Mercer, Sarah. 2012. The complexity of learner agency. *Apples: Journal of Applied Language Studies* 6(2). 41–59.

Miles, Matthew & Michael Huberman. 1994. *Qualitative data analysis: an expanded sourcebook*, 2nd edn. Thousand Oaks/London/New Delhi: Sage Publications.

Mishina-Mori, Satomi. 2011. A longitudinal analysis of language choice in bilingual children: the role of parental input and interaction. *Journal of Pragmatics* 43. 3122–3138.

Montanari, Simona. 2009. Multi-word combinations and the emergence of differentiated ordering patterns in early trilingual development. *Bilingualism: Language and Cognition* 12(4). 503–519.

Noguchi, Mary G. 1996a. *Adding biliteracy to bilingualism:teaching your child to read English in Japan.* Bilingualism National Special Interest Group of the Japan Association of Language Teachers.

Noguchi, Mary G. 1996b. The bilingual parent as model for the bilingual child. *Policy Science*. 245–261.

Obied, Macleroy. 2010. Can one-parent families or divorced families produce two-language children? An investigation into how Portuguese–English bilingual children acquire biliteracy within diverse family structures. *Pedagogy, Culture & Society* 18(2). 227–243.

Ochs, Elinor. & Bambi Schieffelin. 2011. The theory of language socialization. In Alessandro Duranti, Elinor Ochs, Bambi B. Schieffelin (eds.), *The handbook of language socialization*, 1–21. Oxford: Wiley Blackwell.

Okita, Toshie. 2002. *Invisible work: bilingualism, language choice and childrearing in intermarried families*. Amsterdam: John Benjamins.

Oliphant, Amy & Leon, Kuczynski. 2011. Mothers' and fathers' perceptions of mutuality in middle childhood: the domain of intimacy. *Journal of Family Issues* 32(8). 1104–1124.

Olszewski-Kubilius, Paula. 2008. The role of the family in talent development. In Steven I. Pfeiffer (ed.), *Handbook of giftedness in children: psychoeducational theory, research, and best practices*, 53–70. New York: Springer.

Palviainen, Åsa. 2020. Future prospects and visions for family language policy research. In Andrea C. Schalley & Susana A. Eisenchlas (eds.), *Handbook of home language maintenance and development: social and affective factors*, 236–256. Berlin: de Gruyter Mouton.

Patton, Michael. 1999. Enhancing the quality and credibility of qualitative analysis. *HSR: Health Services Research* 34(5). Part II, 1189–1208.

Pavlenko, Aneta. 2004. The making of an American: negotiation of identities at the turn of the XX century. In Aneta Pavlenko & Adrian Blackledge (eds.), *Negotiation of identities in multilingual contexts*, 34–67. Clevedon, UK: Multilingual Matters.

Pérez-Báez, Gabriela. 2013. Family language policy, transnationalism, and the diaspora community of San Lucas Quiaviní of Oaxaca, Mexico. *Language Policy* 12(1). 27–45.

Piller, Ingrid. 2001. Identity constructions in multilingual advertising. *Language in Society* 30(2). 153–186.

Pole, Christopher & Marlene Morrison. 2003. *Ethnography for education*. Berkshire, England: McGraw-Hill Education.

Pratt, Chris. & Robert Grieve. 1984. The development of metalinguistic awareness: an introduction. In William Tunmer, Christopher Pratt & Michael Herriman (eds.), *Metalinguistic awareness in children: theory, research, and implications*, 2–11. Berlin Heidelberg: Springer-Verlag.

Quay, Suzanne. 2001. Managing linguistic boundaries in early trilingual development. In Jasone Cenoz & Fred Genesee (eds.), *Trends in bilingual acquisition*, 149–199. Amsterdam: John Benjamins.

Ren, Li & Guangwei Hu. 2013. Prolepsis, syncretism, and synergy in early language and literacy practices: a case study of family language policy in Singapore. *Language Policy* 12(1). 63–82.

Revis, Melanie. 2016. A bourdieusian perspective on child agency in family language policy. *International Journal of Bilingual Education and Bilingualism* 22(2). 177–191.

Reyes, Iliana. 2004. Functions of code switching in schoolchildren's conversations. *Bilingual Research Journal* 28(1). 77–98.

Riain, Seán. 2009. Extending the ethnographic case study. In David Byrne & Charles C. Ragin (eds.), *The SAGE handbook of case-based methods*, 289–306. London: Sage Publications Ltd.

Romaine, Suzanne. 1995. *Bilingualism*, 2nd edn. Oxford: Basil Blackwell.

Rose, Elisabeth, Sabine Weinert & Susanne Ebert. 2017. The roles of receptive and productive language in children's socioemotional development. *Social Development* 27(4). 777–792.

Said, Fatma & Hua Zhu. 2019. "No, no Maama! Say 'Shaatir ya Ouledee Shaatir'!" Children's agency in language use and socialisation. *International Journal of Bilingualism* 23(3). 771–785.

Saunders, George. 1988. *Bilingual children: from birth to teens*. Clevedon, Philadelphia: Multilingual Matters Ltd.

Saville-Troike, Muriel. (1987). Dilingual discourse: the negotiation of meaning without a common code. *Linguistics* 25(1), 81–106.

Sayer, Peter. 2013. Translanguaging, TexMex, and bilingual pedagogy: emergent bilinguals learning through the vernacular. *TESOL Quarterly* 47(1). 63–88.

Schieffelin, Bambi & Elinor Ochs (eds.). 1986. *Language socialization across cultures*. Cambridge: Cambridge University Press.

Schwandt, Thomas & Emily Gates. 2018. Case study methodology. In Norman Dezin & Yvonna Lincoln (eds.), *The SAGE handbook of qualitative research*, 5th edn. 341–358. Thousand Oaks, California: SAGE.

Schwartz, Seth, Jennifer Unger, Byron Zamboanga & José Szapocznik. 2010. Rethinking the concept of acculturation: implications for theory and research. *American Psychologist* 65(4). 237–251.

Schwartz, Mila. 2010. Family language policy: core issuaf of an emerging field. *Applied Linguistics Review* 1(1). 171–192.

Schwartz, Mila & Anna Verschik. 2013. Achieving success in family language policy: parents, children and educators in interaction. In Mila Schwartz & Anna Verschik (eds.), *Successful family language policy: parents, children and educators in interaction*, 1–20. Netherlands: Springer.

Shin, Sun-young. 2010. The functions of code-switching in a Korean Sunday school. *Heritage Language Journal* 7(1). 91–116.

Shin, Sarah. 2017. *Bilingualism in schools and society: language, identity, and policy*, 2nd edn. New York: Routledge.

Siiner, Maarja, Francis Hult & Tanja Kupisch. 2018. Situating language acquisition planning. In M. Siiner, Francis Hult & Tanja Kupisch (eds.), *Language policy and language acquisition planning*, 1–10. New York: Springer.

Silva-Corvalán, Carmen. 2014. *Bilingual language acquisition: Spanish and English in the first six years*. Cambridge: Cambridge University Press.

Silverman, Linda & Alexandra Golon. 2008. Clinical practice with gifted families. In Steven I. Pfeiffer (ed.), *Handbook of giftedness in children: psychoeducational theory, research, and best practices*,199–222. New York: Springer.

Skutnabb-Kangas, Tove. 2000. *Linguistic genocide in education-or worldwide diversity and human rights?* Mahwah, NJ: Lawrence Erlbaum.

Smagulova, Juldyz. 2014. Early language socialization and language shift: Kazakh as baby talk. *Journal of Sociolinguistics* 18(3). 370–387.

Smith-Christmas, Cassie. 2014. Being socialised into language shift: the impact of extended family members on family language policy. *Journal of Multilingual and Multicultural Development* 35(5). 511–526.

Smith-Christmas, Cassie. 2016. *Family language policy: maintaining an endangered language in the home*. Basingstoke: Palgrave Macmillan.

Smith-Christmas, Cassie. 2017. Family language policy: new directions. In John Macalister & Seyed Hadi Mirvahedi (eds.), *Family language policies in a multilingual world: opportunities, challenges, and consequences*. London: Routledge.

Smith-Christmas, Cassie. 2020. Child agency and home language maintenance. In Andrea Schalley & Susana Eisenchlas (eds.), *Handbook of home language maintenance and development*, 218–235. Berlin: de Gruyter Mouton.

Smith-Christmas, Cassie. 2021a. 'Our cat has the power': the polysemy of a third language in maintaining the power/solidarity equilibrium in family interactions. *Journal of Multilingual and Multicultural Development* 42(8). 716–731.

Smith-Christmas, Cassie. 2021b. Using a 'Family Language Policy' lens to explore the dynamic and relational nature of child agency. *Children & Society* (00). 1–15.

Song, Kwangok. 2016. "Okay, I will say in Korean and then in American": translanguaging practices in bilingual homes. *Journal of Early Childhood Literacy* 16(1). 84–106.

Spolsky, Bernard. 2004. *Language policy*. Cambridge: Cambridge University Press.

Spolsky, Bernard. 2009. *Language management*. Cambridge: Cambridge University Press.

Spolsky, Bernard. 2012. Family language policy–the critical domain. *Journal of Multilingual and Multicultural Development* 33(1). 3–11.

Spolsky, Bernard & Elana Shohamy. 1999. *The languages of Israel: policy, ideology, and practice*. Clevedon: Multilingual Matters.

Stavans, Anat. 2012. Language policy and literacy practices in the family: the case of Ethiopian parental narrative input. *Journal of Multilingual and Multicultural Development* 33(1). 13–33.

Stavans, Anat & Charlotte Hoffmann. 2015. *Multilingualism*. Cambridge: Cambridge University Press.

Stuart-Smith, Jane, Eleanor Lawson & James Scobbie. 2014. Derhoticisation in Scottish English: a sociophonetic journey. In Chiara Celata & Silvia Calamai (eds.), *Advances in sociophonetics*. John Benjamins, Amsterdam, The Netherlands.

Student, Refugee, Kathleen Kendall. & Lawrence Day. 2017. Being a refugee university student: a collaborative auto-ethnography. *Journal of Refugee Studies* 30(4). 580–604.

Swain, Merrill. 1972. *Bilingualism as a first language*. Irvine: University of California dissertation.

Takeuchi, Masae. 2006. The Japanese language development of children through the 'one parent-one language' approach in Melbourne. *Journal of Multilingual and Multicultural Development* 27(4). 319–331.

Tannen, Deborah. 2004. Talking the dog: framing pets as interactional resources in family discourse. *Research on Language and Social Interaction* 37(4). 399–420.

Tannenbaum, Michal. 2012. Family language policy as a form of coping or defense mechanism. *Journal of Multilingual and Multicultural Development* 33(1). 57–66.

Taeschner, Traute. 1983. *The sun is feminine: a study of language acquisition in bilingual children*. Berlin: Springer-Verlag.

Tseng, Vivian & Andrew Fuligni. 2000. Parent-adolescent language use and relationships among immigrant families with east Asian, Filipino and Latin American backgrounds. *Journal of Marriage and the Family* 62(2). 465–476.

Tuominen, Anne. 1999. Who decides the home language? A look at multilingual families. *International Journal of the Sociology of Language* 140(1). 59–76.

Van Mensel, Luk. 2018. 'Quiere koffie?' The multilingual familylect of transcultural families. *International Journal of Multilingualism* 15(3). 233–248.

Van Mensel, Luk & Maartje De Meulder. 2021. Exploring the multilingual family repertoire: ethnographic approaches. *Journal of Multilingual and Multicultural Development* 42(8). 693–697.

Vygotsky, Lev. 1986. *Thought and language*. Cambridge, MA: MIT Press.

Vygotsky, Lev. 2004. Imagination and creativity in childhood. *Journal of Russian and East European Psychology* 42(1). 7–97.

Vygotsky, Lev. 2016. Play and its role in the mental development of the child. *International Research in Early Childhood Education* 7(2). 3–25.

Williams, Sarah & Björn Hammarberg. 1998. Language switches in L3 production: implications for a polyglot speaking model. *Applied Linguistics* 19(3). 295–333.

Wray, Alison, Kate Trott & Aileen Bloomer. 1998. *Projects in linguistics: a practical guide to researching language*. London: Arnold.

Wolcott, Harry. 1990. *Writing up qualitative research*, 3rd edn. Newbury Park/London/New Delhi: Sage Publications, Inc.

Yamamoto, Masayo. 2001. *Language use in interlingua families: a Japanese-English sociolinguistic study*. Clevedon: Multilingual Matters.

Yin, Robert. 2011. *Qualitative research from start to finish*. New York: Guilford Press.

Yip, Virgin & Stephen Matthews. 2007. *The bilingual child: early development and language contact*. Cambridge, UK: Cambridge University Press.

Zentella, Ana. 1990. Integrating qualitative and quantitative methods in the study of bilingual code switching. *Annals of the New York Academy of Sciences* 583. 75–92.

Zhan, Ying. 2018. Trilingual competence of a two-year-old: language awareness and language choice. *Japan Journal of Multilingualism and Multiculturalism* 24. 49–69.

Zhan, Ying. 2019. Cross-linguistic influence in an English-Japanese-Mandarin trilingual child's verb and prepositional phrase constructions. *Japan Journal of Multilingualism and Multiculturalism* 25. 19–43.

Zhan, Ying. 2021. The role of agency in the language choices of a trilingual two-year- old in conversation with monolingual grandparents. *First Language* 41(1). 21–40.

Zhu, Hua. 2008. Duelling languages, duelling values: codeswitching in bilingual intergenerational conflict talk in diasporic families. *Journal of Pragmatics* 40. 1799–1816.

Zhu, Hua & Wei Li. 2016. Transnational experience, aspiration and family language policy. *Journal of Multilingual and Multicultural Development*. 1–12.

Index

academic ability 6, 17, 106, 130, 146, 184
accommodating parent 43
agentive strategy 5, 186
argumentative essay 4, 172–173
audio and video recording 28

Baker, Colin 1, 16, 53, 56, 70, 127, 155
bicultural 104, 117–118, 124–125
bidirectional impact 8
bilingual first language acquisition 59
bilingual mode 66, 128
body language 31, 46, 67, 86, 89, 91, 93, 111, 123

child agency 3, 5, 8–9, 10, 13, 18–19, 21–26, 40, 85, 130, 133, 185–186, 189
child ethnographer 4
child teacher 47, 187
child-centered policy 43–44
Chinese character 2, 7, 35, 57, 72–74, 78, 85, 106, 111, 116, 121, 139, 141–144, 146–147, 164, 169, 182
Chinese dialect 7, 97, 145
classic novel 3, 152
code-switching 29, 42, 44, 50–53, 55, 61–62, 64–66, 72–73, 84, 86, 91–92, 103, 106, 168
cognitive development 9, 45, 51, 108, 132, 137, 187
co-maker and co-manager 5
communication skill 6, 23
community language 51, 77, 91, 106, 120, 122, 128–129
contextual factor 62, 108, 128
conversational context 20, 45, 47
creative writing 143, 154–155, 170, 176
creativity 10, 131–132, 134, 185, 188
cross-linguistic association 145
cross-linguistic influence 53, 125

developmental error 125, 128
diary entry 26, 28, 30, 35–36, 48, 78, 99, 111, 156, 161–162, 165, 168, 170, 183
diary study 13, 28, 30

dictionary 2, 58, 143, 156, 164, 169, 184
discourse strategy 9, 12, 20, 43–44, 79–80, 83–84, 87, 92, 107, 128
dual-lingual conversation 66–67, 89, 92

early literacy 5, 16, 131
eliciting 44–47, 83, 88, 147
ethnographic case study 8, 26
ethnography 26–28

family bond 9, 44, 51, 73–74
family communication 13, 31, 44, 74, 183
family environment 5, 105, 129, 132, 134, 188
family intimacy 107, 167
family language ideology 12
family language management 8–9, 12, 75
family language policy 1–2, 5, 8–10, 13, 17–18, 74, 130, 189
family language practice 8, 14–15, 20–22, 29, 75
fiction and non-fiction book 3, 6, 147
field note 26–28, 32, 35–37, 39, 184
Fogle, Lyn Wright 12, 19–21, 24, 103, 107

generational positioning 24, 25, 40
guided writing 156

heritage language 1, 14–16, 17, 21, 40, 51, 72, 75, 102–103, 107, 114, 118, 120–121, 137–138, 146, 168
hiragana 7, 35, 52, 111
home environment 1
home language 5, 24, 44, 51, 54, 75, 83, 106–109, 118–120, 128–129

identity 2, 9, 13–14, 17, 22, 34, 86, 102, 107–109, 114–117, 120, 124, 130, 143
imagination 3, 131, 135, 148–149, 182
imitating 165
immigrant families 1, 11, 12, 17, 25, 95, 105, 120, 142
immigrant parent 1, 95
indexing 45–47, 68

infant trilingualism 5
intergenerational transmission 11
interviews 28–29
invisible ideology 106
IPA 2, 73, 82, 140–141

Japanese sign language 3, 10, 138, 141, 181, 185, 187

kanji 7, 144–146, 182
katakana 7, 35, 143–144
King, Kendall & Lyn Wright Fogle 1, 12–13, 19–20, 22, 29, 40, 59, 77, 79, 102–104, 106

language ability 9, 115–117, 159
language acquisition 1, 12–13, 25, 28, 30, 112–113, 150, 172, 186
language activity 1, 85, 101, 108
language and culture 1, 15, 36, 40, 107, 121, 124–125, 138
language background 4, 6, 76, 135
language broker 25, 95
language choice 1, 9, 11, 20–21, 24–25, 27, 29–30, 40, 48, 50, 56, 65–66, 74–76, 78–79, 81–88, 91–93, 102–103, 107, 120–122, 127, 186
language development 4–5, 9–10, 12–13, 18–19, 39, 43, 59–60, 74, 79, 83, 88, 102–103, 107, 123, 127–128, 131, 140, 149, 180, 185–186, 188
– child 12–13, 19, 39, 59, 79, 107, 141, 188
language differentiation 13, 59
language dominance 125, 127–128
language exposure 41
language ideology 4, 9, 11
language input 13, 32, 40–41, 45, 104, 114, 128, 149
– environment 60
– pattern 79
language maintenance 107, 124, 146
language management 8–9, 11–12, 27, 36–38, 75, 77
language policy 2, 11–12, 15, 16, 19, 20, 27, 29, 33–34, 36–38, 40, 44, 50, 57, 65, 67, 71, 81, 133, 165, 181
language practice 12, 15, 19, 21–22, 27, 29, 33–34, 36–38, 40, 44, 50, 57, 65, 67, 71, 75, 77, 79, 81, 83, 85, 101–104, 116, 118, 120, 122, 125, 129, 181
language preferences 118, 128
language proficiency 15–16, 43, 64, 77, 105, 109, 113
– perceived 116
– relative 111
language skill 1, 29, 32, 79, 90, 94, 110, 115, 124, 182
language socialization 5, 8, 12, 18–19, 21, 25, 30, 33, 43, 67, 92, 123, 130–131, 187
language use 5, 8–9, 12–13, 17–18, 20, 22, 27–30, 32, 34, 38, 40, 45, 67, 74–77, 81, 83, 85, 92–93, 106, 118–119, 128, 130, 162, 182
Lanza, Elizabeth 12–13, 20, 24, 44, 59, 76–77, 79–80, 83–84, 88, 91
lingua franca 5–6, 15, 26, 78, 104, 107
linguistic competence 24, 104, 111, 113
linguistic repertoire 1, 9, 40, 44, 52–53, 56–67, 92, 102, 162, 164
literacy development 5, 55, 57, 146, 186–188
literacy skill 7–8, 16, 18, 41, 104, 112, 137
literacy-driven practice 9, 141, 181
loanword 7, 51, 93, 143–144

meaning-making 13, 55, 70, 72, 90
metacognitive ability 163, 168
metalinguistic awareness 9, 28, 93, 102, 130, 137, 163
metalinguistic conversations 26, 30, 35–37, 118
metalinguistic knowledge 65, 168
minority language 16, 22, 24, 50, 76, 80–81, 107, 121, 180, 182
monolingual and monocultural society 6
multilingual children 1, 9–10, 53, 95, 102, 108, 121, 133, 186
multilingual families 1, 4, 12–13, 17, 69, 107, 133, 186
multilingual practice 13, 21, 53, 90, 161
multilingual repertoire 13, 71, 133
multilingual space 44, 178, 181, 183, 186–187
multilingual speaker 13, 39, 55, 59, 64, 131, 166
multilingualism 1, 9, 14, 43, 68, 75, 88, 103, 105, 108, 123, 127

– harmonious 105, 119
multiliterate 16, 78, 141, 154, 178

named language 73, 76, 165
non-community language 57, 77
non-societal language 17, 75, 119, 123, 154, 185–186

OPOL 9, 17, 28–29, 50, 52, 66, 76–79, 85–86, 101, 107–108, 114, 133, 146
one-situation-one-language 78, 85–86

paraphrasing 45, 48, 50, 68, 70
parental ideology 13, 21, 103
parental modelling 68, 77, 125
parent-child interaction 13, 18, 33, 77, 82–83, 90
parent-child intimacy 23, 71, 75
parent-child relationship 22, 156
parents' attitude 9, 76, 105, 117
parents' authority 9, 12, 122
participant observation 26–30, 37, 184
pīnyīn 57–58, 79, 94–95, 106, 130, 140, 142, 145, 147
preschooler 6, 119, 148, 154, 161, 165, 181

reading and writing skill 17, 43, 106, 113, 140
recasting 49
rephrasing 45, 48–49, 71, 80, 88

school language 53–54, 107, 120, 182
script 7–8, 140–141, 144, 147, 169

self-learning skill 178
Smith-Christmas, Cassie 12, 14, 23–25, 27, 66–67, 81
social context 122
social network 119–120
social relationships 8, 17, 18
socializing agent 8
societal language 1, 16, 24, 75, 83, 102–104, 107–108, 121, 123
sociolinguistic environments 6, 8, 23, 130
Spanish 2–3, 6, 10, 17, 20, 90, 138, 141, 158, 178–181, 185, 187
speech community 11, 78
speech system 7
spoken and written form 130, 138, 165
Spolsky, Bernard 4, 11–12, 40, 75, 77, 102–103, 107, 115

target language 20, 25, 43, 67, 76, 125, 129, 137
translanguaging 44–45, 53–54, 55, 56, 70–74, 83, 95, 137, 154, 156, 165, 167–168, 178, 182
translating 44–45, 53, 67–68, 70–71, 152, 154, 163
translation equivalent 48, 68–69, 90
transnational family 20, 25, 103, 125
trilingual children 29, 91, 186
trilingualism 2, 5, 79, 104–105, 128, 155, 165, 183
triliteracy 104, 154

well-being development 43, 135, 181
writing system 7, 142–143

www.ingramcontent.com/pod-product-compliance
Lightning Source LLC
Chambersburg PA
CBHW050524170426
43201CB00013B/2080